# BLITZ

## ON BRITAIN 1939–45

*The bombs have shattered my churches,*
*have torn my streets apart,*
*But they have not bent my spirit*
*and they shall not break my heart.*
*For my people's faith and courage*
*are lights of London town*
*Which still would shine in legends though*
*my last broad bridge were down.*

*Greta Briggs*, London Under Bombardment

Other books by the same author

*Instruments of Darkness*
*Battle of Britain The Hardest Day, 18 August 1940*
*Battle of Britain Day, 15 September 1940*
*The Spitfire Story*
*Spitfire at War* (three volumes)
*Battle Over the Reich*
*Aircraft versus Submarine*
*Last Year of the Luftwaffe, May 1944 to May 1945*
*Luftwaffe Data Book*
*Sky Battles*
*Sky Warriors*
*Focke Wulf 190 in Combat*
*Luftwaffe in Camera* (two volumes)
*The History of US Electronic Warfare* (two volumes, with third in preparation)

Books co-authored with the late Jeff Ethell

*Target Berlin, USAAF Mission 250, 6 March 1944*
*World War II Combat Fighting Jets*
*One Day in a Long War, Air Action over North Vietnam, 10 May 1972*
*Air War South Atlantic, 1981*

ALFRED PRICE

# BLITZ
## ON BRITAIN 1939–45

SUTTON PUBLISHING

First published by Ian Allan in 1977

First published in this edition in the United Kingdom in 2000
Sutton Publishing Limited
Phoenix Mill · Far Thrupp · Stroud · Gloucestershire

British Library Cataloguing in Publication Data
A catalogue record for this book is available from the British Library.

ISBN 0-7509-2356-3

Typeset in 11/12 pt Ehrhardt.
Typesetting and origination by
Sutton Publishing Limited.
Printed and bound in England by
J.H. Haynes & Co. Ltd, Sparkford.

# Contents

*The author with Generalmajor Dietrich Peltz, who directed the air attacks on Britain during 1943 and 1944, seen here in 1975 while this book was being researched.*

# Prologue

My intention in writing this book has been to describe the bomber attacks on Great Britain between 1939 and 1945 and the operations of the defences to counter them. For reasons of space I have omitted more than passing references to the other forms of bombardment during this period: the ground-launched V1s, the V2s and the German long-range guns that fired across the Channel. I have made no attempt to mention every single bomber attack. Instead, I have selected actions I consider to be representative of the period covered by each chapter, and concentrated my attention on two of these. In the case of the Battle of Britain, for example, I endeavoured to show in detail what happened on two days, 18 August and 15 September 1940.

*Blitz on Britain* would not have been possible without the wholehearted co-operation of many people both in Britain and in Germany. From the Royal Air Force, Air Chief Marshal Sir Hugh Saunders, Air Commodore 'Toby' Pearson, Group Captain R. Oxspring, Group Captain R.C. Haine, Prince Emanuel Galitzine and Mr D. Hayley-Bell; from the Luftwaffe, General Major Dietrich Peltz, General Roderich Cescotti, Oberst Horst von Riesen and Horst Goetz, Erich Sommer, Adolf Dilg, Helmut Wenk, Rudi Prasse, Otto Schmidt, Wilhelm Raab and Guenther Unger. Also many good friends have generously lent me material and photographs, in particular Hanfried Schliephake, Wolfgang Dierich, Jim Oughton, Franz Selinger, Derek Wood and John Taylor. Peter Cornwell and A.K. Stone have provided invaluable advice on the manuscript.

I am indebted to the staffs of the Air Historical Branch, the Public Record Office in London and the Bundesarchiv in Freiburg for much of the information used in this book. I am also grateful to the Imperial War Musuem, the Bundesarchiv Bildarchiv at Koblenz and Herr Walter Brieke, the keeper of the Kampfgeschwader 76 Archive, for the use of photographs. Thanks are also due to Peter Elstob for permission to use his graphic account of the bombing of London.

The first edition of this book appeared in 1977, before the release of detailed information on the decrypts by the code-breakers at Bletchley Park. This revised account covers this aspect of the story in so far as it affected the RAF intelligence picture on Luftwaffe units operating against Britain.

Also during the twenty-two years since the publication of the first edition, new information on the Battle of Britain and later attacks has become available to the author. This material is also included in this revised and expanded edition.

In this book, where applicable, dimensions have been translated into British units, rounded up or down if appropriate. Times have been adjusted to GMT.

Alfred Price
Rutland
December 1999

*Line-up of Spitfires of No. 19 Squadron at Duxford, May 1939.*

# CHAPTER 1

# More Worry than War, September 1939–June 1940

In approaching the prospects for a successful air campaign either against Great Britain alone, or against both Great Britain and France, there is one conspicuously favourable factor which will tend to influence Germany's judgement and encourage her to hope for success, and that is the exposed position and vulnerability of London . . . France offers to German attack no such favourable objective. Nothing that either France or ourselves can attack in Germany can have quite the immediate and decisive results that Germany may hope to gain by an overwhelming attack on London.

*Marshal of the Royal Air Force Sir Edward Ellington, Chief of the Air Staff, speaking before the war*

At 11.45 a.m. on Sunday 3 September 1939, Prime Minister Neville Chamberlain began his sombre broadcast to the British people:

This morning the British Ambassador in Berlin handed the German Government a final note stating that unless we heard from them by 11 o'clock that they were prepared at once to withdraw their troops from Poland, a state of war would exist between us. I have to tell you now that no such undertaking has been received, and that consequently this country is at war with Germany. . . .

The Prime Minister spoke for about a quarter of an hour, during which time he stressed that he had done all he could to maintain peace but Hitler would have none of it.

Within minutes of the end of Mr Chamberlain's speech, air-raid sirens sounded their warbling note through London and several other cities in Great Britain. For the citizens the prospect of air attack so soon after the outbreak of war came as no great surprise. For almost a decade previously there had been a stream of writers and speakers predicting, in the most grisly terms, the effects of the aerial 'knock-out blow' which they felt would mark the opening of any future world war.

## THE FEARED KNOCK-OUT BLOW

It is the task of military planners to calculate 'worst case' scenarios for what might happen if an enemy launched different forms of attack. However, if planners run two or more 'worst case' scenarios together in series, the resultant prognosis can be truly dreadful. This was the case when, before the war, they had calculated the number of casualties to be expected from an all-out German air attack on Britain.

The pre-war estimates of the weight of bombs the German bomber force could put down on British cities, and in particular London, varied greatly. In December 1938, during a speech intended to justify the appeasement of Hitler, the Lord Chancellor had stated that 'The Germans had it in their power to let loose 3,000 tons of bombs in a single day.' Writing shortly afterwards in his book *The Defence of Britain* the respected commentator Liddell Hart stated, more cautiously, that the weight of bombs German bombers could carry in a sustained offensive on Britain amounted to about 600 tons per day, yet:

> The seriousness of that threat can be gauged by comparison with the fact that during the whole of the last war only 74 tons of bombs were dropped on England by hostile aeroplanes. That quantity, dispersed in time and space, killed 857 people, wounded 2,058 and caused material damage which in monetary cost amounted to approximately £1,400,000. On such a basis of comparison, nearly a quarter of a million casualties, and over £100,000,000 worth of damage, might be anticipated in the first week of a new war.

In the spring of 1939 the British Air Staff put the German long-range bomber strength at about 1,600 aircraft. It was estimated that over the first two weeks of a future war this force could deliver about 700 tons per day on London, with the weight of the attack tapering thereafter. Using slightly different figures to those employed by Liddell Hart in his calculation, they produced a 'worst case' casualty figure of fifty people killed or wounded for each ton of bombs dropped on a built-up area. Taking both of these 'worse case' figures together, Ministry of Health officials calculated that during the first six months of an aerial bombardment there would be 600,000 people killed and 1,200,000 wounded. It was a daunting prospect. To what extent were the fears justified?

From the German records we know that on 2 September 1939 the Luftwaffe possessed 1,180 twin-engined bombers with the range to attack targets in England from airfields in Germany (about a quarter less than the British Air Staff's 'worst case' estimate) of which 1,008 were serviceable. The bulk of the bomber force, nearly 800 aircraft, was made up of Heinkel 111s; some 750 were the latest H and P sub-types, while the remainder were obsolescent variants. Virtually all the remaining twin-engined bomber units were equipped with the Dornier 17, either in its modern Z sub-type form or earlier models. From airfields in north-western Germany to London meant a round trip of 760 miles flying round Holland, or 720 miles flying over it. The maximum bomb load of the Heinkel 111 was 4,400 pounds and that of the Dornier 17 was 2,200 pounds. The British Air Staff, lacking exact performance figures for the German bombers, had credited both

*Early production Heinkel 111, the J variant. At the beginning of 1939 several versions of this bomber were in service and they made up more than half the twin-engined bomber strength of the Luftwaffe.*

types with the ability to carry their full bomb loads to London from airfields in Germany. In fact, with an operational allowance of fuel to allow for formation assembly, route flexibility and a safety margin in case aircraft had to be diverted, neither type could attack London with its full load of bombs.

Thus 400 tons per day – not 700 tons – was nearer the maximum the German bomber force could carry to the British capital as a sustained daily average. Allowing for strays and bombs that failed to explode, the figure fell to a realistic maximum of about 300 tons of exploding bombs on the target for a maximum effort daylight attack and 100 tons for a similar attack at night (when the proportion of stray bombs would have been substantially greater).

The weight of bombs the Luftwaffe could put down on London had been greatly exaggerated; yet this over-estimation was dwarfed by the parallel over-estimation of the effect these bombs might have. The 'fifty casualties per ton' rule was based on official British figures issued after the German bombing attacks during the First World War. But during these attacks the German bombers had *carried* a considerably greater weight of bombs than those *known to have exploded*, which were chronicled in British records. In fact about 110 tons had been carried, which meant that the figure of 74 tons quoted by Liddell Hart was too low by about one-third. Actually, the number of casualties per ton of bombs *carried* to urban areas in Britain during the First World War was about twenty-six. This alone made the Air Staff 'worst case' estimate in error by almost as much again. Moreover, the First World War figures of 'casualties per ton' had been grossly distorted by a few 'lucky' hits before there was a proper warning system or provision of shelters. During the first aeroplane attack on London, by 17 Gotha bombers on 13 June 1917, 162 people had been killed and 432 injured by a total of only 4½ tons of bombs, some of which failed to explode. This meant an average of 132 casualties per ton. During the early Gotha raids many people had been standing in the streets, gawking at the enemy planes flying above, when they were killed or wounded. Once the public learned the folly of such behaviour, air-raid casualties fell dramatically.

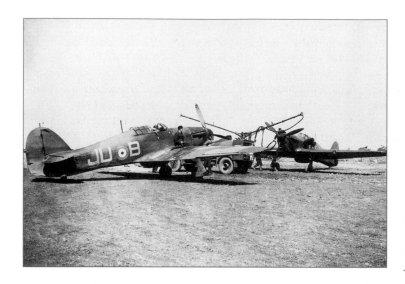

*Hurricanes of No. 111 Squadron refuelling at Wick, early in the war. This type equipped the majority of RAF fighter squadrons during the first year of conflict.* (IWM)

## THE DEFENDERS' RIPOSTE

So much for the predicted weight of attack on Britain, and the actual weight the Luftwaffe was capable of delivering. Now let us examine the ability of the air defences to parry an attempted 'knock-out blow'.

In September 1939 RAF Fighter Command possessed a total of 747 aircraft in 39 front-line squadrons, with about 400 aircraft in reserve. This figure was split as follows (reserve aircraft in brackets): Hawker Hurricane, 16 squadrons with 347 aircraft (22); Supermarine Spitfire, 10 squadrons with 187 aircraft (71); Gloster Gauntlet, parts of 2 squadrons with 26 aircraft (50); Gloster Gladiator, 4 squadrons with 76 aircraft (126); Bristol Blenheim, 7 squadrons with 111 aircraft (about 40). The newer German bomber types could attain brochure maximum speeds of about 250 mph, but flying at this pace guzzled fuel and it was rarely used in normal war operations. Usually, the need to conserve fuel and maintain formation meant bombers cruised at speeds of about 180 mph. They were, therefore, within the interception capability of even the slowest British fighter types.

The most modern of the British fighters, the Spitfire and the Hurricane, were armed with eight .303 inch Browning machine guns; the older Gladiator carried four of these weapons and the Blenheim carried five (plus a sixth gun in the rear turret for self-defence). The rifle-calibre Browning fired ball, incendiary or armour-piercing rounds, each weighing just under half an ounce, at a rate of 1,150 per minute per gun. This fast-firing weapon was very effective against unarmoured aircraft (at the outbreak of the war German bombers did not carry armour). The Gauntlet carried an obsolescent armament comprising two slow-firing Vickers guns and would have been ineffective against German bombers; at the outbreak of war this fighter was on the point of going out of front-line service.

The Commander-in-Chief Fighter Command, Air Chief Marshal Sir Hugh Dowding, calculated that a minimum of 46 squadrons with 736 fighters would be necessary to defend the spread of targets from Portsmouth to the Clyde from air attack on the scale expected. By 'defend' he meant the ability to inflict a loss rate of 13 per cent of the raiding force for each attack, a rate of attrition no air force could accept during a protracted offensive.

Dowding's figure of forty-six squadrons was a realistic minimum requirement to defend Great Britain from the size of attack he had been told to expect. In fact, when war broke out, he had not forty-six squadrons but thirty-nine. And of the latter, four were dispatched to France soon afterwards. This meant Dowding's force was below strength by about one-quarter. But because the British intelligence estimate of the strength of the German bomber force was exaggerated by a similar amount, the number of fighters available in the summer of 1939 can be considered sufficient to inflict unacceptable losses on any attack the Luftwaffe could have mounted from bases in Germany.

To attack Britain from bases in Germany, the bombers would have to operate far beyond the reach of any fighter escort. In the light of what happened subsequently, there can be little doubt that even the small number of fighters available would have been capable of dealing severely with any attempt in September 1939 to mount an aerial 'knock-out blow' on London or any other target in Britain by day. Lacking adequate radar, British fighters were virtually ineffective by night. But by night the bombers, too, would have found it difficult to locate targets and the weight of attack would be greatly reduced.

## FIGHTER COMMAND'S 'SYSTEM'

The fighters were the 'teeth' of Fighter Command. But scarcely less important were the 'eye' and 'brain' organisations, and the 'nervous system' to carry information between the three, to position the 'teeth' to snap at the enemy to greatest effect.

Before the war British scientists had hurriedly prepared for service a chain of rudimentary radar stations which, by the summer of 1939, was able to detect

*The Chain Home radar stations, erected along the eastern side of Britain immediately before the war, were Fighter Command's long-range 'eyes'. These stations could plot aircraft flying more than 100 miles away, at medium or high altitudes. The transmitting aerials were strung between four 350-foot high towers. The transmitter was housed in the camouflaged building in front of the base of the centre tower.*

*Interior of the Chain Home radar receiver room.*

aircraft approaching at medium or high level at a distance of about 100 miles. These stations were Fighter Command's long-range 'eyes'. When war came there were eighteen radar stations, code-named Chain Home (CH), in operation giving cover along the eastern and southern coasts of Britain between Portsmouth and Aberdeen. (The term 'radar' was not coined until after the American entry into the war in 1941; but because of its universal use now, it is used in this account rather than RDF – Radio Direction Finding – which was in use at that time.) To see how this radar information was used, let us follow a typical engagement of a 'raiding force', as practised during the Fighter Command exercises just before the war.

The first sign of the approach of the 'enemy' was usually from one of the coastal radar stations. The grid position, altitude and estimated strength of the incoming force were passed by landline to the Filter Centre at Fighter Command Headquarters, at Bentley Priory near Stanmore. There filter officers checked the plots against the known movements of friendly aircraft. The plots, treated as 'hostile' until identified, were passed to the Fighter Command operations room and by landline to the Group and Sector operations rooms dotted round the country. The controller at the Group operations room was responsible for ordering off fighters to meet any hostile incursion likely to enter his Group's area. As the 'raiders' neared the coast, he allocated responsibility for controlling the engagement to the fighter Sectors. The headquarters at Bentley Priory, and the Group and Sector operations rooms, were the 'brains' of Fighter Command. The plethora of landlines linking all of them with the radar stations and observer posts constituted the 'nervous system'.

Once fighters were off the ground, they were the responsibility of the Sector controller directing the interception. He ordered the fighters to the raiders' altitude, and passed a stream of vectors to bring about an interception. To enable the Sector controller to keep track of his fighters, one pilot in each formation of fighters switched his radio to 'Pip-Squeak'. This automatically switched his transmitter on for 14 seconds in each minute, during which the three ground

*The plots on aircraft approaching the shores of Britain were passed direct from the radar stations to the Filter Room at Stanmore, seen here. In this room the plots were checked against the known movements of friendly aircraft; plots on unidentified and hostile aircraft were then passed to the Group and Sector operations rooms, from which the air battles were controlled.*

*The author standing outside the No. 11 Group fighter control bunker at RAF Uxbridge, open for public viewing.*

*The plotting table at No. 11 Group headquarters, with the WAAF staff moving blocks representing units into place.*

*Fighter controllers' positions at No. 11 Group headquarters, viewed from the plotting table.*

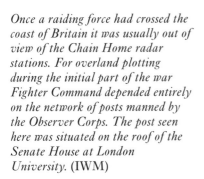

*Once a raiding force had crossed the coast of Britain it was usually out of view of the Chain Home radar stations. For overland plotting during the initial part of the war Fighter Command depended entirely on the network of posts manned by the Observer Corps. The post seen here was situated on the roof of the Senate House at London University.* (IWM)

direction-finding stations in each Sector took bearings on the signals. The bearings were passed to the Sector operations room, where they were correlated to give a fix on the fighters.

As the 'raiding force' neared the coast it came within a view of the Observer Corps posts, situated at 5-mile intervals across the southern and eastern part of the country. These were Fighter Command's short-range 'eyes'. The individual posts passed to their own Group operations rooms details of the position and estimated height and heading of the incoming force, together with an indication of the numbers of aircraft and, usually, their types. The Observer Group Headquarters would relay this information to the fighter Group and Sector operations rooms, where it was used to update the air picture. As the 'raiding force' moved inland it was tracked by the Observer Corps, since the radar stations were sited to look only out to sea.

When the leader of the fighter formation sighted the 'enemy' he called 'Tally Ho', indicating that he was taking control of the engagement and required no further help from the ground. Once the interception was complete, the Sector controller passed the fighters' vectors to take them back to their base or, if this was no longer usable, to a suitable airfield.

By the outbreak of war the Fighter Command control and reporting system, with its chain of radar stations and ground observer posts, was just about ready. During the final air exercises in peace its value had been proved. However, the acid test of actual combat remained.

## AA GUNS AND SEARCHLIGHTS

For the close defence of potential targets in Britain, in September 1939 the Army Anti-Aircraft Command operated a total of 425 modern heavy guns (out of a requirement of 2,232) and 253 light guns (out of a requirement of 1,860). Thus

*The backbone of the British anti-aircraft gun defences against high-flying raiders in 1939 was the 3.7-in gun, seen here in its mobile version; this weapon could fire a maximum of ten 28-pound shells per minute. Normally it was fired from a revetted position but in this posed photograph, taken shortly before the war, it is seen in the open with its range-finder (centre) and predictor (left). (IWM)*

the anti-aircraft gun defences had less than one-fifth of the weapons considered necessary for their task.

The purpose of ground anti-aircraft fire was three-fold: first, to destroy or damage hostile aircraft; secondly, to assist in breaking up enemy formations so that fighters could engage more effectively; and thirdly, to reduce bombing accuracy by forcing aircraft to attack from high altitude. Although they were rarely successful in securing the first two of these objectives, strong gun defences were to prove consistently successful in bringing about the last of them.

The modern heavy anti-aircraft weapons in service in the British Army in 1939 were of two types, the 3.7-inch and the 4.5-inch. The 3.7-inch fired 28-pound shells at a maximum of ten per minute to an effective engagement ceiling of 25,000 feet. On exploding, the splinters from the time-fused shell were lethal against aircraft within about 15 yards. The 4.5-inch gun fired 55-pound shells at a maximum of eight per minute to an effective engagement ceiling of 26,000 feet and was lethal against aircraft up to about 20 yards from the point of detonation. In addition there were 270 of the lower performance 3-inch guns, a First World War weapon with an effective engagement ceiling of 14,000 feet.

*The heaviest type of anti-aircraft gun in service at the beginning of the war was the 4.5-in, which could fire a maximum of eight 55-pound shells per minute. (IWM)*

*Lacking radar for the detection of bombers coming in at night or above cloud, during the first year of the war the gunners had to rely on acoustic sound locators.* (IWM)

Heavy anti-aircraft guns were usually deployed in groups of four. However, sites with two, six or even eight guns were not uncommon. Each site had its own range-finder and predictor. To engage aircraft with heavy anti-aircraft guns, accurate prediction was essential. Fired at an aircraft flying at 17,000 feet, a 3.7-inch shell took about 10 seconds to reach the target; but during that time a bomber moving at 180 mph covered half a mile. Thus the gunners needed to aim their weapons at, and fuse their shells to explode in, a position 880 yards in front of the target's observed position.

There were two prediction devices in service in the British Army at this time, the Vickers and the Sperry. An analogue computer in the predictor calculated, from information on the aircraft's previous flight path, where it *would be* at the time the shells reached it. It then disgorged this information, in the form of azimuth and elevation settings for the guns and time–flight fuse settings for the shells. This information was passed electrically to the individual guns, whose crews tracked the predicted position of the target, fused the shells and fired their weapons by salvoes on the orders of the site commander. Of course, the bomber crew could easily upset the gunners' aim by flying a weaving path. But the guns were sited to cover the approaches to the targets and any 'jinking' during the bombing run usually resulted in bombs landing well clear of the aiming point. The prevention of accurate bombing, it will be remembered, was one of the purposes of anti-aircraft fire.

By night the aircraft were picked up first by sound locators, which assisted searchlights to find and illuminate the target. With the aircraft thus in view, the optical fire-control devices could track it and the engagement could take place as by day. The standard type of searchlight in service at the beginning of the war was the 90-cm, with a carbon projector giving 210 million candle power. Apart from assisting guns and fighters to locate targets at night, the searchlight constituted an effective defence in its own right: by dazzling enemy bomb aimers it could obscure the target. And it could have a profound morale effect on enemy crews

*For defence against low-flying raiders, Anti Aircraft Command employed the 40-mm Bofors gun, which fired at a maximum rate of 120 2-pounder shells per minute. Although a formidable weapon, the Bofors was in critically short supply during the first year of the war. (IWM)*

simply by rendering their aircraft conspicuous, even if there were no fighters or guns immediately available to engage.

At the outbreak of war the gunners' sole method of detecting bombers at night was by means of sound locators. By collating the angles from two or more locators, it was hoped to work out the present and future positions of individual raiders accurately enough for the guns to engage. The main problem with sound locators, however, was that by the late 1930s their capability had been outstripped by the modern bomber. At the locator's maximum range of 6,000 yards, aircraft engine noises took 18 seconds to reach the instrument. Thus, if the aircraft was moving at 180 mph, the bearing found by the locator lagged the position of the aircraft by about a mile. During peace-time trials the locators seemed to provide a moderate chance of engaging unseen bombers with predicted fire. It was, in any case, the best that could be done with the equipment available.

For the defence of targets against low-flying aircraft there was the 40-mm Bofors gun, an excellent weapon that fired 2-pound impact-fused high-explosive shells at a maximum rate of 120 per minute. The gun had an effective engagement ceiling of 12,000 feet. The Bofors could be fired over open sights or, with greater accuracy, using a simple predictor. In 1939 the only thing to be said against the Bofors was that there were hardly any of them: a mere 253 were deployed at the beginning of the war, compared with a requirement of 1,860 for the defence of targets in Britain.

## BARRAGE BALLOONS

The final element of the defence was the barrage balloon, of which a total of 624 were available at the beginning of the war out of a requirement of 1,450. The balloon was designated the LZ (Low Zone); just over 62 feet long and 25 feet in diameter at its widest part, it had a hydrogen capacity of about 19,000 cubic feet.

The LZ balloon was flown from a mobile winch and was designed for a maximum flying altitude of 5,000 feet.

A barrage balloon supporting a mile of cable anchored to the ground did not constitute a lethal obstacle to aircraft in service in the late 1930s. At impact speeds of 2,000 mph and greater, the shock of the collision was usually sufficient to sever the cable without causing undue damage to the aircraft. Immediately before the war govern-ment scientists examined several methods of making balloon cables lethal. One of these, the so-called Double Parachute Link, was considered effective and put into production (see diagram on p. 14). During a trial with the Double Parachute Link a Wellington bomber struck the cable with one wing and the system worked according to plan. Unfortunately, however, the safety cutters failed to sever the cable before the parachutes were fully deployed. The resultant yawing load on the aircraft was so great that the fuselage broke midway

*A barrage balloon flying from the grassed area immediately to the south of the Houses of Parliament.*

along its length. The Double Parachute Link system went into service towards the end of 1939 and by mid-1940 the majority of the LZ balloons had it.

To provide protection from low-level attack, a barrage of 450 balloons was required for a target the size of London. With balloons positioned randomly over the area at a density of nine per mile there was a one-in-ten chance of an aircraft with a wingspan of 60 feet striking one of the cables.

Although the LZ balloon was designed to operate in winds of up to 60 mph, the weather was to prove a continual hazard to these ungainly gasbags. On 15 September 1939, for example, an unexpectedly severe electrical storm caused the destruction of 78 balloons in the London area before the remainder could be pulled to safety.

In September 1939, although there were insufficient anti-aircraft guns and balloons, the British air defences as a whole would have been capable of inflicting a heavy cumulative loss on bombers making repeated daylight attacks without fighter escort. Taking all factors into account, it is clear that it was beyond the German capability to sustain the feared aerial 'knock-out blow' at the beginning of the war. Winston Churchill later noted that before the war governments had been greatly misled by gory tales of the death and destruction to be expected from air raids: 'This picture of aerial destruction was so exaggerated that it depressed the statesmen responsible for the pre-war policy, and played a definite part in the

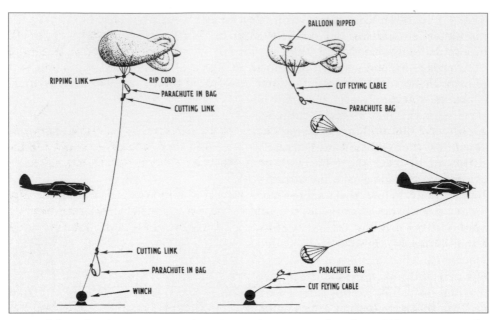

*In air defence few things are as simple as they might appear at first glance. When it was armed with the Double Parachute Link, the LZ balloon was no exception. When an aircraft struck the cable, the latter was severed at the top and the bottom by two cutting links. The aircraft thus carried away the main portion of the cable and an 8-foot diameter parachute opened at each end of the wire. Together the parachutes exerted a drag about six times as great as the engine thrust of a bomber, sufficient to stop it almost dead in its tracks. The aircraft then fell out of the sky and crashed. As the cable parted from the balloon, a wire ripped off a patch which allowed the hydrogen to escape; the balloon then descended slowly to the ground.*

desertion of Czechoslovakia in August 1938.' So we now know that in September 1939 the Germans lacked the means to deliver the 'knock-out blow' against Britain; but did they ever intend to try?

## THE GERMAN INTENT

From German records there is clear evidence that Hitler had no intention of mounting a 'knock-out blow' against Britain early in the war, although he extracted the maximum diplomatic mileage from the threat of such attacks during the final year of peace. Until the war in Poland had been brought to a successful conclusion his bomber force would be required there. And when Poland had been defeated it might be possible to present the Western Allies with a *fait accompli* and, having achieved his immediate aims, secure peace. Either way, he felt there was little to be gained from unleashing his bombers against Britain at that stage.

Later, strategic bombing attacks on Britain might be necessary. Hitler wished to keep this option open. At the end of the top-secret 'Directive No. 1 for the Conduct of the War', dated 31 August 1939, the Fuehrer stated:

Any favourable opportunity of an effective attack on concentrated units of the English Navy, particularly on battleships or aircraft carriers, will be exploited. The decision regarding attacks on London is reserved to me. Attacks on the English homeland are to be prepared; though it should be borne in mind that inconclusive results, due to the use of insufficient forces, are to be avoided in all circumstances.

During the months that followed, Hitler would reiterate his refusal to allow air attacks on civilian targets in Britain. For the time being the cities would remain inviolate. Yet the threat was ever-present, and vigorous steps were taken to strengthen the defences.

The 'raider' that had caused the sirens to wail in London at midday on the first day of war was, it soon became clear, a civil aircraft coming in from France; shortly afterwards, the 'All Clear' was sounded. There was a similar false alarm on the following day, 4 September.

## THE 'BATTLE OF BARKING CREEK'

At 0630 hours on the morning of 6 September there were signs that, at last, the Germans really were coming in force. The Chain Home radar station at Canewdon near Southend began passing plots on a force of some twenty aircraft approaching the Thames Estuary from the east. When both Bomber and Coastal Commands reported they had no aircraft operating in this area, the Fighter Command Filter room designated the force 'Hostile'. At 0645 hours a preliminary warning was issued and fighters were scrambled. During the next few minutes the number of separate 'Hostile' forces being plotted rose from five to twelve, each with between 'six plus' and twelve aircraft. By 0650 hours the incoming force was plotted heading up the Thames, giving all the indications of a massed attack on London. Air-raid warning 'Red' was issued. In London, the sirens wailed for the third time since the beginning of the war.

By 0655 hours No. 11 Group had seven flights of fighters airborne, either in or making for the Thames Estuary. No. 12 Group was warned that it might also be required to provide fighters to reinforce the defences of the capital. An anti-aircraft gun site near Clacton reported it was engaging enemy twin-engined aircraft. Shortly afterwards Spitfires of No. 74 Squadron gave a 'Tally Ho' call and went into action.

It was nearly an hour before the air situation over the Thames Estuary was finally resolved. And when it was, it became clear that the Luftwaffe had been nowhere in the area. By the time the so-called 'Battle of Barking Creek' reached its inglorious conclusion, the Royal Air Force had lost three aircraft destroyed and one pilot killed. The 'twin-engined aircraft' engaged by the anti-aircraft gunners turned out to be Blenheim fighters of No. 64 Squadron, one of which was shot down. The 'enemy aircraft' engaged by No. 74 Squadron turned out to be Hurricanes of No. 56 Squadron, two of which were shot down.

The root cause of the 'battle' had been a technical fault at the radar station at Canewdon. As a result, echoes from aircraft flying to the west of the radar in the

# HE THOUGHT HE COULD JUST DO IT

IT wasn't far—just a fev yards across the road. He wante to catch the 'bus home, so he took chance and ran for it. Death happened t get in his way. It was nothing very unusual literally hundreds of people are killed or injured i the black-out every week. **Nearly 1,200 road death in December alone.** Remember the new speed limit canno alter the fact that you can see the car before the driver can se you. How often do you hurry and 'just' do it'? Will the luck hold

**Remember these** 1 When you first come out into the black-out, stand still for a minute to get yo
**Four Safety Rules** eyes used to the darkness.
2 Look *both* ways before stepping off the pavement.
3 Where there are traffic lights, always cross by them. It is worth going out of yo way to do this.
4 Throw the light of your torch down on to the ground, so that you do not dazzle driver

## LOOK OUT IN THE BLACK-OUT !

*During the first months of the war, the matter of crossing a road in the black-out constituted a far greater hazard to the citizens of Britain than anything caused by the Luftwaffe. As this government-sponsored advertisement shows, there were nearly 1,200 road deaths during December 1939 alone; this was more than four times the monthly average for 1999, when a vastly greater number of vehicles was on the roads.*

'back beam' were not filtered out. Instead, they appeared on the screen looking exactly like those from aircraft approaching the radar station *from the east*. As more fighters had taken off to engage, their echoes added to those of the phantom raiding force which became progressively larger. Once the existence of the 'raiding force' was established in everyone's mind, the misidentifications and shooting were only to be expected from a defensive system inexperienced in war and over-quick on the trigger. It was the first time that friendly aircraft were mistaken for 'hostiles' on a radar screen and it would certainly not be the last. The problem of differentiating between friend and foe in a confused aerial situation remains to this day. The report of the subsequent inquiry stressed the need for far greater care before aircraft were identfied as 'hostile'. And the production of radar Identification Friend or Foe (IFF) equipment for RAF aircraft was to be given the highest priority.

During the weeks that followed the 'Battle of Barking Creek' the false alarms became far less common. And the British people lacked even this diversion to remind them they were at war. After what had been said during the previous decade, there was a clear feeling of anticlimax.

## EFFECTS ON CIVILIAN LIFE

In the event, the institution of the pre-war contingency plans to meet the expected 'knock-out blow' had a far greater effect on people's lives than the war itself during this period. The scheme to evacuate the young and the sick from the cities went ahead. From London alone, the exodus involved more than 650,000 schoolchildren and teachers, very young children and mothers, expectant mothers and invalids. The migration to the countryside was conducted swiftly and, considering the scale, more or less efficiently. Yet, in the absence of the feared air attacks, the will to remain away from home quickly dissipated. As early as mid-September, only two weeks after

*Spitfires of No. 19 Squadron flying in the tight formation of vics employed early in the war.*

the outbreak of war, Minister of Health Walter Elliot found it necessary to appeal to mothers not to return: 'The fact that up to the present no air raids have taken place in the large towns does not affect the position.' This injunction fell on deaf ears, and during the months that followed there was a steady drift homewards. By the end of the year about a third of the schoolchildren and most of the very young children and mothers had returned.

If the evacuation scheme was considered by many an unnecessary irritation that could be put right, the same could not be said of the effects of the black-out. With the street lights extinguished and cars restricted to driving with just sidelights, during the closing months of 1939 road casualties in Britain accounted for far more deaths than the sporadic fighting. By the end of December 1939 more than 4,000 people had been killed, about a third more than in the same period in 1938. This was in spite of the fact that half a million cars had been laid-up by mid-December due to the imposition of petrol rationing. So long as it existed, the black-out was to make night-time travel a serious hazard for motorist and pedestrian alike.

## FIGHTER COMMAND TACTICS

Of course, Air Chief Marshal Dowding had no way of knowing that Hitler did not intend to launch the expected 'knock-out blow' soon after the outbreak of war. And the very speed of the Blitzkrieg in Poland had demonstrated the ability of the German Army to undertake rapid thrusts deep into enemy territory. This undermined the comfortable assumption that a German aerial bombardment of Britain would be made only by unescorted bombers. In November 1939 Dowding wrote to his senior commanders:

> In the training of Home Defence Fighters, it has hitherto been assumed that the fighter aircraft of any probable continental enemy will be unable to reach

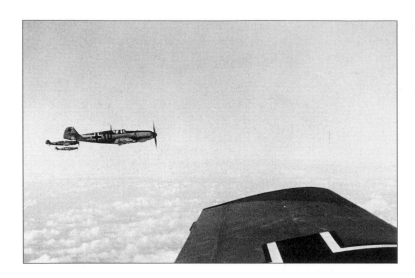

*Messerschmitt 109s flying in the loose Schwarm tactical formation that was far superior to that used by Fighter Command.*

this country, and that therefore his bombing raids will be unescorted. The possibility cannot be excluded, however, that the enemy might over-run the Low Countries at a very early stage of the war and, using aerodromes or refuelling grounds in Holland and Belgium, might be able to send over fighter escorts with his bombing raids . . .

In the light of what was to happen, this was a prophetic statement. Yet in the autumn of 1939 it made little impact.

In any case there were serious doubts as to whether high-speed dogfighting between modern fighters was possible. The Royal Air Force Manual of Air Tactics, 1938 edition, solemnly stated: 'Manoeuvre at high speeds in air fighting is not now practicable, because the effect of gravity on the human body during rapid changes of direction at high speed causes a temporary loss of consciousness, deflection shooting becomes difficult and accuracy is hard to obtain.' To launch escorted bomber attacks, the Germans would need to capture airfields in Holland or Belgium, both of which were neutral at the time. The possibility that France might be forced out of the war and occupied was beyond the bounds of serious discussion at this time, so it is hardly surprising that British tactics were tailored to meet the main, unescorted bomber, threat.

In the bomber formations in general use, the usual element was the 'V' of three aircraft. The optimum element to engage these was, therefore, a section of three fighters. Thus the formation recommended for an RAF fighter squadron of twelve aircraft comprised four 'V's, each 'V' consisting of a section of three aircraft. The squadron commander flew in the middle of the leading 'V' and the other three 'V's flew behind in line astern. The fighters flew in close formation with one wingspan, about 10 yards, between them. The use of such a tight formation had definite advantages for the penetration of cloud, an important factor to be considered in planning air operations over Britain.

Directed by radio from the ground, the squadron commander was to lead his formation into position on one flank of the enemy bomber formation. Once there he ordered his sections into echelon, and took his section in to attack. Each fighter pilot was to position himself behind an enemy bomber where in the words of the 1938 RAF Manual of Air Tactics: '. . . he stays until either he has exhausted his ammunition, the target aircraft has been shot down, or he himself has been shot down or his engine put out of action'. The other sections were to queue up behind and attack after the section in front had broken away. Since these actions were to be fought beyond the range of enemy fighters, the attackers could concentrate their entire attention on the enemy bomber formation.

The tactical formation and the type of attack outlined above were not the only ones used by the Royal Air Force, but they were representative of the rigidity of tactical thinking present in all of them. It must be stressed, however, that against unescorted bombers these tactics were appropriate.

## TURRET FIGHTER, THE DEFIANT

A major area of uncertainty at the end of the 1930s concerned the effectiveness of the defensive crossfire from a formation of bombers. Would this be sufficient to beat off attacks by enemy fighters? As an insurance against this possibility, the RAF issued a specification for a two-seat fighter carrying its four-gun armament in a power-operated turret mounted amidships. The new fighter was named the Defiant; in December 1939 No. 264 Squadron became the first to receive it.

In view of what was to happen to the Defiant when the air war began in earnest, it is important to appreciate the role for which it was designed. The turret fighter was intended exclusively as a *bomber destroyer*. Against an enemy bomber formation, it was felt that even a few such fighters would provide a powerful addition to the defence. The turret fighter could formate below, to the

*Defiant fighters of No. 264 Squadron, the first unit to receive the type. This aircraft, designed to operate against unescorted bomber formations, carried its armament of four .303-in machine-guns in a power-operated turret amidships.* (IWM)

side or even in front of its target and bring the latter under sustained fire. It could choose the best position for the gunner to 'outflank' any armour protection the bomber carried and at the same time remain outside the bomber's return fire. The Defiant's four .303-inch Brownings could traverse through 360 degrees and elevate from the horizontal almost to the vertical. The fact that the guns could not be depressed below 17 degrees up when aimed forwards, to prevent the unsynchronised weapons shooting holes in the propeller blades, was not considered to detract seriously from the tactical role envisaged for the fighter.

Like so much of the equipment in use in Fighter Command – radar, the ground control system to direct fighters into battle, even the monoplane fighter itself – the operational value of the turret fighter could not be proved or disproved until the air war over Britain itself hotted up. Meanwhile, No. 264 Squadron's Defiants were declared operational early in 1940; and by that time a second squadron, No. 141, was re-equipping with the type.

The use of turret fighters to 'outflank' it was one way of defeating the armour protection fitted to a bomber. Another way round the problem, the 'frontal approach', was to fit fighters with a weapon considerably more powerful than the .303-inch Browning. The gun selected was the French Hispano 20-mm cannon, which had the best armour-penetration capability of any weapon of that calibre available at the time. During the closing months of 1939, a Spitfire and a Hurricane were flying, each fitted with a prototype installation for two cannon. If the operational trials proved successful, the Hispano gun was to go into large-scale production. We shall follow the progress of the cannon later in this account.

## IMPROVEMENTS TO FIGHTER COMMAND'S 'SYSTEM'

Throughout the final months of 1939 there was a steady improvement in Fighter Command's control and reporting system. Considering the haste with which it had been erected, the system was working surprisingly well. There had been failures both in equipment and operation, as the 'Battle of Barking Creek' had demonstrated. But as personnel gained experience, the weaknesses in the system were eradicated. Yet the greatest flaw in the system remained beyond the ability of the operators to cure: the poor performance of the Chain Home radar in tracking aircraft at altitudes below about 5,000 feet.

Fortunately for Fighter Command the prototype of a radar partially able to conquer this problem already existed at the beginning of the war. The Coastal Defence radar, designed to observe movements of shipping, proved considerably better than the Chain Home system in observing the movements of low-flying aircraft. If the height of its scanner was 50 feet above sea level and the sea was calm, it could detect aircraft flying at 500 feet 18 miles away. Aircraft at 1,000 feet could be seen 22 miles away and aircraft at 2,000 feet could be seen 35 miles away. Aircraft flying at 10,000 feet could be observed at a range of 90 miles. The new radar received the designation Chain Home Low (CHL), and was ordered into production at the highest priority. The first CHL station became operational in November 1939, followed during the next four months by eight others along the east coast of England. The CHL radar worked on a much shorter wavelength than the CH type; and instead of the fixed wide beam of the latter, it employed a narrow rotating beam (as used by modern search radars). As a result, the plotting accuracy and powers of discrimination of the CHL were much better than those of the earlier set. The CHL could provide useful confirmatory and amplifying information on aircraft tracked by CH stations. Like those from the CH stations, plots from the CHL stations were passed direct to Fighter Command Headquarters by landline, where they were filtered and disseminated through the system.

## THE PROBLEM OF THE NIGHT RAIDER

We have observed that at the beginning of the war British fighter defences were virtually impotent against night raiders. Work was in progress to improve the position but it was far from reaching fruition. An obvious answer was to fit a lightweight radar set into a fighter, so its crew could find targets for themselves. However, this technical requirement proved easier to state than to meet. At the beginning of the war the prototype of an airborne radar was undergoing trials in a Blenheim, but its performance was so poor it was unsuitable for service use. The maximum range of the set was a little over a mile. Its minimum range, 330 yards, meant that at night an enemy aircraft being overtaken by the fighter disappeared off the radar screen some time before the fighter pilot was close enough to see it visually. (Radar minimum range: while the radar transmitter is radiating its high-powered pulse, the receiver has to be switched off to prevent its being damaged. Thus echo signals returning from short range while the receiver is switched off are not displayed on the radar screen, and the radar is 'blind' to them.) Clearly, the development of the radar-equipped night fighter had a long way to go before it was likely to cause problems for an enemy.

## THE NEED FOR MORE FIGHTERS

Whatever the nature of the air fighting when the war eventually did hot up, one thing was clear to

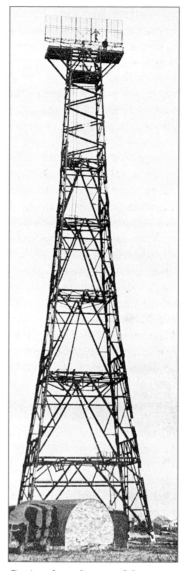

*During the early part of the war there existed a 'gap' in the radar cover below 5,000 feet, through which raiders could fly unseen. To plug part of this gap the Chain Home Low radar entered service at the end of 1939. Mounted on towers up to 185 feet high, or a lower gantry overlooking a cliff, this set could detect aircraft flying over the sea at 500 feet at ranges of up to 18 miles.*

the British Air Staff: more fighter squadrons were needed. Air Chief Marshal Dowding was pressing for twelve more squadrons for Fighter Command, to make up for those sent to France and also to bring his force to the level judged to be necessary for the defence of Great Britain. Other fighter squadrons were required by Coastal Command for convoy protection work; others still were needed to support the British Expeditionary Force in France.

The Chief of the Air Staff, Marshal of the Royal Air Force Sir Cyril Newall, could not pull fully trained and equipped fighter squadrons out of a hat like a magician. Although plans for the large-scale increase in the size of the service were being pushed ahead with all speed, these long-term measures would take years to reach fruition.

The prospects for an early increase in the strength of the fighter force were not encouraging. During the early months of the war production of Spitfires and Hurricanes was running at about 100 machines per month. Once the wastage in training and from the sporadic air fighting in France had been made good, almost all that were left were required to re-equip squadrons already in existence which operated obsolescent types.

In addition to the shortage of modern fighters there was another, potentially as serious in its effect on operations, of trained ground crews. As a short-term expedient Newall ordered the formation of eighteen new fighter squadrons which he equipped with any aircraft available, whether suitable for air fighting or not: Battle and Blenheim bombers and Gladiator biplane fighters. When the necessary modern fighters became available, the organisational framework would exist to receive them. By December 1939 all eighteen new 'fighter' squadrons existed in some form or other. Re-equipped with modern fighters, the majority of these would take their place in the front line of Fighter Command during the first half of 1940.

## THE ATTACK BEGINS

Although Hitler had no wish to initiate attacks on Britain's cities during the opening months of the war, he had given permission for the Luftwaffe to exploit 'any favourable opportunity of an effective attack on concentrated units of the Royal Navy'. Accordingly on 16 October 1939, following a reconnaissance report that the battle cruiser *Hood* was in the Firth of Forth, nine of the new Junkers 88 bombers of I. Gruppe of Kampfeschwader 30 took off to attack her (for the designations of Luftwaffe combat units, see Appendix A). The crews had strict orders to confine their attack to warships at sea. Only precision dive-bombing attacks were permitted and on no account were bombs to be released if there was a chance of their falling on land.

The German bombers arrived over the Firth of Forth to find *Hood* inside the harbour at Rosyth, where she was 'off limits'. There were, however, several smaller warships in the Firth and the Ju 88 crews turned their attentions to these. The German commander, Hauptmann Helmut Pohl, attacked the cruiser *Southampton* as she lay at anchor. (For equivalent ranks, Luftwaffe and Royal Air Force, see Appendix B.) One 1,100-pound armour-piercing bomb scored a direct

*The Junkers 88A-1, similar to the aircraft that took part in the Firth of Forth attack. This aircraft, fast, manoeuvrable and stressed for dive bombing, was the best all-round medium bomber in service in 1939.* (via Schliephake)

hit on her port side and perforated three decks before emerging out of the ship's side and exploding below the water; the ship suffered structural damage. The cruiser *Edinburgh*, anchored nearby, came under attack from another Ju 88; she suffered minor splinter damage.

Soon afterwards Leutnant Horst von Riesen made his attack, on the destroyer *Mohawk*. He scored a near miss. As the bombers pulled out of their dives, the Spitfires of Nos 602 and 603 Squadrons caught up with them. Pohl was chased out to sea and eventually shot down, as was a second of the raiders. As von Riesen sighted the British fighters, he pushed his Junkers into a high-speed descent to a few feet above the sea. But it was no good; within minutes the Spitfires had caught up with him. He later recalled:

> Now I thought I was finished. Guns were firing at me from all sides, and the Spitfires behind seemed to be taking turns at attacking. But I think my speed gave them all a bit of a surprise – I was doing more than 400 kilometres per hour [250 mph], which must have been somewhat faster than any other bomber they had trained against at low level – and of course I jinked from side to side to make their aim as difficult as possible. At one stage in the pursuit I remember looking down and seeing what looked like rain drops hitting the water. It was all very strange. Then I realised what it was: those splashes marked the impact of bullets being aimed at me from above!

Von Riesen did have one ally, however – time. As the panting Jumo motors carried the bomber further out to sea, the Spitfires were drawn further from their base. About a hundred miles from the coast: an accurate burst struck the bomber's starboard engine, riddling the cooling system. As the needle of the temperature gauge swung 'off the clock', von Riesen shut down the steaming engine and feathered the propeller.

*Leutnant Horst von Riesen, whose account of the Firth of Forth attack appears below.* (Von Riesen)

Deprived of the speed that had saved them until now, the German crew could hope only that the end would come swiftly. Yet when von Riesen turned round, expecting to see the fighters curving in for the kill, there was no sign of them. They had broken off the action.

Afterwards Pilot Officers Morton and Robertson of No. 603 Squadron reported having chased an enemy aircraft 'thought to be a Heinkel 111' out to sea at very low level. When they broke off their attack the British pilots observed that the starboard engine of the bomber was 'not running'.

The German crew had shaken off their pursuers. Yet the threat of death was still present. The bomber was only a few feet above the sea, flying at just above stalling speed; there was no power to climb away. Moreover, there was a risk that the overworked port engine might give up at any moment. The chances of getting back to base at Westerland seemed slim. Von Riesen considered the possibilities:

> During our training we had been told that a Ju 88 would not maintain height on one engine – and we were only barely doing so. Should we ditch there and then? I thought no; it was getting dark, nobody would pick us up and we would certainly drown or die of exposure. An alternative was to turn round and go back to Scotland, and crash land there. One of my crew suggested this but one of the others shouted over the intercom 'No, no, never! If we go back there the Spitfires will certainly get us!' He was right. The thought of going back to that hornets' nest horrified us.

The German crew decided to continue eastwards and hope for the best. To assist von Riesen to hold the aircraft steady the observer took off his belt, fixed it round the left rudder pedal and pulled for all he was worth. At the same time the gunner hand-pumped some 400 gallons of fuel from the tanks on the starboard side into those on the port side, where it could be used by the good engine. Gradually, as fuel was burnt and the Junkers became lighter, it became possible for von Riesen to coax it higher. Even so when, after 3½ hours' flying, Westerland was sighted, the bomber was still below 2,000 feet. Its relieved crew made a landing which was, in the circumstances, uneventful.

On the following day Kampfgeschwader 30 sent four Ju 88s to attack the fleet anchorage at Scapa Flow, only to find that almost all the warships were away. For the loss of one of their number to anti-aircraft fire, the raiders inflicted severe damage on the depot ship *Iron Duke* and she had to be beached. During the attack a bomb fell on land near Hoy, but fortunately nobody was hurt.

## MINING THE PORTS

In November the Luftwaffe began laying magnetic mines off ports along the east coast of Britain, to supplement those laid by U-boats. The minelaying began on the night of the 20th, when Heinkel 115 floatplanes of the 3. Staffel of Kuestenfliegergruppe 906 planted their weapons off Harwich and the mouth of the Thames. The air-dropped mine weighed 1,200 pounds, of which 660 pounds was high explosives; the He 115 could carry two such weapons. Released from low altitude, the mines descended slowly by parachute to the surface. Then the parachute was released and the weapon sank to the sea bed. When a steel ship passed within range, its magnetic field actuated the firing mechanism and caused the mine

*A Heinkel 115 floatplane of Kuestenfliegergruppe 906. This unit began mine-laying operations in the waters off Britain in the late autumn of 1939. (via Schliephake)*

to detonate. Striking from underneath, the shock wave would often lift a ship high out of the water and break its back.

Two nights after the start of the aerial mine-laying, on the night of 22 November, there was an unexpected windfall for the Royal Navy. Two mines, dropped into the sea near Southend, came to rest in shallow water where they were exposed at low tide. Lieutenant-Commander J. Ouvry of the torpedo establishment at HMS *Vernon* was called to the scene. He succeeded in dismantling the firing mechanism of one of the weapons and revealing its secrets.

*Wellington bombers converted to carry magnetic coil equipment to explode magnetic mines. This photograph shows the aircraft in the three-aircraft close formation normally employed to clear a channel of suspected mines.*

*The prototype cannon Spitfire, flown by Pilot Officer Proudman during the action on 13 January 1940.*

Now the problem was precisely defined, work began on a host of measures to make the magnetic mines less effective. Most of these were naval in character and fall outside the compass of this volume. However, one countermeasure did involve aircraft: the fitting of a small number of Wellington bombers with a large magnetic coil energised by a separate engine mounted in the fuselage, to explode the magnetic mines as the aircraft flew low overhead. During the final days of 1939 the prototype airborne minesweeping installation was successfully test flown against the firing mechanism taken from the mine found at Southend.

By the third week in February 1940 four Wellingtons had been modified to carry the magnetic coil equipment. On 22 February they opened their operational career by exploding two mines. During the months that followed the odd-looking Wellingtons became a familiar sight flying low over the east-coast shipping routes.

## THE HISPANO CANNON GOES INTO ACTION

While the problem of countering the magnetic mines was being solved, the only action for the air defences was the occasional engagement of German aircraft on armed reconnaissance missions which ventured imprudently close to the coast. During one of these actions, on 13 January 1940, the Spitfire carrying the prototype Hispano cannon installation went into combat for the first time. Afterwards, Pilot Officer G. Proudman reported:

> On the morning of 13 January 1940, No. 72 Squadron having left Drem and No. 609 Squadron having not yet taken over, I attached myself to a flight of Hurricanes from No. 111 Squadron, which took off to intercept a raid. At 20,000 feet, 5 miles East of Fifeness, a Heinkel 111 aircraft appeared followed by three Spitfires from No. 602 Squadron who were carrying out a No. 1 attack. The Heinkel commenced to dive and No. 2 of the Spitfire section

received a bullet in his windscreen, causing him to break away prematurely and leaving a gap before No. 3 could carry on the attack. I then filled in the gap and carried out an attack. At about 12,000 feet I was in range at 300 yards and I opened fire. Almost immediately a piece of shining metal dropped from the Heinkel's fuselage and is believed to be one of the undercarriage wheels. Only one round of HE ammunition was fired, as the starboard gun stopped. The port gun stopped after 30 rounds of ball ammunition had been fired. I broke away at about 5,000 feet, having fired my rounds in two bursts.

The Heinkel was finished off by conventionally armed Spitfires and Hurricanes, and crashed into the sea.

The action showed that the Hispano cannon was effective – when it worked. The trouble was that the weapon had been designed for mounting along the top of the engine of the fighter, so the latter's weight could absorb the recoil forces. The gun did not take kindly to being fired from less-rigid mountings out in the wings, which was the only place where there was room for it in the Spitfire and the Hurricane. During firing the recoil shook the weapon and its feed system to such an extent that almost invariably there was a stoppage.

A further difficulty with the Spitfire installation was that, in order to house the cannon's large sixty-round drum magazine inside the wing without making too large a bulge, the gun was canted on its side. This gave rise to several problems, including that of getting a clean ejection for the belt links and the empty cartridge cases. In action a further problem was revealed: if one cannon suffered a stoppage, the unbalanced recoil forces when the remaining gun was fired caused the aircraft to yaw and this made accurate aiming difficult. All in all, a great deal of development work would be necessary before the Hispano was ready for large-scale service.

In March 1940 the German bombers visited Scapa Flow for a second time, when on the 16th they inflicted further damage to *Iron Duke* and scored a hit on the cruiser *Norfolk*, which put her out of action for three months. During this attack several small bombs fell on land, killing one civilian and wounding seven others and injuring seven sailors. The dead civilian, council employee James Isbister, was the first fatal casualty in Britain as a result of an air attack during the Second World War. His death to a stray bomb occurred some six months after the beginning of a conflict which, by pre-war British calculations, would by then have seen more than half a million such victims.

The first large-scale damage on mainland Britain as a result of enemy air action occurred, again accidentally, on the night of 30 April 1940. A mine-laying Heinkel 111, hit by anti-aircraft fire, crashed on a housing estate at Clacton and its mines exploded. The crew of four and two civilians were killed, and a further 156 civilians were injured.

## THE 'PHONEY WAR' ENDS

Thus far the German bomber force had abstained from making deliberate attacks on Britain. But the lull that had existed in the West since the beginning of the war was fast drawing to a close. On 9 April, German forces invaded Denmark and

*A Handley Page 42 and an Ensign airliner, impressed into service in the RAF, seen at Tangmere on 10 May 1940 as No. 501 Squadron prepared to fly to France following the start of the German offensive. The drain on Fighter Command's resources during the next four weeks would leave the force seriously weakened.*

Norway. Unable to resist effectively, the former capitulated almost immediately. The fighting in Norway was to continue for nearly two months, before the Germans took the entire country. By then, however, events were moving much closer to home for the British. On 10 May the German Army marched into Holland, Belgium and Luxembourg. Three days later it launched a massive armoured thrust into France.

The effect of this on the air defences of Britain was immediate. Two squadrons of fighters had been sent to Norway. Following the invasion of Holland and Belgium four more squadrons of fighters were dispatched to France. They were joined, within the next two days, by thirty-two Hurricanes and pilots (the equivalent to two squadrons) as replacements for casualties. Already Dowding's slender force had been depleted by the equivalent of eight squadrons. And there was every sign that the drain would continue. He later wrote: 'I was responsible for the Air Defence of Great Britain, and I saw my resources slipping away like sand in an hour glass. The pressure for more and more assistance to France was relentless and inexorable.'

## THE DRAIN OF HOME DEFENCE FIGHTERS

On 14 May the French Prime Minister, Paul Reynaud, acknowledged receipt of the RAF fighter squadrons already dispatched and requested that ten more be sent to cover a planned counter-attack against the German thrust. Dowding saw what was happening and objected in the most vigorous terms. On the following day he was allowed to plead his case before the War Cabinet. He said the losses in pilots and aircraft suffered by the fighter squadrons sent to France greatly exceeded the outputs from the training schools and the factories. If losses continued at that rate, Dowding continued, in two weeks '. . . we shall not have a single Hurricane left in France *or in this country*'. Someone, he said, had to give a clear decision on the minimum number of fighter squadrons required to defend Britain if the battle in France was lost. Once that number had been reached no more should be sent '. . . no matter how desperate the situation might become in

France'. The War Cabinet agreed that no further squadrons of fighters were to be sent to France '. . . for the present'.

Some accounts have suggested that the drain on Fighter Command's resources ceased with the Cabinet meeting on 15 May. This was not the case. When the next meeting of the War Cabinet was convened, on the following morning, the situation in France was far from clear. The latest information was that the Germans had broken through the French line only in limited strength, and bold action might still save the day. Accordingly it was decided to send the equivalent of a further four squadrons of fighters to France immediately, and prepare for the dispatch of two more. In addition, late on 16 May, Dowding received orders that six squadrons were to operate over France from bases in southern England, landing at French airfields to refuel and rearm between sorties and returning home each evening.

Meanwhile, in France itself, the situation deteriorated rapidly. By 19 May it was clear that an evacuation of forces from northern France might be necessary. And it was finally agreed that whatever happened, no more fighters should be sent to France. On the following day German spearhead units reached the coast near the mouth of the Somme, to drive a wedge between the Allied forces in the north and those in the south. Now the front line had moved back so far that the RAF fighter squadrons could operate over the battle area as effectively, and with a good deal more security, from airfields in southern England. Accordingly, their withdrawal began. Dowding later commented that the arrival of these fighter squadrons back in England '. . . converted a desperate into a serious situation'. Nevertheless, out of the 261 Hurricanes sent to France, only 66 were to return. The remaining 195 were either destroyed in action or had to be left behind. The loss amounted to about a quarter of Britain's strength in modern fighters.

On 26 May Allied troops in the Dunkirk bridgehead began to be evacuated, and when this came to an end just over a week later, more than 300,000 men had been snatched to safety. But as the air fighting continued, so did the losses to Fighter Command. About a hundred fighters and eighty pilots were lost during the covering operations. When the evacuation was complete Dowding had only three day fighter squadrons that had not been committed to action. And twelve squadrons were in the line for a second time, having been withdrawn to re-form.

On 14 June German troops entered Paris; on the 25th the French Army laid down its arms. In less than two and a half months the situation regarding the air defence of Great Britain had changed completely. Instead of having to face attacks only from due east, the defenders now had to meet them from any direction between north-east and south-west. Fighter Command was left with a strength well below that considered necessary to meet unescorted attacks by the German long-range bomber force. But now, with bases within 100 miles of London and other large cities, the Luftwaffe could operate its twin-engined bombers with their full bomb loads and even send short-range dive bombers against targets in the extreme south. Most important of all, in the battle now unfolding, the attackers could provide fighter protection for bomber units operating over the southern part of England.

If Britain now chose to fight on, her air-defence system would face an attack scenario far worse than any 'worst case' postulated before the war. In the next chapter we shall observe how it met that challenge.

# CHAPTER 2

# Battle is Joined, June–August 1940

*Not by rambling operations, or naval duels, are wars decided, but by force massed and handled in skilful combinations.*

*Alfred Mahan*

The speed of the advance through France, leading to the Armistice on 25 June, had come as a surprise to the German High Command and to Hitler himself. They expected to be victorious, but not so quickly, so dramatically and, considering what had been achieved, at so low a cost. During the final part of June and the first half of July Hitler waited patiently for word from London, for a sign that the British government accepted that further resistance would be futile. If they would see sense and sue for peace, much bloodshed would be avoided. Hitler could even afford to be generous in his peace terms. But the Fuehrer neither knew nor understood the new British Prime Minister, Winston Churchill. He waited in vain.

On 2 July Hitler took the first hesitant step along the path to be followed if the British remained recalcitrant. In a directive to the High Command he stated that a landing operation against England might be required and that plans should be made '. . . for a possible operation'. During the fortnight that followed his feelings hardened and on 16 July he informed his High Command: 'Since England, in spite of her hopeless military situation, shows no signs of being ready to come to an understanding, I have decided to prepare a landing operation against England and, if necessary, to carry it out.' The preparations for such a landing were to be completed by the middle of August. The part to be played by the Luftwaffe during the preparatory phase was stated simply: 'The *englische Luftwaffe* must be so reduced, morally and physically, that it is unable to deliver any significant attack against an invasion across the Channel.'

Three days later, on 19 July, Hitler issued 'a final appeal' for Britain to make peace; it was firmly rejected. On the 21st the Fuehrer decided that only a threatened or an actual invasion would bring the British government to its senses. Preparations were accelerated. On the same day Reichsmarschall Hermann Goering, the Commander-in-Chief of the Luftwaffe, summoned senior commanders to his residence at Karinhall for a conference. He informed them of details for the 'final phase' of the operations against Britain which, he said, would begin in a week or so. In the meantime the small-scale attacks on shipping, the mine-laying of the approaches to harbours and the light probing attacks on targets in Britain were all to be stepped up.

The Luftwaffe units earmarked for the operations against Britain were divided geographically between three Luftflotten. Those in Holland, Belgium and northern France, east of the Seine, came under Generalfeldmarschall Albert Kesselring's Luftflotte 2 with its headquarters at Brussels. Those based in northern France to the west of the Seine came under Generalfeldmarschall Hugo Sperrle's

*Generalfeldmarschall Albert Kesselring, the commander of Luftflotte 2 during the Battle of Britain.*

Luftflotte 3 with its headquarters at Paris. The relatively weak forces based in Denmark and Norway came under Generaloberst Hans-Juergen Stumpff's Luftflotte 5 with its headquarters at Oslo.

*Generalfeldmarschall Hugo Sperrle, right, the commander of Luftflotte 3 during the Battle of Britain. He is seen with officers of I./KG 51 during an inspection of the Gruppe. (Dierich)*

*Generaloberst Hans-Jurgen Stumpff, commander of Luftflotte 5 based in Norway.*

## LUFTWAFFE PROBLEMS

Some commentators have suggested that the Luftwaffe might have achieved decisive results had it begun large-scale operations against Britain immediately after the end of the Dunkirk evacuation. Then, it has been argued, the strength of RAF Fighter Command was at its nadir and the defences could have been overwhelmed. However, such a notion takes no account of the very real problems faced by the Luftwaffe at this time. During the six weeks of hard campaigning that had led up to the Armistice in France, German flying units suffered serious losses. These amounted to 459 fighters, 147 dive bombers and 635 twin-engined bombers, to which had to be added the many hundreds of planes damaged and unfit for immediate operations. The fighting had left the twin-engined bomber force particularly badly off and at the end of June many operational units had less than half their establishment of aircraft serviceable.

One replacement pilot joined the III. Gruppe of Kampfgeschwader 1, based at Rossiers in France, that July. He later recalled that instead of spending three months at his Ergaenzungskampfgruppe (bomber tactical training unit) he was there for only two days before he was summoned to the front-line unit. Out of the nine crews in his Staffel, six were newcomers like himself. The business of bringing the flying units up to full strength for the forthcoming battle placed a heavy training load on the operational Gruppen. The new crews needed time to learn to handle their aircraft effectively under combat conditions.

Meanwhile, the Todt Organisation put in hand a massive programme to prepare the newly captured airfields in France, Holland, Belgium and Norway for all-weather operations against Britain. The replenishment of the German flying units and the preparation and provisioning of their forward bases would occupy most of the three weeks between the end of the campaign in France and the middle of July. On 20 July, shortly after Luftflotten 2, 3 and 5 were brought to readiness for the attack on Britain, their strengths were as follows:

| LUFTFLOTTEN 2 AND 3 | STRENGTH | AIRCRAFT SERVICEABLE |
|---|---|---|
| *Long-range bombers* | 1,131 | 769 |
| *Dive bombers* | 316 | 248 |
| *Single-engined fighters* | 809 | 656 |
| *Twin-engined fighters* | 246 | 168 |
| LUFTFLOTTE 5 | | |
| *Long-range bombers* | 129 | 95 |
| *Twin-engined fighters* | 34 | 32 |

## FIGHTER COMMAND PROBLEMS

To meet this formidable array Air Chief Marshal Dowding had, on 9 July, a total of 48 operational squadrons of Spitfires, Hurricanes and Defiants with about

*Lieutenant A.G. Blake, one of the Fleet Air Arm pilots transferred to Fighter Command by the Admiralty in July 1940. He flew with No. 19 Squadron during the Battle of Britain and was credited with 6½ victories, but was killed near the end of the battle.*

600 serviceable aircraft. In addition there were six squadrons of Blenheims with about 50 serviceable aircraft of doubtful value during the day against escorted bombers. Four fighter squadrons were non-operational at this time; two were forming, one was re-forming and one was re-equipping. Thus the total number of single-engined fighter squadrons available to Dowding was little greater than that which, prior to the war, had been considered the minimum necessary to defend Britain against attacks by *unescorted* twin-engined bombers operating from bases in Germany.

Clearly, Fighter Command's strength fell far short of that necessary to meet the challenge now thrust upon it. Yet in the short term there was little prospect of any increase in its strength. Fighter production was running at a level sufficient to make good the losses likely to be suffered during a major battle: in May 325 single-engined fighters were delivered, with 446 in June and 496 in July. The limiting factor, however, was the shortage of trained pilots. There were three reasons for the shortage. First and foremost, the loss of nearly 300 fighter pilots killed, wounded or captured in the fighting in France and during the evacuation. Secondly, the over-rapid, if essential, expansion of the fighter force during the early months of the war had cut reserves to the bone. And thirdly, the output of fighter pilots from the training schools had been lower than expected, due partly to severe weather during the previous winter and partly to the diversion of resources from operational training units to the new fighter squadrons. An important and welcome acquisition for Fighter Command was the loan of fifty-eight trained pilots from the Royal Navy. These helped fill some of the gaps in the ranks of the operational squadrons. To form further fighter squadrons Dowding had to look to pilots trained beyond Britain's shores. One squadron of Canadians was nearly ready, and two with Polish pilots and a further two with Czech pilots were forming.

The German capture of airfields along the entire coastline from southern Norway to Brittany, from which the whole of the United Kingdom could be threatened with attack, forced Dowding to reposition forces to cover the newly threatened areas. By the third week in July his redeployment was complete. London and the south-east received the strongest defences: No. 11 Group with nineteen squadrons of single-engined fighters. The Midlands up to north Yorkshire was protected by No. 12 Group, with fourteen squadrons. Northern England and Scotland were the responsibility of No. 13 Group, with twelve squadrons. And south-western England and Wales were covered by the newly formed No. 10 Group, with seven Squadrons.

## The Opposing Fighter Types

Since the outcome of the forthcoming battle would depend on the ability of one side's fighters to overcome those of the other, it is of interest to consider the relative merits of the types involved. The bulk of the British day fighter squadrons were equipped with the Spitfire and the Hurricane, both powered by the Rolls Royce Merlin engine. The Luftwaffe fighter Gruppen were equipped with the single-engined Messerschmitt 109 and the twin-engined Messerschmitt 110, both powered by the Daimler Benz 601 engine. Up to 20,000 feet the Spitfire was faster than either German fighter. At ground level the Hurricane was as fast as the Messerschmitt 109, but as height increased it became inferior; up to 20,000 feet the Hurricane was faster than the Messerschmitt 110. In the climb the Spitfire had the edge over the Messerschmitt 109 up to 15,000 feet, though the latter was certainly superior to the Hurricane in this respect. Both British fighters could outclimb the Messerschmitt 110. Above 20,000 feet the German fighter types had a definite edge over the British types. At all levels, at speeds up to their maximum in horizontal flight, the British fighters were more manoeuvrable than those of the Germans. Set against this, however, if manoeuvres were attempted involving negative 'G' – for example nosing over into a dive – the float valve in the carburettor of the Merlin would shut off the fuel and the engine would cut out. The Daimler Benz, with direct fuel injection, did not suffer from this failing.

The Messerschmitt 109E was armed with two Oerlikon MG/FF 20-mm cannon and two Rheinmetall Borsig 7.9-mm machine-guns. The 110 also carried two cannon but had four fixed 7.9-mm machine-guns firing forwards and one firing rearwards for self-defence. The Oerlikon was a slow-firing cannon with a low muzzle velocity, and its performance was greatly inferior to the Hispano cannon under development for the RAF. On the other hand, the German weapon was considerably more reliable than the Hispano at this time. The Rheinmetall Borsig machine-gun was broadly comparable with the Browning. Although for the destruction of bombers, the German mixed cannon and machine-gun armaments were better than the battery of eight rifle-calibre machine-guns fitted to the British fighters, the low performance of the Oerlikon and the differing ballistics between it and the machine-gun meant it was inferior for the engagement of fighters. The Oerlikon had a slight theoretical range advantage over the Browning machine-gun. But in combat, firing against a turning target using a simple reflector sight, this advantage was illusory except for the few ace pilots who could judge the deflection angle correctly.

With self-sealing fuel tanks and armour being fitted to German bombers, Fighter Command had an urgent requirement for a cannon-equipped fighter. We have already seen that during its initial operational trials the Hispano cannon suffered severe teething troubles. By the summer of 1940, however, the installation was judged to be working well enough for an operational unit, No. 19 Squadron, to be issued with two-cannon Spitfires. Before this installation was put into large-scale production, Sir Hugh Dowding had to be certain that its faults had been eradicated and it was an improvement over what it replaced. As he wrote to the Secretary of State for Air, Sir Archibald Sinclair, on 24 July:

> The present situation is that the guns of about six Spitfires in No. 19 Squadron are working satisfactorily, and the defects in the others will probably be rectified in about a week or ten days.
>
> I quite realise that information concerning the fighting qualities of the cannon Spitfire is required as early as possible, and I will take the first opportunity of getting it into action; but I am not at all keen on sending it up against German fighters since it will be extremely badly equipped for that task . . . I say the cannon Spitfire is badly equipped to meet German fighters because it has only two guns and even the Me 109 has two cannon and two machine guns. Furthermore, it has fired off all its ammunition in five seconds.
>
> So you will see that the existing cannon Spitfire is not an attractive type, but it has been necessary to produce it as an insurance against the Germans armouring the backs of their engines. They have not done this yet, their engines are still vulnerable to rifle-calibre machine gun fire and, therefore, the eight gun fighter is a better general fighting machine than one equipped with two cannons only.

Technically, the solution would have been to use the cannon-fighters against bombers and those with machine-guns against fighters. But *tactically*, against escorted formations, this would be difficult to arrange. Whether it was necessary would depend on the success in battle of No. 19 Squadron compared with units flying fighters equipped only with machine-guns.

## AIR FIGHTING TACTICS

In terms of equipment and general flying training, the RAF and the Luftwaffe were fairly evenly matched. But for fighter-versus-fighter combat the close formation tactics employed by the RAF were deficient in several respects. Just how deficient, can be seen if they are compared with the German fighter tactics at this time.

Profiting from experience gained during the Spanish Civil War, the German fighter pilots had evolved a loose formation based on the 'Rotte', or widely spaced pair of aircraft. In the battle area the two aircraft flew almost in line abreast, with the leader slightly ahead, about 200 yards apart. Each pilot concentrated his search towards his partner, so that each covered the other's blind areas behind and below. In combat against enemy fighters it was the wingman's task to watch his leader's tail, so the latter could concentrate his attention on the enemy in front.

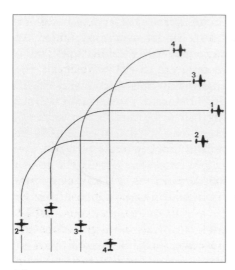

*The cross-over turn.*

Two Rotten made up a 'Schwarm' of four fighters, with the leading rotte one side and slightly ahead of the other. When searching for the enemy the Schwarm formation was approximately 600 yards wide, which meant that it was impossible for the aircraft to hold position in the formation during a tight turn at high speed. The answer was the 'cross-over' turn, in which all the fighters turned as tightly as they could and simply swapped sides in the formation. A 'Staffel' battle formation comprised twelve fighters in three Schwarm, either in line abreast or in line astern. To penetrate cloud, the formation would simply close up and open out again ready for battle when in clear skies.

Three factors should be considered when examining the effectiveness of a tactical formation for fighters. First, the ability of the formation to manoeuvre with cohesion. Secondly, the visual coverage of each aircraft's blind areas to prevent surprise attack. And thirdly, the ability of each aircraft to receive support if it came under attack. By each of these criteria, the loose German formation was greatly superior to the tight formation employed by the RAF.

Using the 'cross-over' turn, the Schwarm could turn as tightly as the individual aircraft; so could the Staffel. In the tight formation 'V's, on the other hand, the leader had to slacken his turn to allow for the minimum turning radius of the men on the inside. When opened out, the Schwarm allowed each pilot to spend most of his time searching for the enemy and covering his partner's blind areas. In the tight formation of 'V's only the squadron commander could spend time searching for the enemy, while his men were busy holding position behind him. The all-important rear sector went uncovered for much of the time. If an aircraft in a Schwarm was approached from behind by an enemy, the spacing of the aircraft was such that a simple turn would result in the attacker being 'sandwiched' between his intended victim and the aircraft next to it, with the latter in a firing position. If the rear section in a tight formation of 'V's was attacked, the action was usually over before it could receive help from any of the others.

When the air war hotted up in the late spring of 1940, it became clear that the RAF fighter tactics were inadequate. But now there was no time for any radical change. Fighter Command would have to fight its decisive battle making the best of the inflexible tactics in which its pilots had been trained. The 'V's were widened out slightly, to allow pilots to spend more time searching for the enemy instead of maintaining exact formation of their neighbours. And one section, led by an experienced pilot, was stationed about 1,000 feet above the formation and flew a weaving course keeping watch on the rear. These steps greatly improved the search and mutual support capabilities of the RAF fighter formations, though they did nothing to improve their ability to manoeuvre with cohesion. Fighter Command Tactical Memorandum No. 8, outlining the tactics recommended for use by day fighter squadrons within the Command, is given in full in Appendix C. Issued in June 1940, this memorandum was not superseded until November 1940, after the Battle of Britain ended.

## BATTLE MANAGEMENT

We have observed that the tactical formation in use in Fighter Command was much inferior to that used in the Luftwaffe. However, the tactical formation is only one aspect of air fighting tactics. Another element was the technique we now call 'Battle Management', and in this the RAF enjoyed a major advantage. Thanks to Air Chief Dowding's system of fighter control, his controllers could adjust their response to meet the changing tactical situation as this developed. Fighters could be concentrated to meet the enemy, and positioned up-sun and with an altitude advantage over the force they were to engage. In contrast, when a German fighter unit crossed the coast of England it was on its own, and its pilots knew only what they had been told at their briefing or what they or others in that unit saw and reported by radio.

## GROUND ANTI-AIRCRAFT DEFENCE SYSTEMS

The fighters would provide the primary means of defence for targets in Britain, but other forms of defence would also have a part to play. By the end of July there were twice as many heavy and light anti-aircraft guns available as at the beginning of the war: 1,280 heavy guns of all types were deployed (out of a 1939 requirement of 2,232) and there were 517 light guns (out of 1,860). Nevertheless, it can be seen that there was still a serious shortage, particularly in light anti-aircraft guns. As a temporary expedient, for the protection of targets likely to come under attack from low-flying aircraft, a few obsolete 3-inch heavy guns were deployed in the low-level air-defence role. These weapons were aimed without predictors, using open sights.

In a further effort to make up for the chronic shortage of light anti-aircraft guns, the unconventional Parachute-and-Cable device was pressed into service for the protection of airfields and important factories. The device consisted of a simple rocket, fired vertically to carry aloft a furled 38-inch diameter parachute connected to 480 feet of steel cable. At the other end of the cable was a bag containing a similar parachute, to which was connected a further small parachute to stabilise the wire during its upward travel. Fired when low-flying enemy aircraft were approaching the area, the rocket took about 5 seconds to position the top of the cable 600 feet above the ground. The rocket then fell clear, the upper parachute opened, and the erect cable fell slowly towards the ground. If the aircraft collided with the cable, the shock of the impact released the second, lower, drag parachute and the aircraft was left with both of them in tow.

Although these parachutes were much smaller than those fitted to the LZ balloon cables, they could still cause a lot of trouble. If the cable caught on

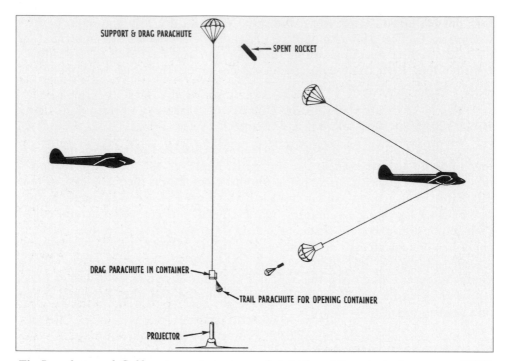

SUPPORT & DRAG PARACHUTE

SPENT ROCKET

DRAG PARACHUTE IN CONTAINER

TRAIL PARACHUTE FOR OPENING CONTAINER

PROJECTOR

*The Parachute-and-Cable system, set up at several airfields and factories in the summer of 1940 to provide a defence against low-flying raiders. The rockets were fired vertically upwards in salvoes of eight or nine in lines, with 60 feet between rockets, as the raiders approached. The rockets carried the top of the cable to a height of 600 feet, where a parachute opened to suspend the cable in the sky. If an aircraft collided with the hanging cable, the shock of impact released a second parachute and the aircraft was left to tow away the cable and the two parachutes. The system was acknowledged to be less efficient than the Bofors gun as a method of low-altitude defence, but insufficient of the latter were available.*

the wing there was a good chance that the asymmetric drag would cause the aircraft to fall out of control. Or, if it survived this, the latter's performance would be reduced to such an extent that it would probably fall as easy prey to fighters or anti-aircraft guns. The Parachute-and-Cable launchers were set up close to the target, in groups of twenty-five. Each group was subdivided into three banks, one bank with nine launchers and the other two banks with eight; the banks of rockets could be fired individually. The launchers in each bank were arranged in a line with 60 feet between them (the wingspan of a typical bomber). The second bank was positioned 10 feet behind the first, the third was positioned 10 feet behind the second. The rockets were fired electrically, by an operator in a control post close to the installation. During the summer of 1940 more than forty Parachute-and-Cable installations were laid out, the majority of them at fighter airfields.

The final part of the ground defences, the balloon barrage, was almost at full strength with a total of 52 squadrons with 1,466 balloons available at the end of July.

## THE CIPHER-BREAKERS PLAY THEIR PART

By the late spring of 1940, the British Government Code and Cipher School (GC and CS) at Bletchley Park was delivering a productive stream of information from decrypted German radio traffic. This source, code-named 'Enigma', provided many useful gems of information. However, during the Battle of Britain, it had only limited value for several reasons. First, only a small proportion of the signals could be read at this time. Secondly, the system was in its early stages and the decryption process often took several days. On several occasions, the operation referred to had taken place before the signal ordering it could be read. Thirdly, the signals referred to individual targets by their Luftwaffe target number, a four- or five-figure number, or by a code-word (*Logge* was London). It took a long time, and numerous air attacks, before the cipher-breakers were able to link a sizeable proportion of those numbers and code-words to actual targets. Fourthly, most high-level communications to and from Luftwaffe airfields in France, Holland and Belgium went by landline. The only notable exceptions were those units based at airfields in north-west France which had yet to be connected to the network. For much of the unfolding battle these units transmitted and received messages by wireless. From time to time the latter's signals were decrypted, but often there was no way of knowing whether the message referred to a limited part of the force or to all of it. Fifthly, orders for major operations were often delivered to flying units by courier. The cryptographers at Bletchley Park had often to derive what clues they could from the amendments to those orders, transmitted by radio.

## DISCOVERY OF KNICKEBEIN

At the beginning of the war there had been little concern in RAF intelligence circles that the Luftwaffe could launch effective night attacks. It was thought that the same darkness that hid the bombers from the defences would also hide the targets from the bombers. By the late spring of 1940 there were ominous signs that this comfortable assumption might not be justified. Dr R.V. Jones, head of the Air Ministry Scientific Intelligence Service, began to receive individually insignificant clues that pointed to some form of radio system that guided Luftwaffe bombers to their targets.

In March 1940 a paper found in the wreck of a Heinkel mentioned 'Radio

*Dr R.V. Jones, head of the Scientific Intelligence Service at the Air Ministry, who played a major part in the discovery of Knickebein.*

*The Knickebein beam transmitter at Stollberg in Schleswig Holstein, one of the first to be detected by British Intelligence. The aerial was about 100 feet high and was rotated on to the bearing of the target by railway bogies running on a track 315 feet in diameter.*

beacon Knickebein from 0600 hours on 315°'. Shortly afterwards a prisoner mentioned that Knickebein ('bent leg') employed a beam so narrow that it could reach from Germany to London without a divergence of more than 1 kilometre. This Jones found hard to believe: the distance from London to the nearest point in Germany was 260 miles, which meant that the beam had to be only one-seventh of a degree wide. If this was the case, the Germans had developed their beam technology far beyond anything that was possible in Britain. Not the least mysterious aspect of the puzzle was the fact that German aircraft examined by British intelligence appeared to carry no special equipment to receive beam signals. Jones made a careful study of the information known about German aircraft radio sets already captured. He noted that the Lorenz airfield blind-approach receiver carried by bombers was far more sensitive than necessary for its essentially short-range task. Could it be that the bomber crews were using the Lorenz receiver to pick up the beam signals?

On 5 June an 'Enigma' decrypt provided a further clue. The signal read: 'Knickebein at Kleve is confirmed [or established] at point 53°21 N, 1°W.' The coordinates gave a position near Retford, which suggested that the beams might have been laid on that point. On 18 June Jones received fresh evidence from the papers in a German bomber shot down in France some weeks earlier. These mentioned a Knickebein transmitter near Bredstedt in Schleswig Holstein and another near Kleve. The first seemed to tie in with Jones's first report in March, for a bearing of 315 degrees from Bredstedt pointed directly to Lerwick in the Shetland Isles, an area in which German bombers had been active. At almost the same time the radio operator's log from a shot-down Heinkel 111 was recovered intact and contained the entry 'Knickebein Kleve 31.5'. The Lorenz blind-approach receiver worked on three frequencies: 30, 31.5 and 33.3 megacycles, and

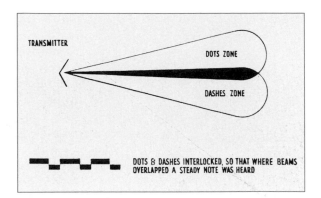

TRANSMITTER

DOTS ZONE

DASHES ZONE

DOTS & DASHES INTERLOCKED, SO THAT WHERE BEAMS OVERLAPPED A STEADY NOTE WAS HEARD

*The Knickebein beam.*

the paper had mentioned one of them. A further radio-operator's log captured on 20 June stated that the Knickebein at Stollberg (which was near to Bredstedt) had been radiating on 30 megacycles and that at Kleve was on 31.5 megacycles. Gradually the pieces in the jigsaw puzzle were beginning to fit together. But still Knickebein signals had yet to be identified.

By the morning of 21 June, when he was summoned to a meeting at 10 Downing Street with Mr Churchill in the chair, Jones was able to establish with reasonable certainty the positions and operating frequencies of two Knickebein transmitters. He put to the Prime Minister the evidence he had collected, and this convinced those present that here was a threat that had to be taken seriously. If the German bomber crews really could find targets at night or under conditions of bad visibility, they could 'outflank' Air Chief Marshal Dowding's carefully prepared system of day fighter defences.

That evening Flight Lieutenant H. Bufton and Corporal Mackie took off in an Anson from Wyton for the third of the special radio-monitoring flights over East Anglia to search for beam signals (two earlier flights had been unsuccessful, the first because of equipment failure and the second because the Luftwaffe was not operating). Shortly after 2200 hours, while Mackie was searching the frequency band between 30 and 33.3 megacycles, he found what he was looking for: at 31.5 megacyles a series of dots, sixty to the minute, piercingly clear in his earphones. As the Anson continued northwards the dots were heard to merge into a steady note signal. A little later, the note broke up, though not into dots but into dashes at the same steady rate of sixty to the minute. Bufton turned southwards to regain the steady note signal, then flew along it to determine its direction. After he landed Bufton reported:

1. There is a narrow beam approximately 400–500 yards wide, passing through a position one mile south of Spalding, having dots to the south and dashes to the north, on a bearing of 104° to 284° True.
2. That the carrier frequency on the night of 21–22 June was 31.5 Mc/s, modulated at 1150 c/s and similar to Lorenz in characteristics.

*Wing Commander E.B. Addison was appointed to command No. 80 Wing, the RAF unit formed in the summer of 1940 to counter the German beam systems.* (Addison)

The beam that Bufton and Mackie had found emanated from the Knickebein transmitter at Kleve. For reasons not entirely unconnected with the location of the Rolls Royce aero engine factory, it was aligned on Derby.

## FORMATION OF NO. 80 WING

The discovery of the Knickebein signals was the first and most important step in the battle to counter the system. Within hours Wing Commander Edward Addison received orders to set up a special jamming organisation to counter it, under the code-name 'Headache'. At the same time Dr Robert Cockburn, a young scientist who had joined the staff of the Telecommunications Research Establishment at Swanage a few weeks earlier, was given a team and told to begin work on the design and production of a special transmitter to jam Knickebein.

In addition to the task of running 'Headache', Addison's unit, designated No. 80 Wing, received a further commitment: the operation of the 'Meacon' system designated by Post Office engineers, to mimic navigational radio beacons. The German beacons radiated in all directions, and were quite different from the highly directional Knickebein beam transmitters. The Meacon was a subtle piece of knavery, and comprised a transmitter and a receiver. The receiver was fitted with a directional aerial set up to pick up only the emissions from the German beacon it was to mimic. When these emissions were picked up they were amplified, then passed by landline to the Meacon transmitter some distance away from which they were re-radiated *exactly in step with the emissions from the German beacon.*

If the German aircraft was nearer to the beacon than the Meacon, its radio compass would give bearings on the real beacon. If the aircraft was midway between the beacon

*Dr Robert Cockburn, who headed the team at the Telecommunications Research Establishment responsible for the design and development of jamming equipment.* (Cockburn)

and the Meacon, the needle of the radio compass would waver between the direction of the beacon and that of the Meacon. But if the bomber was nearer to the Meacon than to the beacon, the direction finder would give a beautifully steady, but quite misleading, bearing on the Meacon. And, unless they had established their position by other means, *the German crew would have no way of knowing that the bearing indicated was not that of the beacon selected.*

During the early summer of 1940 the hastily forming No. 80 Wing prepared to out-smart the German radio navigational systems. From his headquarters at Bentley Priory, Air Chief Marshal Dowding observed the German preparations unfolding for the expected all-out attack on Britain. The light probing attacks by night had begun early in June, then there was a lull of ten days before pressure resumed on the 17th.

## FIRST BLOOD TO THE NIGHT DEFENDERS

The Luftwaffe launched its first large-scale attack on inland targets in Great Britain on the night of 18/19 June 1940. Some seventy bombers from Kampfgeschwader 4 set out to attack the airfields at Leconfield and Mildenhall, oil storage tanks on Canvey Island and other targets.

Believing there was little to fear from night fighters, the raiders crossed the coast at altitudes below 10,000 feet and headed for their targets. It was a brilliant moonlit night with clear skies, however, and that made the bombers vulnerable. Several Blenheims, Spitfires and Hurricanes took off to engage the intruders. On patrol near Felixstowe, Flight Lieutenant 'Sailor' Malan of No. 74 Squadron caught a Heinkel 111 and promptly shot it down. The Spitfire pilot resumed his patrol and a few minutes later observed searchlight activity near Southend. He headed into the area, and soon afterwards saw a clutch of searchlights holding another Heinkel in their beams. Malan delivered an accurate attack and saw the bomber crash near Chelmsford.

Spitfires of No. 19 Squadron were also active, vectored to engage enemy aircraft reported in the Newmarket area. Flying Officer John Petre sighted a Heinkel and was closing in to engage, when suddenly he had to pull away to avoid a Blenheim going after the same bomber. Petre realigned himself on the intruder and opened fire. He saw his tracer rounds strike one of the engines, which immediately caught fire. At that moment, however, his own aircraft was lit up by a searchlight. That allowed the German rear gunner to get in an accurate burst, which set fire to the Spitfire's fuel tank. Petre bailed out of the fighter with severe burns to his face and hands. The battle continued until both the Blenheim and the Heinkel went down out of control and crashed.

Flight Lieutenant Wilfred Clouston, also from No. 19 Squadron, sighted yet another Heinkel illuminated by searchlights near Southend. It took 5 minutes to get into a firing position, but then his accurate bursts scored hits on both engines. The Heinkel crashed on land near the Thames Estuary. Elsewhere that night Blenheim fighters shot down a further Heinkel, and damaged another so seriously that it was wrecked during the crash landing near Calais. Altogether, the action cost the Kampfgeschwader six Heinkel 111s destroyed.

These early attacks caused little damage, but they resulted in a level of disruption out of all proportion to the size of the forces involved or the threat they posed. On the night of 24 June, for example, all districts south of the line Liverpool to Hull were alerted when only Bristol was threatened. On the following night the sirens sounded in practically all industrial areas apart from Lancashire, though only Stoke-on-Trent was under attack. Unless a dozen German bombers were to keep the whole of the United Kingdom awake and running for shelter night after night, a new policy regarding the sounding of sirens was essential. One was soon in operation. The War Cabinet decided that in future there was to be far greater caution in the sounding of sirens. The risk had to be accepted that the odd bomb would arrive unannounced. The effect of this decision was noticeable on the first night on which the new policy was put into operation, 26 June. The sirens sounded only in Middlesbrough, Ipswich, Norwich and Portsmouth, although there were as many German bombers over Britain as on the previous nights.

During the night of 26 June the defending squadrons fought another successful action. A Heinkel fell to the guns of Pilot Officers R. Smith and R. Marples of No. 616 Squadron. Flight Lieutenant H. MacDonald of No. 603 Squadron got another. A third bomber fell to Flying Officer A. Johnstone of No. 602 Squadron and Flying Officer Haig of No. 603 Squadron, possibly with some help from AA gunners.

The Luftwaffe learned its lesson from those costly early night attacks on Britain, however. Henceforth, bombers operating over the British Isles at night usually flew at altitudes above 10,000 feet, almost beyond the reach of the low-powered searchlights. There the raiders could operate with near impunity, though crews found it more difficult to find their targets and as a result the bombing was less accurate.

In the following weeks, Spitfires flew numerous night interception patrols. But never again would they repeat their earlier level of success. Often pilots flying these sorties had a hard fight against the elements, and sometimes the latter won. In the following account Flying Officer Trevor Wade of No. 92 Squadron described the problems he encountered during one such patrol:

> Soon after getting settled down on the patrol line over the Swansea area – marked, incidentally, by an invariably invisible triangle of lights at each end – 10/10ths cloud at about 8,000 feet and a thick ground haze up to 1,000 feet effectively cancelled out any idea of maintaining position.
>
> Having already warned Control that conditions were deteriorating, I felt fully justified in calling the whole thing off and repeating my request to be allowed to return to base, the first occasion on which I had done so having been turned down by higher authority. I might just as well have not wasted my time. My radio decided to go on strike, because whilst I could hear with ever-decreasing clarity the Controller's ever-increasing concern for my well-being, he could hear nothing. For me, very lost and very lonely, it was a very unsatisfactory state of affairs. After flying around for something like an hour on highly inaccurate reciprocal courses, I heard a faint and frantic voice suggest

that I steer south as there was some suggestion of a plot north of base. It soon became obvious that it must have been some other sucker.

By this time I had quite naturally lost faith in relying on communications with the ground, and resigned myself to putting in further night-flying practice in the optimistic hope of benefiting therefrom at a later date. Careful engine-handling enabled me to prolong the agony for a total of three-and-a-quarter hours. Not wanting to hasten my extinction by trying to crash land, left me with only one alternative – which I took. Before doing so, however, I ineffectively tried to get my own back with a final crack at the Controller.

So far as I know, nobody heard my 'Baling out: listening out'. Perhaps it was just as well.

## DEVELOPMENT OF AIRBORNE RADAR

By the summer of 1940, the work to produce an airborne radar suitable for night fighters was beginning to bear fruit. The new Mark III AI (Airborne Interception) radar, now in production, employed a transmitter that developed considerably more power than that of the earlier models. As a result, the maximum range was pushed up to over 3 miles; minimum range remained a problem, however, and was still about 300 yards. By the end of June a total of thirty-one Blenheim night fighters fitted with AI Mk III had been issued to squadrons.

The introduction of the radar-fitted night fighters did not bring any immediate increase in the efficiency of the night defences. Quite apart from the low performance of the equipment, it was unreliable in operation, spare parts and test

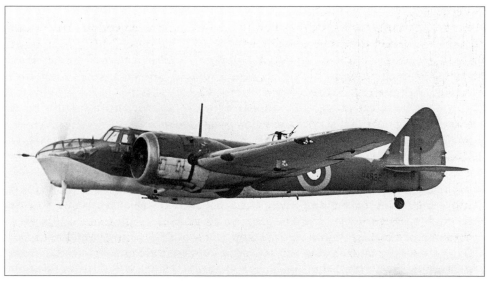

*Blenheim Mark IV fitted with pack to hold four .303-in machine-guns under the fuselage, and AI Mark III radar aerial protruding from the extreme nose. The performance of both the aircraft and the radar fell far short of what was needed to engage with enemy bombers.*

*The AI Mark III was the first night-fighter radar in the world to go into production. This photograph shows the indicator unit with the cathode-ray tubes (left) and the power unit (right), fitted into the radar operator's position in a Blenheim. Compare the crude appearance of this set with that of the later Mark VIII (page 170).*

equipment were either in short supply or non-existent and the training of personnel to operate and service the radar was poor.

Whether they carried radar or not, at this time the night fighters relied on searchlights to illuminate enemy aircraft for the initial contact. During the early night attacks on Great Britain many of the German bombers flew at altitudes below 10,000 feet; there searchlights guided by sound locators were fairly effective in illuminating them for night fighters or anti-aircraft guns to engage.

In none of the twenty-one night-fighter engagements during June did the AI radar play any great part. On the few occasions on which enemy aircraft were observed on the screens, the Blenheim was unable to get into a firing position. Not the least of the night-fighter's problems was the low performance of the AI-fitted aircraft. Burdened by the weight of the radar set and the crewman to operate it and suffering from the additional drag of the aerials, the Blenheim's

*Close-up of the nose-mounted transmitter aerial and the engine-mounted azimuth receiver aerials for AI Mark III on the Blenheim. The elevation receiver aerials were mounted above and below the port wing.*

maximum speed of about 225 mph was quite inadequate for its task. The ideal would have been a ground radar to guide the night fighter to within AI range of the target. But such a precision radar was close to the limits of technology in 1940 and was still some way from service. The Sector control system gave reporting errors of between 3 and 5 miles on enemy forces; by day this was sufficiently good to place a fighter formation within visual range of the enemy. By night, however, the 'area of uncertainty' was usually greater than the maximum range of the night fighter's radar and an interception was largely a matter of chance.

During July the Fighter Interception Unit at Tangmere, responsible for the development of tactics, began operational trials using Chain Home radar to provide information on incoming enemy night raiders. For the reasons outlined above, these operations usually proved frustrating for those involved.

On the night of 23 July, however, there was a rare combination of skill and luck when everything fell into place. Flying Officer G. Ashfield in one FIU Blenheim was patrolling over base at 10,000 feet when he received orders to intercept a small cluster of enemy aircraft about to leave the Sussex coast at 6,000 feet. Ashfield swung on to a southerly heading and pushed down his nose to increase speed. About 2 minutes later the Blenheim's radar operator, Sergeant R. Leyland, made contact with an enemy aircraft about a mile ahead, below and slightly to starboard. Leyland led Ashfield up to the enemy until finally the latter saw his prey silhouetted against the moon; it was a Dornier 17. The Blenheim closed on the bomber and at a range of 400 feet Ashfield opened fire with a long burst from his five machine-guns. The Dornier lurched to starboard and its nose dropped. But as the Blenheim tried to follow, its cockpit perspex was suddenly covered in opaque black oil from its victim. The British crew lost contact and turned on to a northerly heading for the coast, when suddenly a large blaze was observed on the surface of the sea. The pyre marked the end of a Do 17 of Kampfgeschwader 3.

As an historic event, the first-ever kill assisted by airborne radar, Ashfield's victory was significant. Technically, however, the radar-equipped night fighter still had some way to go before it could be considered fully effective as a fighting machine. It was clear that if, in the summer of 1940, the Germans were to launch massed night attacks against Britain's cities, the survival of the latter would depend more upon jamming the radio beams, rather than upon the deterrent effect of the fighter or anti-aircraft gun defences.

From the beginning of July there had also been a steady increase in the scale of the daylight air battles fought over the English Channel and the south coast of England. As well as bombing attacks on British convoys passing through the Channel, and ports along the south coast, the German fighter force launched *Freijagd* (free hunting) patrols over southern England to bring the RAF fighters into battle.

## ATTACKS ON THE COASTAL CONVOYS

As each side probed the strengths and weaknesses of its opponent, there were several scrappy actions. Typical of these was that on the afternoon of 13 July, as a small convoy passed through the Strait of Dover. As half a dozen Junkers 87s from Sturzkampfgeschwader 1 dived to bomb the ships, they came under attack from eleven Hurricanes of No. 56 Squadron. Major Josef Foezoe, leading a Staffel of Messerschmitt 109s from JG 51, described what happened next:

> Unfortunately for them [the Hurricanes], they slid into position directly between the Stukas and our close-escort Messerschmitts. We opened fire, and at once three Hurricanes separated from the formation, two dropping and one gliding down to the water smoking heavily. At that instant I saw a Stuka diving in an attempt to reach the French coast. It was chased by a single Hurricane. Behind the Hurricane was a 109, and behind that, a second Hurricane, all of the fighters firing at the aircraft in front. I saw the deadly dangerous situation and rushed down. There were five aircraft diving in a line towards the water. The Stuka was badly hit and both crewmen wounded, it crashed on the beach near Wissant. The leading Messerschmitt, flown by Feldwebel John, shot down the first Hurricane into the water, its right wing appeared above the waves like the dorsal fin of a shark before it sank. My Hurricane dropped like a stone close to the one that John had shot down.

No. 56 Squadron lost two Hurricanes destroyed and two damaged. Two Junkers 87s were seriously damaged; Jagdgeschwader 51 suffered no losses.

Nearly a week later, on 19 July, nine Defiant fighters from No. 141 Squadron scrambled from Hawkinge to engage an enemy force heading for another convoy. It was the first time the Defiant, with its unusual turreted armament, took part in the Battle of Britain. Near Folkestone Messerschmitt 109s from Jagdgeschwader 51 'bounced' the British two-seaters. The latter had not been designed for the rough-and-tumble of fighter combat, and they suffered accordingly. Attacking from behind and below, the Messerschmitts kept outside the Defiant's return fire, while the unwieldy two-seaters lacked the speed and the manoeuvrability to counter these tactics. Twelve Hurricanes from No. 111 Squadron went to the rescue of the Defiants, but they arrived in time only to save the turret fighters from complete annihilation. Of the nine Defiants only three survived, and one of those had been seriously damaged. Of the eighteen men in the Defiants, ten were killed and two wounded. Only one Messerschmitt was shot down.

Inexorably, the pace of fighting continued to accelerate. On 8 August there was a series of fierce air battles fought over convoy 'Peewit' in the Channel. The Ju 87 Stukas demonstrated the venomous efficiency of their attacks when there was no interference, sinking four and damaging six of the twenty ships in the convoy. In the course of these actions the Luftwaffe lost twenty-eight aircraft and Fighter Command lost nineteen.

## LESSONS LEARNED

In the 34-day period between 10 July and 10 August, the Luftwaffe lost 195 aircraft and Fighter Command lost 88. This gave a ratio of just over 2:1 in favour of the Royal Air Force. Yet this period had seen relatively small-scale actions, in which the average daily loss for both sides totalled only about a dozen aircraft. Neither air force had yet faced a real test.

For both sides there were clear lessons, however. Air Chief Marshal Dowding had carefully watched his system of fighter control as it underwent its baptism of fire, and was pleased with the results. On the other hand it was clear that his Defiant fighters could not survive in combat with enemy single-seaters. He ordered the two Defiant units to the north of the country where they would be safe from this hazard. A second lesson learned from the early engagements was that the German free-hunting fighter sweeps inflicted unacceptably severe losses on his fighters. Accordingly, he ordered Sector controllers to vector fighters to engage only those enemy formations thought to contain bombers. Whenever possible, the enemy fighter sweeps were to be left well alone. For its part, the Luftwaffe learned that unescorted bombers could expect short shrift if they were caught by British fighters.

On 2 August, the Luftwaffe High Command issued operational orders to Luftflotten 2, 3 and 5 for the all-out attacks intended to destroy RAF Fighter Command as an effective fighting force, and thus pave the way for the invasion should this prove necessary. The launch date was set, weather permitting, for 10 August. The code-name for the operation was 'Adler Tag' (Eagle Day). In the next chapter we shall follow the course of Fighter Command's grim fight for survival, against heavy odds.

# CHAPTER 3

# Striking at the Airfields, 11 August–6 September 1940

*Their force is wonderful, great and strong, yet we pluck their feathers by little and little.*

*Sir William Howard*, of the Spanish Armada, *1588*

The precise date of the opening of the Battle of Britain, the large-scale air attack by the Luftwaffe intended to subdue Fighter Command of the RAF, is stated differently in wartime British and German accounts. So far as the RAF was concerned the battle fought round convoy 'Peewit' on 8 August, with the large-scale dogfighting and heavy losses on both sides, appeared to mark the beginning of a new phase in the German air operations against Britain.

At Bletchley Park the decryption experts continued with the formidable task of trying to make sense of the random jumbles of letters arriving from the radio monitoring stations. By 9 August they had noted that several 'Enigma' decrypts bore references to the code-word 'Adler Tag'. But neither the signals themselves, nor any other intelligence source, indicated what 'Adler Tag' meant.

On 11 August the Luftwaffe launched its first large-scale daylight attack on a target in Britain. Following a series of feints by fighters in the Dover area, a force of about seventy Heinkel 111s and Junkers 88s, escorted by nearly a hundred Messerschmitt 109s and 110s, raided the naval base at Portland. Eight squadrons of Spitfires and Hurricanes were scrambled to intercept and in the ensuing action the Luftwaffe lost forty aircraft, the RAF twenty-six.

On 12 August there was a similar heavy attack, this time against Portsmouth, as well as subsidiary attacks by dive bombers against several targets including the Chain Home radar stations at Pevensey, Rye, Dover, Dunkirk (in Kent) and Ventnor. The radar stations were small pinpoint targets, however, and proved difficult to hit and even more difficult to put out of action for any length of time. Following hasty repairs, all the radar stations were operating the following day with the exception of Ventnor. 'Adler Tag', the code-name for the date of the opening of the full-scale air onslaught against Britain, had been provisionally set for 10 August. Then, due to poor weather, the attacks were delayed until the 13th. The earlier attacks, although they had seemed severe enough to the defenders, were but a prelude to the main thrust. It was only on 13 August that the battle, in German eyes, really began. On

*For the Battle of Britain many German Staffeln improvised new unit badges. This example was carried by the Dornier 17s of 2./KG 76. (KG 76 Archive)*

that day the Luftwaffe launched a total of 1,485 sorties against the British Isles, hitting the naval bases at Portland and Southampton as well as the airfields at Detling and Eastchurch. During the day's battles the Luftwaffe lost 19 bombers and 22 fighters in securing the destruction of 14 RAF fighters.

## THE HARDEST DAY

The almost daily battles of the six weeks that followed have been well documented elsewhere, and it is not my intention to describe every one in this account. Each action contained features unique to itself and it would be misleading to describe any of them as 'typical'. Nevertheless, the series of engagements fought on Sunday 18 August 1940 did fit well with the broad pattern of those of the initial phase of the battle, and will serve to illustrate the variety in the methods of attack employed by the German bomber force as well as the defensive tactics used by Fighter Command. We shall, therefore, now look at that day's events in some detail.

During this phase of the battle the Luftwaffe concentrated its main effort against the fighter airfields in southern England; the previous four days had seen large-scale attacks on several of these. On 18 August the Luftwaffe began its activities shortly after dawn, with a series of high-level reconnaissance sorties by individual aircraft. The German High Command needed to know the weather situation over Britain, the whereabouts of convoys moving off the coast and which Fighter Command airfields were active.

Fighter Command's day began early too, as fighters took off to mount standing patrols over the convoys moving through exposed waters to the south and east of England. At about 0700 hours a flight of Hurricanes of No. 257 Squadron had a brush with a Dornier 17 near the convoy they were escorting off Harwich, but the German aircraft escaped without damage. During the mid-morning period No. 11 Group scrambled elements of five squadrons to engage the reconnaissance

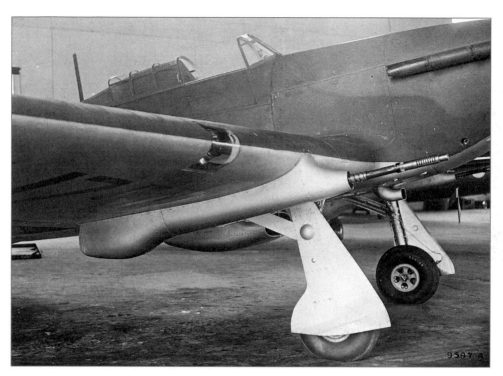

*The sole cannon-Hurricane to take part in the Battle of Britain, serial L1750, was issued to No. 151 Squadron. On 13 August Flight Lieutenant R. Smith shot down a Dornier 17 of KG 2 while flying this aircraft.*

*Rapid turn-around of a Spitfire of No. 19 Squadron during the Battle of Britain. The empty ammunition boxes, recently removed, are on the ground. The full ones waiting to replace them are on the carrying rack in front of the starboard wheel.*

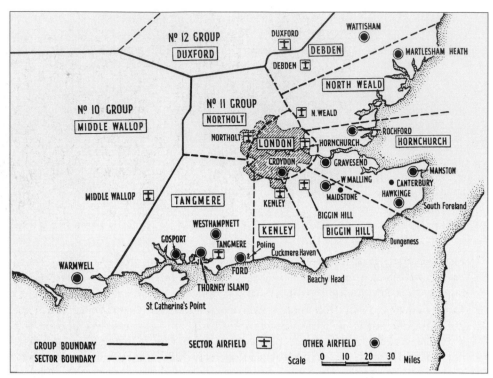

*No. 11 Group and Sector areas, and targets attacked on 18 August 1940.*

aircraft. The only victory went to the Spitfires of No. 54 Squadron which caught a Messerschmitt 110 of Lehrgeschwader 2, at 31,000 feet to the north-east of Manston and shot it down.

The uneasy quiet lasted until shortly after noon, when the Chain Home radar stations in Kent began observing enemy activity building up over northern France. By 1227 hours the Fighter Command Filter room at Stanmore was issuing plots on '60 plus' enemy aircraft near St Omer and '24 plus' to the north of Abbeville. To meet this threat the duty controller at the No. 11 Group operations room at Uxbridge, Wing Commander Lord Willoughby de Broke, now disposed his forces: No. 501 Squadron's Hurricanes were to scramble from Hawkinge and patrol in the Folkestone area; Nos 54 and 56 Squadrons, respectively with Spitfires at Manston and Hurricanes at North Weald, were to patrol between Canterbury and Maidstone; and No. 65 Squadron's Spitfires were ordered from Rochford to patrol the line Manston to Canterbury. Seven other squadrons, three from the Biggin Hill sector, two from Kenley and one each from the North Weald and Debden sectors, were ordered into position to protect their airfields.

This early disposition of the defending fighters was essential if they were to engage bombers attacking from high altitude. With their airfields under continual attack the fighters had to be dispersed round the perimeter in their blast pens.

*Major Adolf Galland, commander of III./JG 26, seated second from left without hat, discussing the next missions with his officers at Caffiers.*

This meant that, allowing time for the pilots to climb in, start up, taxi out and take off, a squadron took about 4 minutes to get airborne. Including this time, from the scramble order a squadron of Spitfires required a minimum of 17 minutes to reach 20,000 feet, while a squadron of Hurricanes required 20 minutes. During these times a formation of German bombers cruising at 190 mph covered 54 or 63 miles respectively, the distance from St Omer to almost the centre of Kent. So, with the warning provided by radar, there was just sufficient time to get the fighters into position to intercept the bombers before they reached inland targets. Because the fighters climbed with a forward speed of about 160mph, it took no longer to reach a position 35 miles from base at 20,000 feet than it took to spiral to overhead base at the same altitude.

The vanguard of the German attacking force comprised a series of freelance hunting patrols by fighters. Leading one of these was Oberleutnant Gerhard

*Heinkel 111s of Kampfgeschwader 55 flying in a typical Gruppe formation as used during the Battle of Britain. A Gruppe was established at thirty aircraft, so at 70 per cent serviceability twenty-one were available for any one attack. The aircraft of the Gruppe Stab unit flew at the head of the formation, followed by those of the three constituent Staffeln. The twin-engined bomber units were based deep in France and assembled in formation close to the ground, before climbing away on course for the target. They were almost invariably at attack altitude before reaching the French coast and did not, as many British accounts have stated, 'form up in full view of the British radar'. (Dierich)*

*When they came under attack by fighters, the German bombers closed formation to concentrate their defensive fire. This photograph, taken from an He 111 of KG 1, shows how close they then flew.*

Schoepfel of the III. Gruppe of Jagdgeschwader 26. As he crossed the coast in his Messerschmitt 109 Schoepfel sighted the Hurricanes of No. 501 Squadron climbing out of Hawkinge. Afterwards he reported:

> Suddenly I noticed a *Staffel* of Hurricanes underneath me. They were using the English tactics of that period, flying in close formation of threes, climbing in a wide spiral. About 1,000 metres above I turned with them and managed to get behind the two covering Hurricanes, which were weaving continually. I waited until they were once more heading away from Folkestone and had turned northwestwards and then pulled round out of the sun and attacked from below.

*This well-known photograph shows a pair of Hurricanes of No. 501 Squadron during a scramble take-off from Rochford on 15 August. It is of interest to this account because these particular Hurricanes, serials P3059 and P3208, were two of the four shot down by Oberleutnant Gerhard Schoepfel of III./JG 26 on the morning of 18 August. (IWM)*

With two rapid bursts Schoepfel dispatched both weavers, unnoticed by their comrades maintaining tight formation below. With its weavers gone, No. 501 Squadron was almost naked and Schoepfel made the most of his opportunity. With his wing-man guarding his tail he pulled into position behind the rear vic of Hurricanes and put a short burst into one of them; it blew apart. And still the remainder of the formation flew on. Schoepfel continued:

> The Englishmen continued on, having noticed nothing. So I pulled in behind a fourth machine and took care of him but this time I went in too close. When I pressed the firing button the Englishman was so close in front of my nose that pieces of wreckage struck my 'windmill'. The oil from the fourth Hurricane spattered over my windscreen and the right side of my cabin so that I could see nothing. I had to break off the action.

*Gerhard Schoepfel pictured later in the war, after his award of the Ritterkreuz.*

Within a space of 4 minutes Schoepfel had knocked out a third of a squadron of Hurricanes, killing one pilot and wounding three others. It was a clear illustration of the failings of the RAF system of depending upon two aircraft as lookouts while the remaining pilots concentrated on holding formation.

No. 501 Squadron's losses were seen avenged, however. A few minutes afterwards the Hurricanes of No. 56 Squadron bounced Messerschmitt 110s of

*Messerschmitt 110 long-range fighters of 1st Gruppe ZG 26.*

*A Dornier 17 of the low-level attack unit 9./KG 76, with the unit's badge under the cockpit. At the base of the nose can be seen the 20-mm cannon carried by aircraft of this Staffel.* (Raab)

II./ZG 26 near Ashford, and shot down four in short order. One of the successful pilots was Flying Officer P. Weaver, who afterwards reported:

> I was leading No. 2 Section and was put into line astern by the Squadron Leader. I observed approximately five Me 110s below us in a defensive circle and singled one out and attacked. I fired for about six seconds and broke away when smoke and bits poured from the starboard engine. I then observed an Me 110 below me and chased it down to about 3,000 feet, full throttle and 12 pounds boost. I eventually closed to 200 yards and as the enemy aircraft was taking evasive action I fired short bursts, with and without deflection. My guns finished firing, the enemy aircraft went into a steep right hand turn and then dived vertically into the ground, bursting into flames, about 8 miles south of Ashford, on the northern bank of the canal.

At 1250 hours the phalanx of bombers 27 Do 17s and 12 Ju 88s of KG 76, followed by 60 He 111s of KG 1, began crossing the coast between South Foreland and Dungeness and headed north-westwards for the fighter airfields at Kenley and Biggin Hill respectively. The four RAF fighter squadrons deployed forwards fought a series of inconclusive engagements around the bombers, but for the most part were unable to penetrate the screens of escorting fighters.

While the defender's attention was distracted by its 'right hook', Luftflotte 2 attempted to slip a 'straight left' to Kenley. Streaking across the Channel, so low that the slipstream of the aircraft left wakes across the surface of the sea, came nine Dornier 17s of the 9. Staffel of KG 76. Flown by crews specially trained for low-level attacks, these Dorniers were fitted with extra armour and a nose-mounted 20-mm cannon. With Staffelkapitaen Hauptmann Roth in the leading aircraft, the bombers crossed the coast at Cuckmere Haven at 1300 hours and continued northwards, so close to the ground that pilots had to ease their aircraft up to clear tall trees.

*The Dornier 17s of 9./KG 76 approaching the south coast of England only a few feet above the waves at midday on 18 August. In the background can be seen the Seven Sisters cliffs and Beachy Head. (Raab)*

In previous operations during the Battle of France these low-flying tactics had enabled the Dorniers to maintain the element of surprise right to the target. On this occasion, however, they were unlucky. The Observer Corps posts in the south of England were as vigilant as ever and even before the bombers crossed the coast, Post K3 situated on Beachy Head had reported their approach. The details were passed to No. 2 Observer Group Headquarters at Horsham, and from there to Headquarters No. 11 Group and the Sector operations room at Kenley. As the raiders penetrated inland and other posts' reports came in, the threat to Kenley became clear.

In the operations room at Kenley the duty controller, Squadron Leader Anthony Norman, moved rapidly to meet the new threat. Kenley's own fighter squadrons, Nos 64 and 615, were already airborne to meet the high-level attack

*Do 17 of 9./KG 76 heading inland for Kenley, soon after crossing the coast. The town in the background is Seaford.*

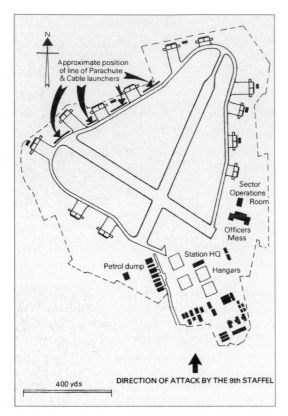

*Kenley was representative of the more important Fighter Command airfields during the Battle of Britain. The two 800-yard runways had been built early in 1940. At the same time twelve dispersal revetments were constructed off the taxi-track; each revetment could hold three fighters, enabling the airfield to accommodate two squadrons each with eighteen aircraft.*

approaching from the south–east. At nearby Croydon, however, there were the twelve Hurricanes of No. 111 Squadron, waiting at cockpit readiness. Normally it was the Group controller's responsibility to order fighters off the ground, and they came under the Sector controller's jurisdiction only when airborne. But with a possible attack on one of the Sector stations only minutes away Norman had no time to ask questions. He ordered No. 111 Squadron to scramble immediately and position over Kenley at 3,000 feet.

While the fighters were starting up and moving out of their dispersals at Croydon, Kenley's own ground defences prepared for action. The airfield's main anti-aircraft defence comprised four modern 40-mm Bofors guns, plus two obsolescent 3-inch heavy guns modified to engage low-flying aircraft. In addition, dotted round the airfield, were eight First World War Lewis machine-guns mounted to engage either a low-flying aircraft or enemy troops.

Finally, along the northern side of the airfield, was a Parachute-and-Cable installation with twenty-five launchers. It was a motley collection of weapons. Whether they were enough to inflict high attrition on a force of bombers attacking at low level would soon be put to the test.

At Kenley it was a warm and sunny day, with a light breeze from the south-west and good visibility. The gunners swung their barrels round to the south, where their field of fire against low-flying aircraft was restricted by the main body of airfield buildings and lines of high trees. Now it was a question of waiting for the enemy to come to them.

As they passed over Godstone, 4 miles to the south of Kenley, the Dorniers climbed to clear the southern face of the North Downs. In front, partially hidden by the trees, the German crews glimpsed the tops of the airfield's hangars. They were within 1 minute of their target and, thanks to their low-level approach, they

*Kenley under attack, taken from one of the low-flying Dorniers. In one of the dispersal revetments stood a Spitfire of No. 64 Squadron. The building under attack on the left of the photograph was a pill-box, from which the defenders had been firing at the German bombers. The photographing aircraft had just flown over the line of Parachute-and-Cable launchers and was about to cross the northern boundary of the airfield. Just visible to the right of the picture are the chimneys of 'Highleigh', the house in whose grounds Oberleutnant Ahrends's aircraft crashed.*

had penetrated 40 miles into enemy territory without interference from the defences. The nine Dorniers were drawn up in three vics of three with Roth in the leading aircraft. As the airfield swung into view the formation loosened with each pilot going for his own target. Then the defending gunners opened up.

With stunning suddenness, the sky round the German bombers was criss-crossed with streaking tracer rounds. Almost immediately Oberleutnant Ahrends's Dornier, at the head of the port vic, suffered a direct hit on the nose from either a Bofors or a 3-inch shell. It curved to starboard out of control. Leading the starboard vic, Oberleutnant Magin was mortally wounded by machine-gun fire from the ground and his observer, Oberfeldwebel Illg, had to lean over him and take the controls.

Each Dornier was loaded with twenty 110-pound bombs, delayed action fused to allow the bombers to get clear before they went off. To give their safety

*Hauptmann Roth (right), the commander of 9./KG 76, with Oberleutnant Lamberty; these two officers flew in the leading aircraft during the low-level attack on Kenley on 18 August. (Raab)*

mechanisms time to operate, the minimum release altitude was 45 feet. Some using their 20-mm cannon to reply to the ground fire, the Dorniers rose to this level and began releasing their bombs. Flying on the extreme port side of the formation, Unteroffizier Guenther Unger had lined up on one of the hangars and his observer was about to let go of the bombs when a burst of Lewis gun fire thudded into his starboard engine. He shut down the engine and struggled to hold his Dornier straight, as the bombs were released in a long stick.

Crouching in the Parachute-and-Cable firing position on the northern side of the airfield, Aircraftsman D. Roberts fingered his firing button. He later reported:

*The Dornier flown by Roth and Lamberty lying in a stubble field at Leaves Green, 6 miles from Kenley, after being set on fire by the ground defences at the airfield.*

I observed twin-engined aircraft flying at a height of about 50 feet over the hangars and as I saw them they released bombs which appeared to drop directly on the hangars. The aircraft them came in a straight line across the landing field slowly gathering height with three of them heading directly for my line of rockets. One was leading, with two others following in 'V' formation. They all seemed to be machine gunning the ground defences. When the leading aircraft was within range I released my first line of 9 rockets and saw it [the aircraft] fly directly into the cables.

It is possible that the leading Dornier, Roth's, was struck by one of the soaring rockets; at about this time one of his fuel tanks was pierced and almost immediately the leaking fuel caught fire. Feldwebel Wilhelm Raab, flying the aircraft immediately to Roth's starboard, was horrified to see the vertical grey columns of smoke from the rockets rising in front of him. He had no idea what they could be, but instinctively he wrenched into a steep bank to starboard to avoid one of the smoke trails. He did not succeed, and felt his aircraft yaw violently as his port wing struck something yielding, then swing back as it pulled itself free. (When he got back to France Raab had difficulty in convincing his superiors that he had indeed struck a 'rocket driven cable'. Only after engineers had examined the dents and scratches on the leading edge of his port wing was the story confirmed.)

Ahrends's Dornier, curving across the airfield out of control, also struck one of the cables and this put an end to the agony. The mortally wounded bomber smashed into trees. The crew of four, together with a war correspondent, were all killed.

As the Dorniers were beginning their bombing runs, the Hurricanes of No. 111 Squadron caught up with them. Flight Lieutenant S. Connors, leading the squadron, went straight into the attack with his flight but was immediately shot down by anti-aircraft fire. (The Kenley Operations Record Book states that the airfield was attacked by 'nine Do 17s and an Me 109'. German crews questioned

*Do 17 of I./KG 76 shot down by Pilot Officer Alan Eckford of No. 32 Squadron on 18 August, going down with one engine on fire. The plane crashed near Oxted.*

on the action are adamant that there were no escorting fighters, and it is almost certain that the 'Me 109' was Connors's Hurricane.) The Dorniers pulled clear of the airfield after attacking and swung starboard for home, the Hurricanes in hot pursuit. Sergeant W. Dymond led Yellow Section after Roth's already blazing aircraft and after a series of attacks it crashed at Leaves Green, a little over a mile from the airfield at Biggin Hill. The proximity of the crash of Roth's aircraft to Biggin Hill led, in some published accounts, to statements that 9./KG 76's low-level attack was against that airfield. In fact, a search of contemporary records reveals no evidence of any low-level attack on Biggin Hill on 18 August. Just before the Dornier struck the ground the local Home Guard unit loosed off a few rounds at it, and some accounts written at the time suggested the riflemen were responsible for bringing it down. It is almost certain, however, that their fire added little if anything to the already severe damage inflicted on this aircraft. Roth and the four-man crew survived the crash, though all suffered burns or other injuries.

Hugging the ground more closely than ever, the retreating Dorniers dodged in and out of trees, barns and houses – anything that would give fleeting cover from the angry Hurricanes. Guenther Unger, nursing his bomber back on one engine, was soon left behind by his comrades and was singled out for attack. He later recalled:

At first they tried attacking from the sides, where my armament was weakest. But by sticking very low, and dodging behind trees and buildings, I was able to make things very difficult for them. Then one of the fighters came in from behind and I felt the impact of his bullets against my wings and fuselage. I struggled to keep the Dornier as low as I could and make the most of the available cover, while my engineer and wireless operator returned the fire. Suddenly he came roaring past us; streaming black smoke the fighter pulled up and the pilot baled out.

*Taken from one of the high-flying Dorniers of KG 76 within a few minutes of the low-level attack by the 9. Staffel, this photograph shows: 1, aircraft parked on the apron; 2, hangars burning; 2a, Ahrends's Dornier burning on the ground; 3, bomb craters on one of the runways.*

Following the action, Sergeant Harry Newton of No. 111 Squadron reported:

Green 2 saw a Dornier 17 flying south from Kenley aerodrome and I dived on it from a height of 5,000 feet. I fired a 5-second burst from dead astern and above closing to 50 yards. I could see my tracers entering the front of the fuselage. A cannon [shell] must have burst on my starboard petrol tank. [In fact the 20-mm cannon fitted to Unger's Dornier could fire only downwards and forwards and was not used against the Hurricane] and my aeroplane caught fire. I managed to climb to 700 feet and turn on my back and bale out.

*One of the hangars of Kenley, wrecked during the attack on 18 August.* (IWM)

*Hurricane of No. 615 Squadron seriously damaged during the attack on Kenley.*

Unused to engaging bombers flying at such low altitudes, the fighter pilots found it difficult to pick out the camouflaged Dorniers against the background of fields. Moreover, the German gunners were able to reply with considerable effect, shooting down another of the No. 111 Squadron Hurricanes and causing a third to crash land. Two RAF pilots were wounded.

Unger managed to shake off the pursuit, but over the Channel his remaining engine failed and he was forced to ditch. Several hours later, close to death from exposure, he and his crew were rescued by a German minesweeper. One further Dornier came down in the Channel after being shot up by fighters and its crew was rescued later. The remaining five Dorniers reached France, four with serious damage or wounded crewmen which forced them to make emergency landings as soon as possible. Thus, of the nine Dornier 17s of 9./KG 76 that had taken off from Cormeilles-en-Vexin to attack Kenley, only one returned there.

While the survivors of the low-level attacking force struggled to escape from the Hurricanes of No. 111 Squadron, the high-level raiders bombed Kenley, West Malling, Biggin Hill and Croydon. Fighting a pitched battle to defend their airfields, RAF fighters shot down two Do 17s, two Ju 88s and an He 111, and caused damage to two Do 17s, a Ju 88 and an He 111. The German escorts defended their charges vigorously, however. No. 615 Squadron from Kenley lost four Hurricanes in rapid succession.

As the last of the raiders withdrew, it became clear that Kenley had been hit hard. More than a hundred bombs had struck the airfield and its buildings. Miraculously, in view of the scale of the attack, only nine station personnel were killed and ten wounded. The runways were cratered in four places and there were six craters in the taxi tracks and the dispersal pens. Kenley's fighters airborne

*The semi-revetted Sector operations building at Kenley, looking much as it did during the Battle of Britain. Some published accounts have stated that the building was demolished during the attack on 18 August. This was not so, as this 1975 photograph shows.*

diverted to Croydon and Redhill. Three out of the four hangars were wrecked. Six Hurricanes, a Blenheim and four training aircraft were destroyed on the ground, three Spitfires and one training aircraft were damaged. Thirty vehicles were destroyed and several airfield buildings were struck, including the station headquarters, the sick quarters and the officers' and sergeants' messes. The all-important Sector operations building was not damaged, but landlines to and from it were severed and the direction of fighters was made impossible. The standby operations room in the nearby town of Caterham was opened and, after a short hiatus, took control of fighter operations in the Kenley Sector. The airfield was out of action while men of the Royal Engineers filled in the more obstructive craters. Just an hour after the attack, a runway was made good for limited operations and within 2 hours the airfield was serviceable again. Twenty-four unexploded bombs were rendered harmless. West Malling, Croydon and Biggin Hill suffered less heavily and were able to continue operating.

Short of destroying every raiding aircraft, anti-aircraft gun defences cannot prevent a determined a low-level attack. All they can do is inflict losses so serious that such attacks are not repeated often. In this the makeshift anti-aircraft defences of Kenley were successful. In a dramatic demonstration of the power of gun defences against low-flying aircraft they shot down one Dornier, inflicted near-fatal damage to another, caused damage to a third (Unger's) which resulted in it ditching, and inflicted lesser amounts of damage to other aircraft of 9./KG 76.

So much had happened, yet the day's action had only just begun. By 1400 hours Chain Home radar stations along the coast of Hampshire and Dorset were passing plots on three incoming enemy formations: '80 plus' to the north of Cherbourg, '20 plus' to the east of Cherbourg and '10 plus' to the north-west of Le Havre. Luftflotte 3 was launching its major attack of the day.

The raiding force comprised 109 Junkers 87 dive bombers, drawn from all three Gruppen of Sturzkampfgeschwader 77 and the I. Gruppe of StG 3. Their targets were the airfields at Thorney Island, Ford and Gosport and the radar station at Poling near Littlehampton. This was by far the heaviest attack on Britain by Ju 87 dive bombers and the fighter escort was correspondingly strong: 157 Messerschmitt 109s drawn from JG 2, JG 27 and JG 53.

As the plots on the raiders were marked on the operations rooms' tables, the Hurricanes of No. 601 Squadron were already airborne on standing patrol over their base at Tangmere. Within minutes other squadrons were roaring off the ground to join them: No. 213 Squadron, with Hurricanes, from Exeter to patrol over St Catherine's Point; No. 152, with Spitfires, from Warmwell to patrol over Portsmouth; No. 43, with Hurricanes, from Tangmere to patrol over Thorney Island; No. 602, with Spitfires, from Westhampnett to patrol overhead base and No. 234 Squadron, with Spitfires, from Middle Wallop to intercept the raiders near the Isle of Wight.

The German formations reached the coast shortly after 1400 hours, having

*Sergeant Herbert Hallowes was one of the pilots who flew Hurricanes with No. 43 Squadron during the massacre of the Ju 87s attacking Thorney Island. He is seen here later in the war, after he had been commissioned.* (IWM)

earlier split into two forces; the westerly force made for Gosport, the easterly one made for Thorney Island, Ford and Poling. As intended, No. 234 Squadron was the first to intercept. It attacked the westerly force off the Isle of Wight but found its way to the dive bombers effectively blocked by the Messerschmitt 109s of JG 27. During the ensuing dogfight, however, the Squadron's Spitfires shot down five Messerschmitts without loss to themselves. In the meantime, the twenty-two Ju 87s of I./StG 3 carried out a set-piece attack on Gosport and withdrew without loss.

The dive bombers of the more easterly force were not so fortunate. Near Selsey Bill they were attacked by nineteen Hurricanes of Nos 43 and 601 Squadrons before their escorts could intervene. Sergeant Herbert Hallowes of No. 43 Squadron afterwards reported:

I followed Blue Leader in line astern but lost sight of him as we engaged the enemy. I caught up with one formation of five Ju 87s in line astern, opened fire at about 300 yards, two people baled out of number five aircraft and a further two from number four machine, both aircraft going into a vertical dive about three to four miles east of Thorney Island. I then carried out a quarter attack on a third Ju 87 without any apparent result. Observing another 87 at about

*A Junkers 87B of Sturzkampfgeschwader 77, the unit that suffered heavily during the action on 18 August.* (Schmid)

200 feet which had released its bombs on Thorney Island, I came up into a position astern and gave it three short bursts; I was closing too fast and had to break away to the right, coming in again for a beam attack on the same machine which broke in two, just in front of the tail fin, and fell in the Solent about half way between the mainland and the Isle of Wight . . .

As the escorting Messerschmitts realised what was going on and dived to defend their charges, the Spitfires of No. 602 Squadron joined the fray. The outcome was a free-for-all around the Junkers 87s, which were themselves engaged in dive bombing their targets.

Oberleutnant Otto Schmidt of I. Gruppe of StG 77 later recalled that after planting his bombs on the hangars at Thorney Island, he pulled out of his dive and levelled off, looking for his comrades:

*Ju 87 shot down by RAF fighters at West Broyle near Chichester, 18 August.*

I noticed the scattered wreckage of an aircraft in the mirror calm Channel – and then behind me, looming ever larger, was a Spitfire trying to get into a firing position. I had to act fast to get out of his way – and turning would not have saved me. So I sideslipped – a tricky manoeuvre for a Junkers. She came out of the slip and the attacking fighter was foiled.

I looked around at my radio operator. He was hanging forward in his straps and his machine gun was pointing aimlessly into the sky. I didn't realise that either he or the aircraft had been hit. In the meantime the Spitfire had turned again and was coming in for another attack. It was quite obvious that he had selected me for his personal target! In that short breathing space, however, I had time to gather my senses and when he came in again I knew what to do. He must have seen my helpless gunner, since he made for my tail; but I sideslipped again and he went screaming past. Then something else happened. One of my comrades low down suddenly plunged into the sea and disappeared, while yet another Ju 87 was shot down – I remember he bounced on the surface of the sea, then disappeared.

Schmidt managed to shake off his pursuer and landed at Caen; afterwards ground crewmen counted more than eighty bullet holes in his Junkers. His gunner, seriously wounded, was rushed to hospital but died a few weeks later.

At Gosport the dive bombers caused heavy damage, with many buildings wrecked and two hangars struck; four aircraft were destroyed and five damaged. At Thorney Island two hangars were wrecked, one aircraft destroyed and one damaged. The radar station at Poling was put out of action for a week. While the repair work was taking place, a mobile station was set up to fill the gap in the radar cover. The airfield at Ford was hardest hit of all. This second-line station was engaged in training Fleet Air Arm crews. Thirteen Shark, Swordfish and Albacore torpedo bombers were destroyed and a further twenty-six planes were damaged. Two hangars, the petrol and oil installations, the motor transport hangar, two stores buildings and numerous accommodation buildings were wrecked. Twenty-eight people were killed and seventy-five wounded.

In achieving this, however, Sturzkampfgeschwader 77 had paid a fearful price. Fourteen dive bombers were shot down, four were damaged beyond repair and a further four returned with lesser hits. Ten of the aircraft shot down and two of those damaged beyond repair had come from the I. Gruppe. General Baron Wolfram von Richthofen, the commander of Fliegerkorps VIII of which StG 77 was part, later commented in his diary: 'A *Stukagruppe* has had its feathers well and truly plucked.' The action marked the virtual end of the Ju 87's career over Britain. During the dogfight around the dive bombers, eight Messerschmitt 109s were shot down for the loss of four Spitfires and two Hurricanes.

By 1500 hours the plotting tables at the RAF Sector operations rooms showed the central Channel area clear of enemy movement, and once again the focus of action shifted to the Straits of Dover. A dozen Messerschmitt 109s ('identified' at the time as Heinkel 113s) carried out a strafing attack on the airfield at Manston, during which they destroyed two Spitfires and damaged six more of No. 266 Squadron, killed one ground crewman and wounded fifteen others. At the same time one of the Dover barrage balloons was shot down by German fighters. There was a lull for nearly an hour, then came the familiar activity behind Calais that always presaged heavy attacks.

In the late afternoon the Luftwaffe launched its third major attack of the day. Fifty-eight Dorniers of KG 2 and fifty-one Heinkels of KG 53 headed, respectively, for the important fighter airfields at Hornchurch and North Weald. Escorting the bombers were about 150 Messerschmitts.

The first signs of the build-up came at 1620 hours, when the Chain Home stations reported '20 plus' enemy aircraft between St Omer and Boulogne. A quarter of an hour later other activity was seen south of Cap Gris Nez. On the British side the No. 11 Group controller took the usual advance action to protect his forward airfields: Nos 501 and 54 Squadrons were scrambled, with orders to patrol over their bases at Hawkinge and Manston respectively.

By 1700 hours it was clear that two separate attacking forces were advancing towards targets north of the Thames Estuary. Seven squadrons of Hurricanes were ordered up: No. 56, from Rochford, to intercept the force approaching Clacton; No. 257, from Martlesham, to patrol over Canterbury at 12,000 feet; No. 32, from Biggin Hill, to patrol to the north of Canterbury; No. 46, from Duxford, to patrol over North Weald; No. 85, from Debden, to patrol overhead base at 10,000 feet; No. 151, from North Weald, to patrol over their base and No. 1 Squadron from Northolt to intercept the enemy force approaching Southend. In addition, elements of six other squadrons were ordered into the air between 1715 and 1745 hours, most of them to cover airfields. The cloud coming in from the north, however, was to provide the British airfields with the best protection of all.

The southernmost of the German formations, comprising 58 Do 17s of KG 2 escorted by Messerschmitt 109s, was engaged by Nos 32 and 501 Squadrons. The action began just to the north of Margate and continued almost to Chatham. Both Hurricane squadrons found the German escorts quick to intervene and nearly all the combats were with fighters. The bombers continued westwards as far as Chatham then, seeing the airfield at Hornchurch blanketed by cloud, turned round and withdrew. On their way out some bombers hit rail lines in northern Kent.

It was a similar story with the raiding force to the north, comprising fifty-one He 111s of KG 53. As the bombers crossed the coast near Foulness, Hurricanes of No. 56 Squadron charged into the formation. Soon afterwards the Spitfires of No. 54 Squadron, and more Hurricanes from Nos 46, 85, 151 and 257 Squadrons, also went into action. The German escorts absorbed much of the force of the attack, and the bombers continued their advance in good order. As the raiders ran in over Essex, however, their leader saw that a blanket of cloud covered the target: the airfield at North Weald. Accordingly, the formation of Heinkels turned around and headed for home without bombing.

By 1800 hours the enemy aircraft counters on the plotting tables at the various Sector operations rooms were all heading eastwards or southwards away from Britain, following an action in which the laurels went to the defenders. About a hundred bombers had been involved in the two attacks but no airfield had been hit and, although Fighter Command lost nine Hurricanes destroyed, only three pilots had keen killed and three wounded. In each case the German escorts had protected their charges well and only two bombers, He 111s of III/KG 53, were shot down. However, Zersteorergeschwader 26, which put up the escorting Messerschmitt 110s, suffered heavy losses in the process: eight of its fighters were shot down and five more were damaged. Of the covering Messerschmitt 109s, only one was shot down.

Following the withdrawal of the afternoon raiders there was an uneasy stillness until dark. Then the Luftwaffe put in harassing attacks on Bristol and targets in South Wales and East Anglia. Also that night Heinkel 115 mine-layers were active, particularly in the Bristol Channel.

So ended 18 August. Fighter Command mounted a total of 822 sorties, of which 56 were standing patrols to cover convoys. As is to be expected, No. 11 Group, covering the south-eastern part of Britain, put up the lion's share of the sorties: 545, of which 37 were convoy patrols. Analysis of the sortie figures sheds an interesting light on the nature of the No. 11 Group's operations. Although the early warning from the Chain Home stations meant fighters could be scrambled in time to meet the bombers first seen over France that were making for inland targets, they had insufficient time to engage bombers attacking targets near the coast. Group controllers had to resort to standing patrols to cover these targets. Thus No. 43 Squadron, which flew more sorties than any other in Fighter Command on 18 August – 63 – mounted almost continuous standing patrols over its airfield at Tangmere throughout the morning and the early afternoon. Only nine of these sorties actually came into contact with the enemy, during the 1400 hours' attack on the Portsmouth area. Between them three forward operating squadrons, Nos 43, 54 and 501, mounted a total of 168 sorties or one-third of all of those put up by the 21 squadrons of No. 11 Group to cover land targets. The radar warnings did not absolve the Group controllers of the need to mount standing patrols altogether, but they saved an enormous amount of wear and tear on the fighters by limiting the need for such patrols to those covering the forward airfields and the convoys.

On the German side, an interesting feature of the day's operations was the relatively small proportion of the bomber force that took part. Even on this hard-fought day only about 350 single-engined and twin-engined bombers were committed; this represented less than one-quarter of the total available. In analysing the Battle of Britain one sees the huge German bomber force putting up only a modest proportion of its strength on any one day, while the fighter force was running almost at full stretch to provide the necessary escorts. Thus the number of available escorts, rather than the overall number of aircraft, was the factor limiting the strength of the German daylight air attacks during the Battle of Britain.

A further constraining factor for the Luftwaffe was the limited range of its only really effective fighter, the Messerschmitt 109. Like the Spitfire and the Hurricane, this aircraft had been designed as a short-range interceptor and its radius of action as a bomber escort was limited to about 125 miles. If German bombers were to penetrate beyond the south-eastern corner of England, they had to do so without cover from Messerschmitt 109s. It had soon become clear that beyond the range of such cover, large-scale operations by day would result in heavy losses from the defending British fighters. By day, except on rare occasions, the useful attack radius of the German bombers was limited to the effective escort radius of German single-engined fighters.

Altogether, the attacks on 18 August cost the Luftwaffe a total of twenty-seven bombers shot down, with eight more damaged beyond repair; this represented 10 per cent of those committed, a moderately heavy loss but one which the Luftwaffe could make good from its large reserves. Twenty-seven covering fighters were destroyed and six more damaged beyond repair. The Royal Air Force lost forty-five fighters, of which ten were destroyed on the ground. Ten RAF pilots were killed or missing and a further fifteen were wounded. Both sides greatly overestimated the number of enemy aircraft destroyed in the battle, the Luftwaffe (with 142 claimed) by just over three-to-one, the Royal Air Force (with 123 claimed by fighters and 15 by anti-aircraft guns) by two-to-one.

## TACTICS REASSESSED

On the German side the action fought on 18 August was to have far-reaching consequences. The Junkers 87 was shown, in the face of resolute fighter defence, to be almost impossible to protect. As a result of the losses suffered on 18 August the Ju 87s took little further part in the battle. They represented the most effective anti-shipping force available to the Luftwaffe and had to be conserved to counter the Royal Navy when the invasion got under way. The Messerschmitt 110, like the RAF's Defiant, was vulnerable when engaged by enemy single-seat fighters. But whereas the Defiant represented only a small proportion of Fighter Command's front-line strength, the Messerschmitt 110 constituted about a quarter of the German fighter strength. With the scale of the bomber attacks limited by the number of fighters available to escort them, the German High Command was loath to reduce its fighter force still further. The Messerschmitt 110s were to continue to take part in the battle, though whenever possible they were to be covered by Messerschmitt 109s – an odd situation where the supposed escorts were themselves to be escorted.

*Throughout the Battle of Britain the limited range of the Messerschmitt 109E was a major constraining factor governing German daylight operations. The pilot of this aircraft spent just too long over England, and was lucky to be able to set down his fighter on a beach in France when the tide was out. (Bundesarchiv)*

The Luftwaffe was still experimenting with ways to provide an effective escort for the formations of twin-engined bombers. One bomber pilot recalled:

Initially, the fighters went with us all the way from the French coast to our target. But even during attacks against targets close to the coast this was found to be impractical, since our escorts began to run short of fuel just when they most needed it – on the return flight when the British fighters often engaged us in greatest force. So the next stage was to send the fighters on *Freijagd* (freelance hunting) patrols, to clear our route to the target. The problem was that the British could see what we were doing and would send in a few fighters from one side. When our fighters saw them they thought 'Ah, victories' and dived after them; no fighter pilot gets a *Ritterkreuz* for preventing bombers being shot down. That was usually the last we saw of our fighters; and since their radios did not work on the same frequencies as ours, we had no way of calling them back. Then, shortly afterwards, another British formation would appear and have a fine time shooting down our unescorted bombers.

Goering's answer was to introduce the so-called 'unmittelbar Begleitschutz' (immediate escort). Fighters zigzagged close to the bombers, within 100 to 200 yards, usually in groups of eight, maintaining station above, behind and on each side of the bombers. The fighters had strict orders that on no account were they to leave their charges. They were to go into action only if the bombers they were protecting came under direct attack from enemy fighters. Ideally there would also be a couple of fighters in Staffeln formation operating in the Freijagd role above the group, to break up British attacks before they could develop. But as the demands on the German fighter force became greater the bombers often had to forgo this luxury. By binding his unmittelbar Begleitschutz tightly to the bombers, however, there can be little doubt that Goering reduced the ability of the German fighter force to inflict losses on Fighter Command.

Of course, none of the German decisions was immediately known to Dowding or Park. All they knew was that during the previous eight days' heavy fighting the British squadrons had suffered serious losses in terms of both men and machines. To reduce pilot losses, in future Sector controllers were to direct fighter squadrons to engage enemy formations over land, so that those who baled out would come down on land. To meet low-level attacks, such as that which devastated Kenley, Park ordered that when enemy forces were observed at high level making for airfields, a squadron or a flight of fighters should be positioned over the airfield at low level.

Following the hard battles during the week ending 18 August came six days when the weather prevented large-scale air operations. During this lull Dowding decided to give the Defiant another chance: one squadron, No. 264,

*Air Vice-Marshal Keith Park, the commander of No. 11 Group of Fighter Command during the Battle of Britain. (IWM)*

was ordered south to Hornchurch. In an effort to prevent the sort of fighter-versus-fighter combat that had proved so disastrous just over a month earlier, Park instructed his Sector controllers: 'The Defiants whenever practicable are to be detailed to attack the enemy bombers. They may also attack fighters that are attacking ground targets, but are not to be detailed to intercept fighter formations.'

## THE BATTLE RESUMED

When the Luftwaffe resumed its attack, on 24 August, there were further heavy raids on the Fighter Command airfields. On the 24th the airfield at Manston was put out of action. On the 26th Kenley, Biggin Hill and Debden were all hit hard. On the 28th, in spite of the controllers' attempts to keep them clear of enemy fighters, the Defiants of No. 264 Squadron were caught by Messerschmitt 109s and of the twelve aircraft, four were shot down, and three damaged, without inflicting any loss on the enemy. Shortly afterwards the Defiants were relegated to night operations, for good. On the final day of August, Croydon, Hornchurch and Biggin Hill all suffered serious damage.

So far during the battle No. 19 Squadron's cannon-armed Spitfires had been in action on four occasions, but with little success. During the combat on 16 August both cannon functioned properly on only one of the seven Spitfires engaged; on the 19th on none out of three; on the 24th on two out of eight and on the 31st on three out of six. The unit's commander, Squadron Leader R. Pinkham, bitterly complained:

> In all the engagements so far occurring it is considered that had the unit been equipped with 8-gun fighters it would have inflicted far more severe losses on the enemy . . . It is most strongly urged that until the stoppages at present experienced have been eliminated this Squadron should be re-equipped with Browning gun Spitfires. It is suggested that a way of doing this would be to allot the present cannon Spitfires to an Operational Training Unit, and withdraw Browning gun Spitfires from there for use in this Squadron.

Air Chief Marshal Dowding accepted this suggestion and ordered that the exchange be made immediately. On 4 September No. 19 Squadron delivered its aircraft to No. 7 Operational Training Unit at Hawarden, and in exchange received the latter's elderly but machine-gun fitted 'hacks'. The No. 19 Squadron diarist noted: 'First day with the eight-gun machines, and what wrecks. At least the guns will fire . . .'

September brought no immediate relief for Park's hard-pressed squadrons. On each of the first six days there were large-scale actions round the fighter airfields. Aircraft factories were also hit, though without causing any serious fall in fighter production. During the two weeks from 24 August until 6 September, Fighter Command lost 295 aircraft destroyed and a further 171 seriously damaged. Throughout the same period the output from factories and repair units was only 269 Hurricanes and Spitfires. Even worse, during this period 103 fighter pilots

*Air Chief Marshal Dowding (right), the C-in-C Fighter Command, escorting King George VI and Queen Elizabeth when they visited his headquarters at Stanmore Park on 6 September. (IWM)*

had been killed and 128 wounded. With just under 1,000 pilots in his Command, Dowding was seeing his force wasting away at the rate of about one-tenth of his effectives per week. In August the operational training units turned out about 250 new fighter pilots, but these inexperienced newcomers often fell as easy prey to the enemy before they learned how to survive in battle. But those that survived their initial baptism of fire quickly mastered the essentials of air fighting to become effective combat pilots. The main No. 11 Group airfields, at Kenley, Biggin Hill, Tangmere, Hornchurch and North Weald, had all suffered heavily. Yet, throughout this phase of the action, a programme of running repairs and hasty improvisations kept these airfields in operation.

Meanwhile, however, the Luftwaffe had also suffered serious losses. From 24 August to 6 September the force lost about a 100 twin-engined bombers and over 200 fighters. Moreover, large numbers of aircraft had returned with battle damage and required extensive repairs before they would again be fit for action.

## THE AIRFIELD ATTACKS REVIEWED

During August and the first week of September the Luftwaffe had mounted an intensive 3½-week campaign of attacks with the intention of knocking out Fighter Command's airfields in the south of England. On each day that the weather allowed, there had been attacks by one or two Gruppen of bombers on two or more airfields. In retrospect, it is clear that this campaign was a failure.

Consider first, the destruction of RAF fighters on the ground. Fighter squadrons based in the south of England remained at high states of readiness throughout the daylight hours. Backing them was an excellent control and reporting organisation, using information from radar sites and Observer Corps posts. Almost invariably, these fighters were airborne and well clear of their airfield before an attacking force could reach it. Aircraft able to fly but not fight took off and headed for a safe area to the north until the threat had passed. Aircraft unable to fly were pushed into revetments or otherwise dispersed around

*Reichsmarschall Herman Goering congratulating the men of I./KG 76 who had flown the largest number of missions during the Battle of Britain, at Beauvais-Tille on 18 September. It was one of the rare occasions when Luftwaffe personnel were promoted in the field for this reason. From left to right: Goering, Major Schweitzer (Gruppe commander), Oberfeldwebel Mairose (promoted to Leutnant), Feldwebel Carstens (to Leutnant), Unteroffizier Sobol (to Oberfeldwebel), Feldwebel Scheffel (to Leutnant) and Oberleutnant Hallseleben (to Hauptmann).* (KG 76 Archive)

the airfield, making unsuitable targets for pattern-bombing attacks. During the series of attacks on airfields *less than twenty* Spitfires and Hurricanes from front-line squadrons were destroyed on the ground.

Consider next, the destruction of facilities at airfields. An accurate pattern-bombing attack by a Gruppe of thirty bombers could and did render the landing surface temporarily unusable. But if the runways were damaged, RAF fighters could operate from grass surrounds. After each attack the repair parties would mark out a strip for take-offs and landings, in the least affected part of the airfield. Any bomb crater that interfered with this was filled in first. Usually, airfields were restored to limited operations within a couple of hours of an attack. On no occasion did it take more than 24 hours to restore a Sector station to full operation.

Damage to airfield facilities caused problems, but this was high summer and the buildings were desirable rather than essential. If hangars were wrecked, engineering work on aircraft could take place in the open. After all, that was what happened at the hastily prepared Luftwaffe landing grounds in France and Belgium. The only vulnerable points that were essential to Fighter Command were the operations rooms at the main Sector airfields. The location of these buildings was unknown to the Luftwaffe during the battle, however. When these buildings suffered damage it was the result of chance hits rather than deliberate attacks. And when these control centres were put out of action, substitute operations rooms were quickly set up off the airfields.

Certainly, some airfields did suffer serious damage during the battle. Manston was hit particularly hard and often, and for a time it was relegated to use as a refuelling strip. But Manston was not one of the all-important Sector stations on which the defence hinged. The attacks on the airfields had failed to subdue Fighter Command. So, at the end of the first week in September, the Luftwaffe shifted its attack to London itself. It was hoped that this new phase of the battle, long feared by the British government, would force the latter to sue for peace. In the next chapter we shall follow the course of the actions that brought the battle to a rapid climax.

# CHAPTER 4

# The Attack on London and After, 7 September–1 November 1940

You can squeeze a bee in your hand until it suffocates;
but it will not suffocate without having stung you.

*Jean Paulhan*

Since the final week in August RAF bombers had been conducting night attacks on targets in Germany, including Berlin, in retaliation for stray bombs that had fallen on the outskirts of London. This development enraged Hitler, and the latter ordered a series of heavy attacks on London by way of reprisal.

Saturday 7 September began quietly with scarcely any German air activity over southern England during the morning and early afternoon. The sole exceptions were the high-flying reconnaissance aircraft, observing the weather and photographing damage caused by earlier attacks. It was a fine sunny day which, in view of the intensity of the previous two weeks' operations, made the silence even more ominous.

The uneasy quiet lasted until 1554 hours, when radar stations in the south-east of England began passing plots on an attack building up over the Pas de

*Pilot Officer Bob Doe, left, of No. 234 Squadron, credited with fourteen victories during the Battle of Britain.*

Calais. As the vanguard of the raiders crossed the coast at 1616 hours and came within view of the Observer Corps posts on the ground, its composition became clear to operations officers at Bentley Priory and the Group headquarters. Some 350 bombers, escorted by more than 600 fighters, formed a huge phalanx of aircraft that was advancing along the south of the Thames Estuary towards London, with a frontage some 20 miles wide. To meet this threat the No. 11 Group controller ordered off almost all of his force. The Sector controllers positioned the interceptors in anticipation of yet another attack on the fighter airfields. As a result only four squadrons were in position to intercept the raiding force before it reached London and the powerful escort brushed these aside. The bombers struck their targets, in the dock area of the city, hard.

One of those who had followed the raiders' progress from the War Room of the Home Office in Whitehall was Wing Commander John Hodsoll, the Inspector General of Air Raid Precautions. As the bombs started to fall he made his way to the roof of the Home Office building and later wrote:

> It was indeed an awe-inspiring sight that met our eyes. Huge clouds of black smoke were billowing and spiralling up into the clear blue sky; great spurts of flame were shooting up; there was a dull thud of bombs as they exploded and reverberated in the distance, and an acrid smell of burning was borne in on the wind. The docks looked as if they had been reduced to one great inferno. Above it all, just visible, was the maze of tiny dots with their white tails of vapour, high up in the sky; and here and there the signs of combat, of weaving trails, as our fighters did their best to parry this thrust at the heart of London. The spectacle had an almost eerie fascination, which held us spellbound and

*Spitfires of Nos 222 (ZD) and 603 (XT) Squadrons at Hornchurch, September 1940. Note the steamroller in the background, used to flatten bomb craters in the landing area after they had been filled with rubble and earth.*

*A close shave for Pilot Officer Alan Wright of No. 92 Squadron on 9 September. A machine-gun round from behind pierced his perspex hood, nicked the windscreen frame near the top, bounced off the toughened glass windscreen and smashed his reflector sight; Wright himself escaped without injury.*

immobile, and it was some little time before I could drag myself away and descend into the street. There, too, I found a strange air of unreality. The streets were nearly empty, since the warning had gone; but there were streams of fire engines and appliances speeding to the docks, with fire bells ringing and echoing their message of urgency. Wardens were controlling what other traffic there was, and the few pedestrians in sight seemed dazed now that the long-awaited blow had fallen.

During its first pitched battle over and around London itself, Fighter Command did not get to grips with the enemy. The Luftwaffe lost ten bombers destroyed or damaged beyond repair and twenty-two fighters. The RAF lost twenty-nine fighters destroyed and seventeen pilots killed or seriously wounded. In view of what had been achieved, the German losses seemed surprisingly light.

As the daylight raiders withdrew the German bomber force followed up its success with a powerful night attack on the capital. (The night attacks will be covered in the next chapter.) In the second daylight large-scale attack on the city, on the afternoon of 9 September, cloud prevented accurate bombing. Twenty-seven German planes were destroyed for the loss of nineteen British fighters. Two days later, on the 11th, the Luftwaffe returned to add to the damage inflicted on the dock areas. Fighter Command emerged from that action the loser – in shooting down twenty-three German planes, it lost twenty-nine Spitfires and Hurricanes. Three days later, on 14 September, German bombers attempted a further attack on the capital, only to be defeated by cloud over the target. On that day the losses were exactly equal: twelve planes destroyed on each side.

## ERRONEOUS ASSESSMENT

During each of the first four daylight attacks aimed at London, for one reason or another the British fighter controllers failed to bring a major proportion of their force into action. In the case of the initial attack, the shift of the offensive to the capital had come as a surprise and the fighters had been positioned to block further strikes on airfields. During the next three attacks, the cloud that hindered accurate bombing also impeded the ground observers' efforts to track the German formations, which made it difficult to vector the fighter squadrons on to the raiders. This unconnected series of failures led the German High Command to make an entirely erroneous assessment of the way the battle was progressing.

Examining the evidence of the first four daylight raids on London, Luftwaffe officers noted that in none of them had the bomber formations been engaged with the ferocity and effectiveness that characterised many August actions. It seemed that Fighter Command might indeed be on the point of collapse, long predicted in the German calculations, and required only a few more large-scale actions to finish it as an effective fighting force. If this assessment was correct and Fighter Command really was at its last gasp, the correct strategy was to mount further attacks on the capital, to draw the remaining British fighters into action so they could be cut down by the escorting Messerschmitts.

## 'BATTLE OF BRITAIN DAY', 15 SEPTEMBER

With the aim of bringing the remnants of Fighter Command into battle, for 15 September the Luftwaffe planned the most ambitious daylight action against the British capital it had yet mounted. There were to be two separate attacks, one against a nodal point in the rail system and the other against the docks, with an interval of a couple of hours between each. Every available Messerschmitt 109 unit in Air Fleet 2 was to take part in the escort of the attacks, and many units were to fly double sorties. If successful, the attacks planned for the 15th would advance the German cause in four important ways: they would knock out a focal point in the rail network; they would destroy large quantities of supplies imported from overseas; they would strike at civilian morale by demonstrating London's vulnerability to attack; and lastly, and most significantly, they would impose a further drain on the Royal Air Force's dwindling fighter strength.

The first of these assaults was to be delivered shortly before noon. It involved 21 Messerschmitt 109 fighter bombers of Lehrgeschwader 2 followed by 27 Dornier 17s of Bomber Geschwader 76, escorted by about 180 Me 109s. The fighter bombers were to attack railway targets in the south-eastern quarter of the city. Then the Dorniers were to bomb rail viaducts and the important assembly of lines running through Battersea, which carried traffic from the main-line stations at Victoria and Waterloo.

Almost from the start the operation went badly from the German viewpoint. As it was climbing towards the Pas de Calais to link up with its fighter escort, the Dornier formation ran into a layer of cloud that was thicker than expected which forced the bombers to break formation. The formation leader, Major Alois Lindemayr, had to orbit above the cloud for about 10 minutes to reassemble his force and when it did it was two aircraft short. At the Pas de Calais the bombers picked up their escorts, then turned on to a north-westerly heading for London. But again the weather took a hand in the proceedings: this time there was a

90 mph headwind at the bombers' approach altitude of 16,000 feet, delaying further their arrival at the target.

The small force of Messerschmitt 109 fighter bombers, each carrying one 550-pound incendiary or four 110-pound high-explosive bombs, reached the capital as planned and delivered their attacks without interference. The fighter-bomber pilots aimed their bombs at the rail stations in Lambeth, Streatham, Dulwich and Penge, but caused little damage and few casualties before they withdrew without loss.

During their passage across Kent, the Dornier 17s and escorting Messerschmitts fought a series of skirmishes with fighters from eleven RAF squadrons. The escorts mounted an energetic covering operation, however, and the bomber formation reached the outskirts of the capital intact and without the loss of a single aircraft. Now, however, the effects of the delays incurred over France and the need to battle against the powerful headwind became apparent: the raiders arrived at the capital more than half an hour late. For the escorting Me 109s this delay was crucial. They were running short of fuel before they reached the outskirts of the capital, and one by one the German fighter units were forced to turn for home. By the time the Dorniers began their bombing runs, their escort had disappeared.

Air Vice-Marshal Park was ignorant of the Germans' predicament, but had he known of it he would probably not have fought the action any differently. He assembled twelve squadrons of Spitfires and Hurricanes over the eastern outskirts of London in readiness to meet the attack. Most fighter squadrons flew in pairs, though five of them belonged to Squadron Leader Douglas Bader's 'Big Wing' on its way from Duxford near Cambridge and about to go into action in full strength for the first time.

The German bombers held tight formation, trading blows with their tormentors, and completed their bombing runs. Then, as they turned for home, the repeated fighter attacks started to take effect. After its pilot and two other crewmen had baled out, a Dornier with two dead men aboard continued flying a straight course across the city. Several fighters pounced on the lone raider and delivered further attacks before a Hurricane of No. 504 Squadron rammed it. The main part of the bomber fell into the forecourt of Victoria station. The Hurricane was also wrecked in the collision and crashed in Chelsea. Of the crewmen who had bailed out of the bomber before it was rammed, two were taken into captivity immediately after landing. The third man was less fortunate. He parachuted to earth near the Oval underground station in Kennington and was set upon by enraged civilians. Before soldiers could rescue him the man was badly beaten up, and he died of his injuries shortly afterwards.

As it headed for home the formation of Dorniers was under heavy attack from scores of fighters of No. 11 Group, now joined by the five squadrons of 'Big Wing'. Other bombers were damaged and forced to leave their formation, to be finished off by the angry fighters. Of the twenty-five bombers that crossed the coast of England three-quarters of an hour earlier, six were shot down. Four more limped on alone using the available cloud cover, and most of the fifteen remaining in formation had some damage. Near Maidstone, the Messerschmitt 109s

*Dornier 17 of KG 76 crash-landed in France after the action on 15 September. These rugged planes often regained friendly territory after suffering quite remarkable amounts of battle damage. This example returned with more than 200 hits from .303-in rounds, and was listed as damaged beyond repair.*

assigned to cover the Dorniers' withdrawal linked up with their charges and shepherded the survivors home. Assisting the force on the way out was the same 90-mph wind that had impeded the bombers on the way in.

During the action Kampfgeschwader 76 had taken a fearful mauling. Yet, considering the lack of escorts over the target and the overwhelming concentration of RAF fighters engaging, it is surprising that any Dorniers survived. The fact that three-quarters of the bombers returned to France is testimony of the leadership of Major Alois Lindmayr, the formation discipline and flying skill of his crews and the sturdiness of the Dornier and its ability to absorb punishment.

As the last of the noon raiders left the coast of England, the bombers assigned to the next attack were already airborne, assembled in formation and climbing towards the Pas de Calais. This raiding force was far larger than the previous one, with five separate formations comprising 114 Dorniers and Heinkels. The crews were briefed to attack the Royal Victoria and the West India Docks to the north of the Thames, and the Surrey Commercial Docks to the south.

Shortly before 2 p.m., Air Vice-Marshal Park began scrambling his squadrons to meet the threat, deploying them in much the same way as during the morning action. The vanguard of the German bomber force made its landfall over Dungeness, then wheeled on to a north-north-westerly heading for the capital. Above Romney Marsh the forward-deployed Spitfire squadrons went into action. The initial clash involved Nos 41, 92 and 222 Squadrons, with twenty-seven fighters, which immediately became entangled with the escorting Messerschmitts.

Park scrambled all twenty-one of his Spitfire and Hurricane squadrons. From No. 12 Group, Squadron Leader Douglas Bader was again on his way south at the head of the five-squadron Duxford Wing, while from the west two squadrons from No. 10 Group were moving towards the capital. For the defence of London there were now 276 Spitfires and Hurricanes airborne, slightly more than for the earlier engagement. But this time the German raiding force was more than twice as large as the earlier one, outnumbering the British fighters by more than two-to-one. For every two Spitfires or Hurricanes airborne, there were three Messerschmitt 109s providing cover for the bombers.

With raiders advancing across Kent, a succession of pairs of RAF fighter squadrons joined the action. Again and again the Messerschmitts came diving in to break up the attacks or drive away the Spitfires or Hurricanes. For the Messerschmitt pilots assigned to the close escort this was a particularly frustrating time. They were not permitted to pursue enemy fighters and go for the kill, if that meant leaving their charges. Again and again Messerschmitts had to break off the chase and return to their bombers. Then the British fighters would return and the process would be repeated.

Air Vice-Marshal Park concentrated the bulk of his force immediately in front of London for the main action, as during the noon action. No fewer than 19 fresh squadrons were assembled in the area, with a total of 185 Spitfires and Hurricanes. The Dorniers of Kampfgeschwader 3 came under heavy attack at this time. Feldwebel Heinz Kirsch, gunner in one of the planes, later wrote:

A new call, 'Fighters dead astern!' Something struck our machine. 'Hit on the left elevator!' called the radio operator. Like a couple of shadows two Hurricanes swept over us, they came past so quickly we were unable to 'greet' them. More hits on our machine. And on top of that there was smoke in the cabin. The Tommies were staking everything they had, never before had we come under such heavy attack. After firing, the fighters pulled to the left or right to go past us. Some came so close I thought they were going to ram us.

Over London, Douglas Bader's 'Big Wing' joined the battle. But his five squadrons immediately came under attack from above by free-hunting Me 109s. Bader ordered his three Hurricane squadrons to split up and engage the enemy fighters while, in a reversal of their usual role, the Spitfires were to try to punch their way through to the bombers. Bader's combat report describes the chaos that now ensued:

On being attacked from behind by Me 109 I ordered break up and pulled up and round violently. Coming off my back partially blacked out, nearly collided with Yellow 2 [Pilot Officer Crowley-Milling]. Spun off his slipstream and straightened out 5,000 feet below without firing a shot. Climbed up again and saw E/A twin engined flying westwards. Just got in range and fired a short burst (3 secs) in a completely stalled position and then spun off again and lost more height.

Four German bombers were destroyed on the way to the target, and seven more had suffered damage and been forced to leave formation and head for home. All five bomber formations reached London intact, however, and now prepared to begin their bombing runs on their assigned dock areas.

By now the cloud cover over London had built up appreciably, and most of the city lay under nine-tenths cumulus and strato-cumulus cloud with tops extending to 12,000 feet. The blanket of cloud covered all the bombers' briefed targets. To the north of the Thames the only clear patch of sky was over West Ham. Many Dorniers and Heinkels realigned their bombing runs on that part of the city. Several planes singled out the Bromley-by-Bow gasworks for attack, and a torrent of high-explosive bombs deluged the plant, wrecking large parts of it.

The two formations of Dorniers from KG 2, unable to attack the Surrey Commercial Docks as briefed, turned through a semicircle and headed for home without dropping their bombs. At the time three Hurricane squadrons had been engaging this part of the raiding force. Now the unexpected U-turn came as a sudden and unpredicted delight. The RAF pilots were convinced that by their presence they had scared the German crews into turning away from the capital, and said so afterwards in their combat reports. In fact both Dornier formations had reached the capital intact, having lost only one aircraft on the way in. They could certainly have fought through to their briefed target, if only they had been able to find it. On their way out the Dorniers scattered their bombs over a number of districts.

Several bombers forced to leave their formations, due to battle damage or technical problems, picked their way through the cloudbanks over Kent. These unfortunates had to play a deadly game of hide-and-seek with defending fighters bent on finishing them off. Leutnant Herburt Michaelis of KG 2, flying his Dornier on one engine, emerged from cloud and was immediately spotted by Squadron Leader John Sample of No. 504 Squadron. The Hurricane pilot later wrote: 'I started to chase one Dornier which was flying through the tops of clouds . . . I attacked him four times altogether. When he first appeared through the cloud – you know how clouds go up and down like foam on water – I fired at him from the left, swung over to the right, turned in towards another hollow in the cloud where I expected to reappear, and fired at him again.' Sample's attacks shattered the bomber's glass nose, and one round passed through Michaelis's life-jacket tearing away the pouch containing the yellow dye marker (to identify his position if he came down in the sea). The fine dust flew everywhere and some went into the German pilot's eyes, blinding him temporarily. Michaelis ordered his crew to bail out, groped his way to the escape hatch and followed. The bomber crashed near Dartford.

Despite the extensive cloud cover, the RAF fighter controllers performed their tasks in exemplary fashion that day. During the noon action, twenty-three squadrons of fighters had been scrambled and all except one had made contact with the enemy. During the afternoon action twenty-eight squadrons of Spitfires and Hurricanes were scrambled and every one went into action.

Elsewhere that afternoon, Heinkels of KG 55 attacked the Royal Navy base at Portland and a small force of Messerschmitt 109 and Me 110 fighter bombers of Erprobungsgruppe 210 tried unsuccessfully to hit the Supermarine aircraft works at Woolston near Southampton. Neither attack caused significant damage.

During the hard-fought actions on 15 September the Luftwaffe lost fifty-eight aircraft, against the thirty-one by RAF Fighter Command. The ferocity of the latter's reaction made it all too clear that the force was far from beaten, and the German High Command was forced to recognise that victory no longer lay within its grasp. On 17 September Hitler orderd that Operation 'Sealion', the invasion of Britain, be postponed until further notice. Within days the ships and barges that had been concentrated at ports along the Channel coast started to disperse. From then on, the threat of invasion diminished with each day that passed.

On 18 September there was an unsuccessful daylight attack on the capital, and others on the 27th and 28th. Also during the latter part of the month the Luftwaffe carried out destructive attacks on the Bristol Aeroplane Co. works near Bristol (on 25 September) and the Supermarine works at Southampton (on the 26th). But in spite of these successes, it was clear that the era of the massed attack on targets in England by twin-engined bombers by day was drawing to a close. The outcome of the Battle of Britain had already been decided. From now on it would be merely a question of keeping up the pressure on Britain while Hitler planned his next moves.

## ANALYSIS OF THE BATTLE OF BRITAIN

The hardest-fought part of the Battle of Britain lasted from 8 August until 30 September. A statistical analysis of the British defensive air operations during this period might therefore be of interest. During the 54-day period the average fighting strength of Fighter Command was 50 squadrons with a total of just over 1,000 fighters, of which an average of 720 were available for operations on any one day. The fighters flew nearly 35,000 operational sorties, of which 69 per cent were scrambled with orders to intercept specific enemy attacks, 21 per cent were standing patrols, 7 per cent were standing patrols mounted to protect shipping and the remaining 3 per cent were described as 'miscellaneous patrols'. Fighter Command mounted its maximum effort on 15 August, with a total of 1,254 sorties; on three other days, 30 August and 18 and 19 September, the Command put up more than 1,000 sorties. The daily average for the 54-day period, including periods of light activity, was just under 650 sorties.

On the average, only 23 per cent of the total of Fighter Command sorties actually came into contact with the enemy. If one neglects the shipping patrols and other sorties, which would not normally be expected to go into action, the figure rises to 31 per cent. The fact that less than a third of the Fighter Command sorties found the enemy is significant. It indicates that although the ground control system Dowding had built up was far ahead of that of any other nation, during the Battle of Britain it was still crude and there was considerable room for improvement.

The short warning time provided by the radar chain, compared with what was needed, forced the fighter Group controllers to use part of their forces to mount standing patrols. Even on days of light activity Fighter Command flew a daily average of about 400 such sorties. On days of heavy activity, prior to the shift of the attack to London, the time between the detection of the raiding force and the actual bombing was short – too short for the fighters in No. 11 Group to go into action in forces of greater than single squadrons. This deployment of fighters in several separate formations added to the problems of the Sector controllers, because for

*This dramatic series of photographs (above and opposite) shows a Messerschmitt 110 of III./ZG 26 ditching in the Channel, and the arrival of a Heinkel 59 floatplane to pick up the crew. It is believed that these photographs were taken during the final week of September 1940.* (via Radinger)

technical reasons only four formations of fighters could be tracked simultaneously in any one Sector. The effectiveness of the control of further formations was, therefore, somewhat reduced.

When the Luftwaffe began concentrating its bombers against London, the situation was reversed. To meet these attacks No. 11 Group was able to engage with two-squadron formations and No. 12 Group was able to get even larger formations into action. Against the raids on London an average of nearly 40 per cent of the fighter sorties made contact and on 15 September, this figure reached a triumphant 78 per cent.

During the 54-day period of the battle, Fighter Command lost 746 aircraft destroyed or damaged beyond repair. A further 460 aircraft suffered major damage. These casualties represented a wastage over the period of one fighter lost or seriously damaged for every 30 operational sorties. If only those sorties are considered when the enemy was engaged, the wastage over the period rises to one

*During the final phase of the Battle of Britain the Luftwaffe resorted to high-level attacks by Messerschmitt 109 and 110 fighter bombers on London. The Messerschmitt 109 seen here is carrying a single 550-pound bomb.*

fighter destroyed or seriously damaged for every 6½ sorties engaging. Aircrew casualties over the period were 304 killed and missing, and 265 wounded. This means that Fighter Command suffered one aircrew casualty for every two aircraft lost. That relatively favourable ratio was due in large part to the fact that the battle was fought mainly over land or the immediate coastal waters.

During the same period the Luftwaffe lost about 1,200 aircraft destroyed and a further 400 damaged. Thus the exchange rate during the period of the heaviest fighting came to 17 German fighters or bombers lost for every 10 defending fighters and 5 RAF pilots – a very favourable ratio from the point of view of the Royal Air Force.

## ATTACKS BY FIGHTER BOMBERS

From the latter half of September the Germans made progressively more use of fighter bombers to attack London and other targets in southern England; these attacks continued until well into November. Although the new tactics caused relatively little damage, as intended they provided Air Vice-Marshal Park with a difficult interception problem. Flying at altitudes around 25,000 feet, the bomb-carrying Messerschmitt 109s and 110s could be over the southern part of London within 17 minutes of the first radar warning. From the scramble order to 25,000 feet took a squadron of Spitfires an average of 22 minutes (Hurricanes took 25 minutes), so the only fighters likely to engage such raiders before they reached London were those airborne when the first radar plots were received. To meet the new threat No. 11 Group was forced to mount standing patrols along set lines over south-eastern England. The defending fighters waited at 15,000 feet to conserve oxygen and, when the incoming raiders were detected, the Sector controllers ordered them to climb 30,000 feet and move into position to engage.

Representative of the scrappy actions that characterised this phase of the Battle of Britain, were those on 1 November. At daybreak, 0735 hours, the Hurricanes of

*Messerschmitt 110 fighter bombers of Erprobungsgruppe 210, one of the units taking part in the attacks on London in the closing phase of the battle.*

Nos 253 and 605 Squadrons took off from Kenley to mount a standing patrol in the Maidstone area. Shortly afterwards the Spitfires of Nos 41 and 603 Squadrons left the ground for a similar patrol over Rochford. The first incoming raiding force was observed on radar at 0758 hours, when 20 miles to the east of Boulogne. It was assessed a '9 plus'. A formation comprising about ten high-flying Messerschmitt 109s crossed the coast near Dover at 0805 hours and penetrated to the Sittingbourne area, where they dropped their bombs and made off. A quarter of an hour later a similar formation crossed the coast and made for Canterbury. No. 605 Squadron engaged the raiders and claimed one shot down, two probables and four damaged. During this skirmish the squadron's commander, Squadron Leader A. McKellar, was killed. The circumstances leading to his death are not clear, but his Hurricane was seen to emerge from cloud in an inverted spin before crashing. The pilots of No. 253 Squadron saw the Messerschmitts only as they were heading southwards for home and were unable to catch up. The two Spitfire squadrons also failed to make contact.

The quiet returned and the defending squadrons resumed their patrol lines. At 0905 hours the Spitfires of Nos 74 and 92 Squadrons took off from Biggin Hill to take over the Maidstone patrol. Nothing happened until 1015 hours when the fighters, excepting those of Blue Section of No. 92 Squadron, received the order to return to base. The remaining four were directed to intercept a lone intruder over Kent thought to be at 23,000 feet. At 1020 they caught sight of the enemy aircraft near Dover, a Messerschmitt 110 of Fernaufklaerungsgruppe 22 engaged on reconnaissance at 29,000 feet. Two Spitfires attacked from astern and abeam and Pilot Officer C. Saunders reported hits. Streaming glycol from the cooling system, the Messerschmitt escaped out to sea and limped home with both crew members wounded.

At 1035 hours the Hurricanes of Nos 229 and 615 Squadrons took off from Hornchurch to mount guard over Maidstone. They were there when, soon after 1100 hours, the second raiding force comprising some thirty-five Messerschmitt 109s in two formations crossed the coast near Dover. Hurricanes of Nos 253 and 501 Squadrons took off from Kenley to reinforce the defence and all four squadrons were ordered to intercept. They failed to make contact with the enemy formations, however. At 1120 Nos 74 and 92 Squadrons again took off for the Maidstone patrol line; climbing into position they had an inconclusive brush with German fighters.

In the afternoon there were three further attacks, on south London, on convoys off the mouth of the Thames and on Dover. In each case they inflicted little damage and resulted in similarly inconclusive actions. For the pilots of Fighter Command this was frustrating, with a lot of time spent waiting at readiness in the air and on the ground and little chance to engage the enemy.

## THE ITALIAN AIR FORCE ENTERS THE BATTLE

At the close of October the Italian expeditionary air force, the Corpo Aero Italiano, began mounting attacks against Britain from its bases in Belgium. Following an inconclusive raid on Ramsgate on 29 October, the Italians fought their first, and only, daylight action with Fighter Command on 11 November.

*A Fiat BR 20 bomber of the Italian Air Force. During the latter part of October and the early part of November these aircraft carried out a few small-scale attacks on targets in southern England.* (via Selinger)

*Fiat CR 42 biplane fighters of the Italian 56° Stormo, which operated against Britain from airfields in Belgium. These obsolescent aircraft proved no match for the Spitfires and Hurricanes of the RAF.* (via Ghiselli)

During this attack ten Fiat BR 20 bombers, escorted by forty Fiat CR 42 fighters, targeted Harwich. Three squadrons of Hurricanes took off to intercept and in the unequal combat that followed they shot down three bombers and three fighters without loss to themselves. A Spitfire operating as part of a convoy protection patrol also became involved in the action, albeit inadvertently. In his combat report Pilot Officer E. Wells of No. 41 Squadron afterwards stated:

On a convoy protection patrol east of Orfordness I broke away to investigate a large patch of burning oil on the water north of the convoy. I called to inform Blue Leader. I was at 4,000 feet when I saw some biplanes which I took to be Gladiators.

Immediately the nearest three dived straight down to attack me, firing tracer as they came. I evaded and climbed at full throttle; others from higher up came down in dive attacks in twos and threes. As I gained height I got clear of most of them. I then chose one slightly below me and dived to attack him. As I opened fire he half-rolled very tightly and I was completely unable to hold him, so rapid were his manoeuvres. I attacked two or three more and fired short bursts, in each case the enemy aircraft half-rolled very tightly and easily and completely out-turned me, in two cases as they came out of their rolls they were able to turn in almost on my tail and opened fire on me. To one other I gave a longish burst and saw large black sheets, which I took to be engine cowlings, fly off the front part of his engine, also grey wisps of smoke (or petrol) came out of the root of his top plane where my ammunition was striking. He half-rolled and went into cloud. I got into position on another and saw my de Wilde ammunition hitting the rear part of his fuselage. He also half-rolled and went down into cloud.

The manoeuvrability of the Italian biplanes came as an unpleasant surprise to Wells and he noted 'They seemed to be able to pull their noses up very high to enable them to get in a short burst, without stalling, at a Spitfire climbing at maximum angle.' Even so the action did reveal the basic inferiority of the aircraft he faced. Having exhausted his ammunition, Wells broke off the action without difficulty and returned to Hornchurch with no damage to his aircraft. An estimated twenty Fiat CR 42s were in the area. Had the odds been reversed and there been twenty Spitfires and one CR 42, the fate of the single biplane fighter can hardly have been in doubt.

As the autumn set in, the weather caused a gradual thinning of the air operations over Britain. The daylight bombing attacks did not come to an abrupt halt, rather they petered out over a long period.

## What if the Luftwaffe had Defeated Fighter Command?

So ended the battle that is said to have saved Britain. Yet in concluding this account of the Battle of Britain, it is relevant to ask what Britain was saved from. The main threat was, of course, a German invasion. But even with the Royal Air Force out of the way, could the Germans have carried out a successful invasion of Britain?

Any force invading Britain had to get past the Royal Navy which, in spite of a year of sustained action, was as powerful in the summer of 1940 as it had been at the outbreak of the war. In contrast the far smaller German Navy had suffered heavy losses in ships sunk and, just as important in the short term, in ships damaged. The Norwegian campaign had left the German Navy with an operational force comprising no battleships, 1 heavy cruiser, 3 light cruisers, a maximum of 9 destroyers and some 30 submarines. In contrast the Home Fleet of the Royal Navy had available to combat an invasion 5 battleships, 11 cruisers, 43 destroyers and 35 submarines.

The view has been frequently repeated that, had it gained air superiority over the southern half of England, the Luftwaffe could have redressed this enormous disparity in naval forces. Such a view does not withstand analysis. In 1940 the Luftwaffe had no effective force of torpedo bombers. Not only were there few aircraft equipped for this role, but those that were had a low performance and the German aerial torpedoes were unreliable and generally ineffective. Horizontal

*During 1940 and the early part of 1941 experiments were conducted in Britain in air-to-air bombing as a means of breaking up enemy bomber formations. The Hurricane depicted was carrying two 250-pound anti-aircraft bombs, each fitted with a photo-electric cell to detonate it as it passed another aircraft during its fall. The photo-electric cells proved unreliable for this purpose, however, and the anti-aircraft bombs were never used operationally by the RAF.*

bombing attacks against fast ships manoeuvring in open water were notoriously ineffective and would have been unlikely to embarrass the Royal Navy. Dive bombing would have been a more serious hazard, especially for the warships of cruiser size and smaller which lacked heavy armour. But in 1940 the Luftwaffe had none of the rocket-assisted bombs that later became available. It had no bombs likely to penetrate the heavy deck armour of battleships when released in diving attacks. Moreover, the accurate steep diving attack was impossible without almost clear skies of up to 8,000 feet. The Luftwaffe had no night-attack capability against ships.

In the light of these known deficiencies, the Royal Navy's tactics are easily predictable. From the anchorage at Scapa Flow to Eastbourne, the middle of the planned German invasion zone, would have taken capital ships about 24 hours' sailing. They would arrive at first light, having traversed the final 200 miles to the bridgehead during the hours of darkness. Once in the invasion area, the British warships would have made short work of the German escorts, merchant ships and invasion barges. No less an authority than General-Major Dietrich Peltz, the German dive-bombing expert, has expressed the conviction that even under optimum conditions, with the weapons and equipment available in 1940, the Luftwaffe could not have prevented the Royal Navy from annihilating a German invasion fleet. Vice-Admiral Kurt Assmann, the German naval expert, put it another way: 'Had the Luftwaffe defeated the Royal Air Force as decisively as it had defeated the French Air Force a few months earlier, I am sure Hitler would have given the order for the invasion to be launched – and the invasion would in all probability have been smashed.' The order was never given. The landing operations, precarious even with the Royal Air Force subdued, would have been suicidal if the warships of the Royal Navy had fighter cover.

So, if Britain was safe from invasion in any case, did the RAF victory in the Battle of Britain make a significant contribution to national survival? Without doubt, it did. We have observed the fear generated before the war, of the effects of large-scale air attacks resulting in the *concentrated* bombing of civilian targets. Had Fighter Command been unable to intervene effectively, the Luftwaffe could have employed its entire force of bombers in a series of accurate and devastating daylight attacks on Britain's cities. The nation would have been subjected to a rain of destruction, if not death, on a scale near to that envisaged in the pre-war forecasts. It is possible that this would have forced the British government to accept the German peace terms without the necessity for an invasion. Whether this would have been so remains one of the interesting 'ifs' of history; nobody is going to run an action replay of 1940 to discover the answer.

Fighter Command had demonstrated that it could inflict unacceptably heavy losses on forces of bombers attacking targets in Britain by day. In doing so, it denied the Germans the possibility of securing a relatively quick victory against their remaining enemy in the summer of 1940. However, by night the defences were far less effective. To exploit this weakness, during the latter part of the daylight battle, the Luftwaffe mounted a campaign of night attacks against Britain's industrial centres and major ports. Simultaneously, the German Navy made an all-out attempt to sever Britain's maritime lifeline using U-boats and surface raiders. Adolf Hitler hoped that such a coordinated action might force the British government to sue for peace, though it would take longer. In the next chapter we shall observe the course of the night bombing campaign on Britain, and the various moves by the RAF to assemble an effective system to counter the night raider.

# CHAPTER 5

# Death by Darkness, August 1940–May 1941

A people who are bombed today as they were bombed yesterday, and who know that they will be bombed again tomorrow and see no end to their martyrdom, are bound in the end to call for peace.

*Giulio Douhet,* The Command of the Air, *1921*

Throughout the early summer of 1940, in parallel with its heavy daylight attacks, the Luftwaffe had mounted numerous small-scale night attacks against targets in Britain. For example, during the 8 hours after dusk on 27 August some 200 German bombers had crossed the coast and attacked targets in the following areas: Hull–Leeds–Manchester, Birmingham, Derby–Nottingham–Leicester, Lincolnshire, Norwich and on either side of the Thames Estuary. Also, bombers went in ones and twos to Plymouth, Bristol, Middlesbrough and Aberdeen. Mines were laid off the Humber, Tees and Thames Estuaries and off Yarmouth, Lowestoft and the Isle of Wight. Against such night attacks, the defences were impotent. Fighter Command put up a total of forty-seven sorties but the sole interception ended without a kill. Anti-aircraft guns opened fire on the raiders whenever they could locate them but claimed only one shot down, near Cardiff.

By the end of August there were twelve Knickebein-beam transmitting stations in operation; nine were new ones, set up in France, Holland and Norway from where they could point out targets anywhere in the British Isles. On the night of 27 August at least two Knickebein stations were radiating: those at Kleve and Dieppe provided beams that crossed over Nottingham. On this night No. 80 Wing of the RAF was using hastily improvised jammers to radiate low-powered jamming on the German beam frequencies. In addition, there was Meacon spoofing of the navigational beacons: on the night of 27 August those at Ruddervoorde, Trouville, Walcheren, Cherbourg, Dunkirk, St Malo, Dreux, Givry, Clermont, Fecamp and La Fleche were covered for all or part of the time by No. 80 Wing Meacons at Harpenden, Henfield, Flimwell, Temple Combe and Petersfield.

## NEW BEAM SYSTEMS

The Luftwaffe had not shown all its cards during the early night raids, however. During August it introduced two completely new radio-beam systems to

*A Heinkel 111 of the pathfinder unit Kampfgruppe 100; the two extra aerials for the X-Geraet receiver can be seen on the rear fuselage.* (Sommer)

guide its bombers, code-named 'X-Verfahren' and 'Y-Verfahren' (the X- and Y-systems).

The X-Verfahren employed a pair of ground Wotan I transmitters which radiated complex patterns of fine and narrow beams. For its operation the X-Verfahren employed four of those beams. In a manner similar to Knickebein, there was an approach beam that pointed directly at the target. Three other beams crossed the approach beam at points short of the target. The beams were radiated

*Unteroffizier Horst Goetz standing in the cockpit of a Heinkel of KGr 100; on the nose of the aircraft is the unit's 'Viking Ship' badge.* (Goetz)

on spot frequencies in the 66 to 77 MHz band, and were made up of morse dot and dash signals which came together to form a steady note signal in the central lane. To pick up these signals, each bomber carried an 'X-Geraet' (X-device) receiver system. The bombers flew up the approach beam and at a point 50 kilometres (31 miles) from the bomb-release point they flew through the first of the cross beams which served as a warning that they were approaching the target; at 20 kilometres (12½ miles) from the bomb-release point the aircraft passed the second cross beam and the observer pressed a button to start one hand of a special clock not unlike a stopwatch but with two hands that

*Wotan ground station for transmitting X-Geraet signals.*

rotated independently. When the aircraft was 5 kilometres (3 miles) from the bomb-release point it flew through the third cross beam and the observer again pressed the button on his special clock. The hand that had been moving now stopped and the other hand started rotating to catch it up. The distance from the second cross beam to the third cross beam was three times that from the third cross beam to the bomb-release point, so this second hand travelled three times faster than the first. When both hands coincided, a pair of electrical contacts closed and the bombs were released *automatically*. The combination of clock and beams provided accurate data on the bomber's speed over the ground, one of the

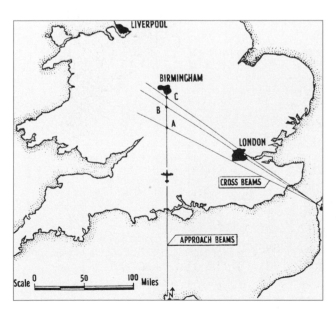

*X-beams aligned on the Spitfire factory at Castle Bromwich, as they were on the night of 13 August 1940. The aircraft flew up the approach beam until they passed the first cross beam (at A), indicating that they were 50 km from the target. As he heard the signals from the second cross beam, 20 km from the target (at B) the observer started his bomb-release clock. When he heard signals from the third cross beam, 5 km from the target (at C), the observer again pressed the button on his clock; the hand which had been moving then stopped and the other hand started rotating to catch it up. When the two hands overlapped, at the previously computed bomb-release point, the bombs were released automatically.*

most important factors necessary for precision bombing once the aircraft was routed (by the approach beam) accurately over the target.

The Y-Verfahren was more complicated. The single Wotan II transmitter radiated a complex beam pattern on spot frequencies in the 40 MHz band, comprising 180 directional signals per minute. That was too fast for human interpretation and the Y-Geraet equipment in the aircraft used a special electronic analyser to calculate its position within the beam. To measure the aircraft's position *along* the beam the ground station transmitted an additional ranging signal, which the aircraft equipment automatically picked up and re-radiated. By measuring the time interval between the transmission and the reception of the ranging signal, the ground operators were able to compute the aircraft's range with great accuracy. When the aircraft was at the previously calculated bomb-release point, its crew received the order to release the bombs. Since it required only one ground transmitting station, and left the minimum latitude for human error, the Y-Verfahren was technically the most advanced of the German systems.

All in all the X- and Y-Verfahren were for their time impressively sophisticated systems, especially if it is borne in mind that the X-Verfahren had been ready before the beginning of the war. Both new systems worked on frequencies somewhat higher than those used by Knickebein, with the result that their beams were thinner and their indications were more precise. On the other hand the X- and Y-Geraet receivers were much more complicated than those necessary to pick up the Knickebein signals; moreover, specially trained crews were required for their operation. As a result the X- and Y-systems were operated only by specialised units equipped with Heinkel 111s, respectively Kampfgruppe 100 based at Vannes in Brittany and III./KG 26 based at Poix, north of Paris.

On 11 August Kampfgruppe 100 began preparing for operations against England. Two days later, on the night of the 13th, the unit carried out a precision

*Crew of KG 4 boarding their Heinkel before a mission. The aircraft carries two 2,200-pound bombs under the fuselage.*

attack against the factory at Castle Bromwich near Birmingham, which was tooling up to produce Spitfires; eleven direct hits were scored on the factory buildings. Before the end of the month the Gruppe had carried out eleven further attacks.

During the middle of August the RAF radio-monitoring service picked up X-beam signals for the first time on a frequency of 74 MHz. In the weeks that followed the dossier on the new German system grew rapidly. Direction-finding stations located the beams' sources in the Cherbourg and Calais areas. Although the new signals differed from those of Knickebein in their frequency, the type of note and the keying rate of the dots and dashes were sufficiently similar for them to be identified as an aid to navigation. At the same time, 'Enigma' decrypts linked with the new system gave azimuth beam setting instructions to within 5 seconds of arc (implying an accuracy of about 12 feet at a distance of 100 miles from the transmitter). This revelation caused considerable anguish in RAF intelligence circles. Dr Cockburn's section at the Telecommunications Research Establishment at Swanage received instructions to begin work on a suitable jammer, as a top priority.

Yet, while the X-Geraet was indeed a clever system for its time, over Britain its accuracy was nowhere near as good as the 'Enigma' decrypts had suggested. As with all long-range beam systems, diffraction could also induce small but significant errors. The Y-Verfahren got off to a bad start. It proved so unreliable that operations had to cease until its 'bugs' had been ironed out. The only redeeming feature of this initial failure was its totality: the RAF monitoring service failed to detect the special Y-beam signals and the element of surprise remained.

## NEW PHASE IN THE ATTACK

With the impotence of the British night defences so clearly demonstrated, the Germans' next step was only a matter of time. Up until now the larger proportion of the Luftwaffe bomber force had remained inactive, because of the shortage of escorting fighters. Used by night to mount attacks against important targets, these bombers could add greatly to the pressure on the British war economy.

The new phase began on the night of 28 August, when 160 bombers attacked Liverpool. During the three nights that followed the city was raided in similar strength. Although the defences were able to force the bombers up to levels from which accurate bombing was difficult, and the jamming caused some bombers to get lost and miss their targets altogether, that was the limit of their success: during the four attacks the Luftwaffe lost only seven bombers.

On 7 September, following the first heavy daylight attack on London, the focus of the night attack shifted to the capital also. A total of 318 German bombers made for the city to launch an attack that would set the pattern for the nights to follow. With little to fear from the defences, raiders converged on London from all directions from south-west to due east. There was no attempt to concentrate the raiding force and the attack lasted from 2010 hours on the 7th until 0430 hours the following morning.

*Smoke rising from fires in the dockland area of London as seen from the roof of one of the buildings in Fleet Street, 7 September.*

With their target clearly marked by the fires started during the daylight assault, the night raiders were able to launch a devastatingly accurate attack. Soon after midnight there were nine fires raging that merited the description of 'conflagration'. (The official definition of a 'conflagration' is 'a major fire which is spreading' and requires more than one hundred pumps to bring it under control). One such blaze, in the Quebec Yard of the Surrey Docks, was the fiercest single fire ever recorded in Britain. In the book *Front Line*, the historian of the London Fire Brigade afterwards wrote:

At Woolwich Arsenal men fought the flames among boxes of live ammunition and crates of nitro-glycerine, under a hail of bombs directed at London's No. 1 military target. But in the docks themselves strange things were going on. There were pepper fires, loading the surrounding air heavily with stinging particles, so that when the firemen took a deep breath it felt like burning fire itself. There were rum fires, with torrents of blazing liquid pouring from the warehouse doors and barrels exploding like bombs themselves. There was a paint fire, another cascade of white-hot flames, coating the pumps with varnish that could not be cleaned for weeks. A rubber fire gave forth black clouds of smoke so asphyxiating that it could only be fought from a distance, and was always threatening to choke the attackers. Sugar, it seems, burns well in liquid form as it floats on the water in dockyard basins. Tea makes a blaze that is 'sweet, sickly and very intense'. One man found it odd to be pouring cold water on hot tea leaves. A grain warehouse when burning produced great clouds of

*A grim-faced Winston Churchill inspects the gutted works of the Silvertown Rubber Works, 8 September.*

black flies that settled in banks upon the walls, whence the firemen washed them off with their jets. There were rats in their hundreds. And the residue of burned wheat was 'a sticky mess that pulls your boots off'.

When the all–clear sounded on the morning of 8 September there were, in addition to the 9 conflagrations, 19 major fires, 40 serious fires and nearly 1,000 smaller fires. A total of 430 Londoners had been killed and some 1,600 were seriously injured.

The London Fire Brigade spent the entire day of 8 September battling desperately with the fires. Those that remained would serve as beacons to guide the German bombers, if they returned that night. In spite of their efforts, however, there was light aplenty for the 207 bombers that returned to the capital after dark. Those fires that had survived the firefighters' efforts were fed afresh and new ones were started. By the morning of 9 September, twelve conflagrations were raging out of control. A further 412 people were killed and 747 seriously injured and for a short time every railway line going southwards from the capital was out of action due to damage to the four main termini. The bombers would be back in force on the following night and the nights to follow.

## THE GUNNERS' PROBLEMS

Faced with these massive and repeated attacks, the London defences proved no more effective than those of the provincial cities in warding off the raiders.

*General Frederick Pile, the commander of Anti-Aircraft Command.* (IWM)

Operating at altitudes of over 15,000 feet, the bombers were often out of hearing of the sound locators. Moreover, if more than one aircraft was passing through the zone between adjacent locators, there could be no certainty that both were tracking the same aircraft.

There was one further German counter to the sound locators, which many who lived in wartime Britain remember to this day. To track aircraft, the sound-locator operators required a steady note from the aircraft engines. This could be denied, however, if the German pilot ran one engine slightly faster than the other. The resultant 'waaam–waaam–waaam' note made aural direction finding extremely difficult. The sound of desynchronised engines was quite distinctive and listeners on the ground could thus distinguish hostile from friendly aircraft at night.

The RAF used similar tactics to throw off sound locators during its raids on Germany, and German civilians also came to distinguish friend from foe in this way.

*A troop of 3.7-in anti-aircraft guns sited in Hyde Park loosing off a salvo against German aircraft over the capital at night. During the autumn and winter of 1940 the British anti-aircraft fire at night was, in Pile's words, 'largely wild and uncontrolled shooting'.* (via Wood)

The breakdown of the gun-control system meant that for much of the time the ninety-two heavy guns round London were unable to fire because they lacked information on the whereabouts of targets. To get the guns firing General Frederick Pile, in charge of Anti-Aircraft Command, gave instructions to battery commanders that in the absence of information they were to fire at enemy bombers heard overhead using any possible method of aiming. As Pile later noted in his official dispatch: 'The volume of fire which resulted, and which was publicised as a 'barrage', was in factor largely wild and uncontrolled shooting. There were, however, two valuable results from it: the volume of fire had a deterrent effect upon at least some of the German aircrews . . . there was also a marked improvement in civilian morale.' That was one way of looking at it. On the other hand, a total of 260,000 heavy anti-aircraft shells were loosed off during September, most of them into thin air. This number was far greater than the meagre results justified and could not be maintained indefinitely without causing a serious depletion of the reserves. And although the citizens of London derived comfort from the sound of gunfire, and the thought that their tormentors were suffering also, the chances of an unaimed shell bursting close enough to knock down an enemy bomber were so small as to be negligible. As Professor Archibald Hill of the Air Defence Research Committee wrote at the time:

> One cubic mile of space contains 5,500,000,000 cubic yards. The lethal zone of a 3.7-inch shell is only a few thousand cubic yards and exists for only about 1/50th of a second. The idea of a 'barrage' of anti-aircraft shells is nonsense. The word ought to be dropped; it gives a false impression, and is based on sloppy thinking and bad arithmetic. Nothing but aimed fire is of any use. In order to give a *one-fiftieth* chance of bringing down an enemy moving at 250 miles per hour and crossing a vertical rectangle ten miles wide and four miles high (from the barrage balloons to 25,000 feet) about *three thousand 3.7-inch shells would be required a second.* (Author's italics.)

Obviously some form of radar control for the guns was necessary if they were to engage the night raiders with any prospect of success. During the summer of 1940 the first hand-built GL (Gun Laying) Mark I radars became available. These had been designed to give only the range of targets previously detected by sound locators, however. They required considerable modification to enable them to measure the bearing and elevation of aircraft. Early in October, the modified GL Mark I sets were pressed into action. The radar was still crude, unreliable and the fire it controlled was far from precise at the best of times and grossly inaccurate at the worst. Yet, as we have observed, any form of aimed fire was a great improvement over unaimed fire. At first Pile had only a few radars, insufficient to provide one for each four-gun site. To enable all guns to be controlled with radar, he had those around London re-sited into groups of eight each with a GL set.

*To render them less conspicuous during the night attacks the sides and under surfaces of the German bombers were daubed with matt black distemper, as in the case of this Ju 88 of KG 1.*

## THE NIGHT FIGHTERS' PROBLEMS

When the night blitz on Britain began, Fighter Command was no better able to fight off the raiders than the gunners had been. *Quantitatively* the force of night fighters available was strong enough to inflict serious losses on the raiders. But *qualitatively* its equipment was poor. The main part of the force comprised six squadrons of Blenheims, low-performance machines fitted with the crude AI Mark III radar. In addition there were two squadrons of Defiants that had been relegated to night operations and lacked any sort of radar, as did the single-seat Spitfires and Hurricanes that flew night patrols. The instructions from the ground on the whereabouts of raiders were so imprecise as to be useless. Although scores of sorties were flown each night, successes were few and largely a matter of luck.

At this time the overland tracking of raiders was the responsibility of the Observer Corps. By day this system worked well enough. But by night the posts were able to give only sound plots which, though useful in a general way, were nowhere near accurate enough for the direction of night fighters. Air Chief Marshal Dowding saw clearly that some form of overland radar-plotting system was essential if his fighters were to master the threat of the night bomber. He persuaded General Pile to part with ten precious GL radars and installed these at selected searchlight sites in the Kenley Sector, astride a frequently used German approach route to London. The radar operators were linked by landline with the Kenley Sector operations room, where the radar plots on the raiders were chalked up at 30-second intervals on a large gridded blackboard. The fighter, tracked by its 'Pip-Squeak' transmissions, was then directed towards its prey by the Sector controller. Guided by radar, the searchlights were to point their beams towards the enemy aircraft. Even if the latter was not illuminated, it was hoped that the line of the beam would give the fighter pilot some assistance in locating the raider. Although it was a makeshift system, it soon demonstrated that the general line of approach was correct. Radar operators in the Blenheims frequently saw returns from enemy aircraft within AI range, though

*A Defiant of No. 264 Squadron preparing to take off for a night sortie. During the attack on London on the night of 15 October, this unit brought down the only German bomber to fall to enemy action. (IWM)*

*Armourers complete the loading of a pair of SC 250 550-pounders on an He 111.*

*The largest type of German bomb dropped on targets in Britain was the SC 2500, the 5,500-pounder nicknamed 'Max'.*

there were few 'kills' because the fighter lacked the performance to catch, and the firepower to knock down, the bombers.

The 90-cm searchlight proved disappointing as a means of providing direct illumination of bombers so that the night fighters could engage. Pilot Officer Dick Haine, who flew Blenheims with No. 600 Squadron at this time, recalled:

It might seem a simple matter for night fighter crews to see the bombers which had been illuminated by searchlights, but this was not the case. If the raiders came on bright moonlight nights, which was usual during this time, the beams of the 90-cm searchlights were not visible at heights much above 10,000 feet. If the searchlights were actually on the enemy bomber the latter could be seen from some way away, but only if the fighter was beneath the bomber and could see its illuminated underside; if the fighter was higher than the bomber, the latter remained invisible to the fighter pilot. If there was any haze or cloud it tended to diffuse the beams so that there was no clear intersection to be seen, even if two or more searchlights were accurately following the target.

Meanwhile, new equipment was in the pipeline to meet Fighter Command's most pressing problems. The first of these, the prototype of the new purpose-built ground radar for the direction of night fighters, the GCI (Ground Controlled Interception), was nearing completion at the Telecommunications Research Establishment. This set would have a range of 50 miles, more than six times that of the gun-laying radars used during the Kenley experiment. To reduce the delays in plotting, the GCI set used the rotating timebase type of display (nowadays this type of display is the most common for radars, but in 1940 it was a major innovation). With both the enemy aircraft and the intercepting fighter shown in plan on his screen, the GCI controller was to radio instructions to position the fighter within AI range of its target.

As important as a new radar to direct the night fighters was a new high-performance machine to replace the obsolescent Blenheim. The Beaufighter, which began to arrive at squadrons in September 1940, had a maximum speed of 323 mph at 15,000 feet. Moreover, it carried the unprecedentedly heavy armament, for a British fighter, of four 20-mm Hispano cannon (which were reliable when mounted upright rigidly in the nose) and six .303-inch machine-guns. To compound its effectiveness, the Beaufighter carried the latest AI Mark IV radar. Better engineered than the old Mark III fitted in the Blenheim, the new set had a higher powered transmitter giving greater range and an improved receiver that made it possible to

*The Beaufighter carrying AI Mark IV radar, which became operational during the latter half of 1940, proved to be the long-term answer to the menace of the night raider.* (BAC)

track targets to a minimum range of 140 yards. Great things were expected from the Beaufighter and its new radar. But in each case production would be slow getting into its stride and, as with any new piece of equipment, there would be teething troubles to overcome.

So the two main elements of the British night-air defences, the anti-aircraft guns and the fighters, were making progress. The same could also be said for the third element: No. 80 Wing formed to jam the various German navigational systems. Early in September the first purpose-built jammers came into operation to counter Knickebein, code-named 'Aspirin'. This device transmitted powerful Morse dashes on the German beam frequencies. The dashes were not synchronised with the German signals, but were superimposed on them. Thus, when a German pilot entered the dash zone he would turn port to where he expected the 'steady note' zone to be. In the 'steady note' zone, however, he continued to hear the dashes and so tended to overshoot. When in the dot zone, he would hear a mixture of dots and dashes which would not resolve themselves into a steady note at all. 'Aspirins' were prescribed for the more important jamming sites, replacing the less-efficient improvised transmitters which had been pressed into service. The latter went to new sites, to extend the area protected by jamming.

During this time there was controversy as to whether it might not be better to build a device to *bend* the German beams so bombers were pushed off course without their crews realising it. Technically, such a beam-bending device was feasible. But such an elegant countermeasure would take a long time to develop.

And with Britain's cities under almost nightly bombardment, time was the one thing No. 80 Wing could not afford. As a result of this situation, Dr Cockburn and his jamming team at Swanage produced the simpler but technically more crude 'Aspirin' jammer.

Perhaps it was a wartime 'plant' by British Intelligence, with the aim of weakening the Germans' confidence in their beams, but to this day many people believe that the RAF was able to bend the German navigational beams and make the raiders release their bombs 'to order'. Even during the war such stories were current and sometimes they caused embarrassment to No. 80 Wing. As the unit's commander, Wing Commander Edward Addison, told the author:

> Whenever anything unusual happened, people thought it was us. At the time we worked in such secrecy that when these funny ideas got around we had no means of correcting them – even had we wanted to. On one occasion a German aircraft unloaded its bombs in the castle grounds at Windsor. The next morning, the Comptroller of the King's Household rang me; he was very cross and wanted to know why we had bent the beams over Windsor – His Majesty might have been killed. It was the usual case of a lost German getting rid of his bombs – and we got the credit or the blame, depending on where they fell.

But if the Knickebein beams were not bent deliberately, they were certainly bent accidentally on occasions. It will be remembered that the dashes from 'Aspirin' were not radiated in synchronism with the beam's dashes. On the other hand, they were not deliberately radiated *out* of synchronism. The result was a continuous drift in and out of synchronism, rather as a man and a woman walking together with slightly different lengths of pace will drift in and out of step. So there were times when the 'Aspirin' dashes synchronised accidentally with the German dots to produce a 'steady note' zone which, instead of being confined to a narrow lane, extended over a wide area; when this happened German crews attempting to fly the beam could have been led off course. It must be stressed, however, that this effect was not deliberate.

No. 80 Wing was never large: in October 1940 it comprised only 20 officers and 200 men, to operate the 15 'Aspirin' sites and the various Meacons dotted throughout southern England. What did the Wing achieve? In theory, the Knickebein beams could have marked out a square with sides 300 yards long in the sky over London – about the size of one of the larger blocks of ministry buildings in Whitehall. Had German bomber crews been allowed to use Knickebein freely, there can be no doubt that the attacks on London and other British cities would have been a good deal more effective than they were. In the event, however, even weak jamming proved remarkably successful in preventing them using this system. One Heinkel pilot recalled:

> At first we were very excited about *Knickebein*, a fine new method of navigation and a big help to find our targets. But after we had used it on operations once or twice, we realised that the British were interfering with it. Initially the jamming was weak and it hardly concealed the beam signals at all. But the fact

*'Like bubbling pea soup' was how one German pilot described the appearance of London during the night attacks in the autumn of 1940. This photograph was taken from one of the raiders and shows the fires burning on the ground and shells bursting overhead.* (Dierich)

that our enemy obviously knew that the beams existed and that they were pointing towards the target for the night, was very disconcerting. For all we knew, night fighters might be concentrating all the way along the beam to the target; more and more crews began to use the *Knickebein* beams only for range and kept out of them on the run up to the target.

By using Knickebein during the small-scale operations over Britain before the main battle, the Luftwaffe had compromised its secrets. When the bomber force really needed its beams No. 80 Wing had the knowledge and the means to 'nobble' the system.

As the night Blitz got under way the other German beam system in frequent use, the X-Verfahren, had also been uncovered by British Intelligence. Dr Cockburn and his jamming team modified a few gun-laying radars into suitable jammers, under the code-name 'Bromide'. By the end of September Kampfgruppe 100 had taken part in some forty attacks on Britain, half of them

*On the evening of 14 October a bomb fell in Balham High Street near the underground station. The resultant crater took the top off the Northern Line tunnel and caused severe flooding. When the bomb exploded this bus was 25 yards from the impact point and heading towards it. The driver had a lucky escape – he was blown from his cab and ended up in a shop doorway with cuts and bruises. Others were less fortunate – sixty-eight people were killed in the incident, many of them taking shelter in the station.*

*One of the greatest hazards faced by German bombers attacking Britain by night in 1940 and 1941 was the landing at the often ill-equipped airfields in France and Belgium. This Ju 88 of KG 1 ground-looped after returning from a sortie.*

on London. The unit often visited targets alone, attempting precision attacks using the X-beams. In almost every case British Intelligence was able to establish the 'Kampfgruppe 100 footprint' after these attacks: the line of bomb craters on a bearing which, extrapolated southwards, led directly to the approach beam transmitter near Cherbourg.

German aircrews had no way of knowing about the various schemes being prepared for their future discomfort. All they knew was that in the autumn of 1940 the British night defences were weak and ineffectual. Unteroffizier Horst Goetz served as a pilot with KGr 100 during these attacks and from his logbook we can observe the rate at which his unit operated during one three-week period: against London on 23 September, once in the morning and once on the evening of the 24th, on the 27th, 28th, 29th, 30th, 2 October and 4th; against Manchester on the 7th and 9th and against Coventry on the 12th. Of this period he later recalled:

> I have no particular memories of individual operations. They were all quite routine, like running a bus service. The London flak defences put on a great show – at night the exploding shells gave the place the appearance of bubbling pea soup; but very few of our aircraft were hit – I myself never collected so much as a shell fragment. On rare occasions one of my crew might catch sight of a British night fighter, but it seems they never saw us and we were never attacked. During our return flights the radio operator would often tune in his receiver to a music programme, to provide some relief from the monotony.

Goetz was an experienced pilot, with more than 1,800 flying hours before he began operating over Britain. He had little difficulty in flying at night. This was not so for the less-experienced pilots, however, and there were frequent accidents at the ill-equipped forward airfields in France, Holland and Belgium.

Meanwhile, night after night, London was reeling under the repeated hammer blows from the Luftwaffe. One of the heaviest attacks began soon after dark on

15 October. Like all large-scale German attacks of this period, it was protracted, beginning at 2040 hours in the evening and ending at 0440 hours the following morning. It was a moonlit night and the raiding force of some 400 bombers approached the city at altitudes of between 16,000 and 20,000 feet. The vanguard came in from Holland and crossed the coast at Essex. Succeeding aircraft came in from Holland and Belgium via the Thames Estuary, and from various points in northern France, crossing the south coast of England between Bognor Regis and Dungeness. German crews reported the anti-aircraft fire over London as varied, with barrage fire extending from 13,000 to 20,000 feet, strongest in the south-eastern and south-western sectors of the capital. A great deal of searchlight activity was also reported.

Guenther Unger, now a feldwebel, flew two sorties in his Dornier 17 against London the night of 15/16 October, one in the evening and the other early in the morning, with just over two hours on the ground between each. On both occasions his target was the dock area. His orders were to remain over the target for as long as possible, to circle and release one bomb every 5 minutes or so and cause the maximum amount of disruption. Displaying a realistic contempt for the so-called 'barrage', Unger spent about 25 minutes circling over London on each occasion.

A total of forty-one fighters took off to engage the raiders but only two succeeded in making interceptions. One was a Blenheim of No. 23 Squadron whose radar operator made AI contact over Tunbridge Wells but, after a long chase, the bomber escaped. The other was a Defiant of No. 264 Squadron which chanced upon a Heinkel 111. Its pilot, Pilot Officer Desmond Hughes, told the author:

It was a bright moonlight night. Suddenly, out of the corner of my eye I saw something move across the stars out to my left. If you are scanning the night sky it is normally completely still, so anything that moves attracts the eye. This just had to be another aircraft. I got Fred [Sergeant Fred Gash, the gunner] to swing his turret round and we both kept an eye on the black shape. We moved towards it and soon caught sight of a row of exhausts. It was a twin-engined aircraft. I slid alongside, below and to the right of him, and slowly edged in 'under his armpit' while Fred kept his guns trained on the aircraft. Then we saw the distinctive wing and tail shape of a Heinkel – there was no mistaking it. I moved into a firing position, within about 50 yards off his wing tip and slightly below, so that Fred could align his guns for an upwards shot at about 20 degrees. Obviously the German crew had not seen us, they continued straight ahead.

Fred fired straight into the starboard engine. One round in six was a tracer, but what told us we were hitting the Heinkel was the glitter of the de Wilde [incendiary rounds] as they ignited on impact. Fred fired, realigned, fired again. He got off two or three bursts. There was no return fire from the bomber – indeed, I doubt if any guns could have been brought to bear on our position on its beam. The engine burst into flames, then the Heinkel rolled on its back, went down steeply and crashed into a field near Brentwood.

The Heinkel belonged to Kampfgruppe 126; two crewmen bailed out and were taken prisoner, the other two were killed.

*Bomb damage in Leicester Square in front of the Headquarters of the Automobile Association, 17 October. The vehicles in the foreground were too badly damaged even for that organisation's talented mechanics to get them running again!*

During the attack London's railway services were hard hit: the termini at St Pancras, Marylebone, Broad Street, Waterloo and Victoria were all put out of action for varying periods. Traffic to Euston, Cannon Street, Charing Cross and London Bridge had to be reduced to less than a third of its normal volume. A bomb on the outskirts of the City burst the Fleet sewer, and the waters from it poured into the railway tunnel between Farringdon Street and King's Cross. Three large water mains were also fractured. The Becton Gasworks, Battersea Power Station and the BBC Headquarters at Portland Place were all hit and there was widespread damage in residential areas. More than 900 fires were reported in the London area, of which six were described as 'major' and nine as 'serious'. A total of 430 people were killed and some 900 suffered serious injuries.

Although London was the main target for the German bombers on the night of 15 October, it was not the only one. Twenty Heinkels of K.Gr 100 attacked Birmingham and eight Dorniers of K.Gr 606 made for Bristol. Simultaneously, bombers in ones and twos attacked Southend, Windsor and Portsmouth, Yeovil, Southampton and Bournemouth, Plymouth, Tunbridge Wells, Hastings, Reigate and Eastbourne. Two four-engined Focke Wulf 200s, maritime reconnaissance bombers rarely used over Britain, attempted to attack the Rolls Royce Works at Hillingdon but failed to find their target.

The nightly attacks on London continued, with but a single completely peaceful night for its citizens, from 7 September until early on the morning of 14 November: sixty-seven nights of bombardment.

## THE ATTACK ON COVENTRY

During the summer and autumn of 1940 Luftwaffe signals personnel worked hard to extend the network of landlines westwards through France. As each unit was connected up, it ceased using the wireless to transmit messages to and receive them from its headquarters. Each time that happened, it shut off one further source of information to the cryptographers at Bletchley Park. As luck would have it, however, Kampfgruppe 100's base in Brittany lay in the far west of France and was among the last to go 'on line'. As a result, the unit's communications provided a stream of useful information for a little while longer.

On 11 November, a decrypt of a message sent two days earlier gave the signals procedures to be used by KGr 100 during an important forthcoming operation, 'Moonlight Sonata'. The signal gave no indication of the target for attack. Nor did it give the date, though the code-name suggested the attack would take place during the full-moon period in the middle of the month.

Examination of Luftwaffe signals decrypts and prisoner interrogations in the days to follow pointed to future operations against several targets that might or might not be linked to 'Moonlight Sonata'. The list included Wolverhampton, Birmingham, Coventry, the Harwich–Ipswich district, the Faversham–Rochester–Sheerness district, and even 'The Industrial District of England'.

*Succeeding Sir Hugh Dowding, Air Marshal Sir W. Sholto Douglas was appointed C-in-C Fighter Command in November 1940 and held the post for two years.* (IWM)

In an attempt to blunt the effect of 'Moonlight Sonata' the RAF drew up a counter-plan, 'Cold Water', to take place once the German operation was under way. 'Cold Water' would have six main features. First, there would be a continuous watch on Luftwaffe radio activity, with No. 80 Wing putting out maximum interference of German navigational beacon and beam transmissions. Secondly, RAF bombers would fly nuisance raids over German bomber airfields in France, Holland and Belgium. Thirdly, there would be a large-scale attack on the airfields at Vannes and St Leger used by KGr 100. Fourthly, bombers were to attack the beam transmitters near Cherbourg. Fifthly, there would be a simultaneous attack on a selected city in Germany. And sixthly, Fighter Command was to send the maximum possible number of night fighters into action against the raiders.

During the mid-afternoon of 14 November, No. 80 Wing listening stations heard the X-beam transmitters come on the air, and established that the pattern of beams was aligned on Coventry. Almost certainly this city was the target for 'Moonlight Sonata' and the attack would be launched that evening. Thereupon, the executive order for 'Cold Water' was issued to the units earmarked for it. It was too late, however, to reposition AA units to assist in the defence of the city.

A total of 449 bombers took part in the raid on Coventry that night. One or two Heinkels of KGr 100 started fires at the target early in the attack, and the remainder of the unit's thirteen planes attacked at intervals at the same time as the rest of the main force. Even without the assistance of KGr 100 it is likely the main force of bombers would have found their target with little difficulty, for it was a bright moonlit night with clear skies. Guenther Unger confirms the ease with which Coventry was located:

> While we were still over the Channel on the way in we caught sight of a small pinpoint of white light in front of us, looking rather like a hand torch seen from two hundred yards. My crew and I speculated as to what it might be – some form of beacon to guide British night fighters, perhaps? As we drew closer to our target the light gradually became larger until suddenly it dawned on us: we were looking at the burning city of Coventry.

The scale of the bombardment that night was one that Londoners had grown used to. But London was a vastly bigger target than Coventry. Parts of the Midland city were razed to the ground and production was brought to a virtual halt; 506 people were killed and 432 seriously injured.

Although it was executed in a timely manner, Operation 'Cold Water' failed to deliver any discernible relief for Coventry. About two dozen Coastal Command aircraft, Blenheims and Hudsons, bombed the airfields at Vannes, St Leger and Rosendail. All returned safely. Bomber Command sent eighty-two Whitleys, Wellingtons and Hampdens to attack Berlin and the airfields at Schiphol and Soesterberg in Holland. Twelve of these failed to return and one crashed on landing, making this Bomber Command's heaviest single night's loss to date. Aircraft attacked two beam-transmitting stations on the Cherbourg Peninsula, and claimed to have inflicted damage to both.

Fighter Command put up 121 fighters to engage the raiders, including 10 Beaufighters and 39 Blenheims carrying AI radar. Yet the results of their efforts were disappointing. AI fighters made contact with radar eleven times, but only one led to a sighting. Non-AI fighters achieved ten sightings, but only one claimed to have damaged a raider. Although it was a moonlit night, lacking effective ground control radar the defending fighters had a difficult task. The bombers flew in long 'crocodiles', with an average of 12 miles between each. They were dispersed some 7 miles to either side of track, flying at altitudes of between 10,000 and 20,000 feet; this meant that on average there was one bomber to 330 *cubic miles* of airspace. There simply was nothing for the night fighters to concentrate on.

The anti-aircraft gunners did a little better and brought down one bomber over Birmingham and another near Loughborough. German losses for the night amounted to less than ½ per cent of the force involved.

## AFTER COVENTRY

The new 'Bromide' transmitters of No. 80 Wing should have been able to neutralise the X-beams to some extent, but in the event their jamming had little effect. What had gone wrong? The jammer had been hastily conceived at a time when too little was known about the X-Verfahren, as a result the tone of the jamming signals was radiated at the 1,150 cycles note used by Knickebein instead of the 2,000 cycles actually used by the X-Verfahren. It was the difference between a whistle and a shriek, but the filter circuits in the German receivers were sensitive enough to pick the beam signals out of the jamming with ease. During the investigation following the Coventry attack this error was discovered and jammers were hastily modified to radiate on the correct tone.

The destruction visited on Coventry appeared to confirm the feared level of effectiveness of the X-beam system combined with KGr 100's target-illumination methods. Following the Coventry raid, other cities outside London came under large-scale attack. Birmingham was raided on the nights of 19 November (with thirteen Heinkels from KGr 100 involved), the 20th (eleven) and the 22nd (nine). Yet that city suffered nothing like the concentrated damage inflicted on its neighbour.

British intelligence circles attributed the apparent reduction in effectiveness of these German attacks to improvements to the Bromide jammer. However, in retrospect it is clear that the German system of marking targets had several weaknesses. During the Birmingham attacks there was cloud cover in the target area, and no bright moon to assist the raiders. The incendiary canisters dropped from the KGr 100 planes were inaccurate weapons, designed to scatter individual bombs over a large area. Even if the fire-raisers released their loads accurately, the incendiaries covered a large area on the ground. Moreover, the effect of the marking was diluted when the main force of bombers arrived and these planes dropped large numbers of incendiary bombs with varying degrees of accuracy. (Later in the war the RAF would use specially developed ground marker bombs, manufactured to fine tolerances to permit accurate aiming, to produce distinctive coloured marking at targets. Only pathfinder aircraft flown by picked crews carried these specialised weapons.)

Meanwhile, the defences were improving in other ways. During the attack on Birmingham on the night of 19 November a Beaufighter with the new AI Mark IV radar made the first kill. Flight Lieutenant John Cunningham of No. 604 Squadron was

*Flight Lieutenant John Cunningham was the first pilot to achieve a kill using the Beaufighter and AI Mark IV. He went on to become the most successful home-defence night-fighter pilot in the RAF. (Wright)*

on patrol south of the target when he spotted a cone of searchlights. He headed towards it and shortly afterwards his radar operator, Sergeant J. Phillipson, observed a firm echo on his screens; Phillipson directed his pilot in behind the aircraft until the latter caught sight of what appeared to be a 'four-engined aircraft'. Cunningham opened fire but was blinded by his muzzle flash and the German aircraft escaped. Some 20 minutes afterwards, however, a Junkers 88 crashed in flames on the south coast near Selsey Bill. Its crew had baled out and were soon captured, and one of them stated that they had been fired at by a night fighter shortly before they reached the target. No other fighter had reported engaging a bomber in that area and it was clear that Cunningham had seen the four exhausts of the Ju 88 and assumed it was a four-engined aircraft. This first kill did not mark the end of the teething troubles of the new fighter or its radar – there would be no further successes for it during the remainder of the year. But the 'kill' did provide a lot of encouragement and showed that when both the fighter and its radar functioned properly, they made a lethal combination.

In the final part of November the Luftwaffe visited London, Southampton, Bristol, Plymouth and Liverpool, as well as repeating its attack on Birmingham. In December there was no major attack on Plymouth, but the remaining cities were all struck again and Portsmouth, Sheffield and Manchester were added to the list. During this month raiding forces comprising more than a hundred bombers operated over Britain on eleven nights.

## TERROR ON THE GROUND

Each raid brought its own brand of terror and tragedy to the city involved. Peter Elstob described vividly what it was like to be on the receiving end of one attack on London:

> One evening after the sirens had sounded their usual warning and nothing had happened, there was a sound like stones being thrown against the house or a number of slates falling off the roof. We ran to the front door and found an incendiary bomb burning brightly on the mat. Roland dashed upstairs for a bucket of sand he kept for just such an emergency; I ran to the kitchen and snatched up a bowl of washing-up water. The suds doused the bomb, snuffing it like a candle.
>
> From the doorway we could see that there were many other incendiaries, some burning out harmlessly in the road or basement areas, some on houses, and one on the back seat of a car, having burned through the roof. Roland dumped his bucket of sand on that one and was pleased that it obediently went out. The bombs were about nine inches long and burned with a white light for three or four minutes, leaving only their tail fins . . .
>
> The daughter of a trapped woman was standing on her doorstep crying hysterically. Roland asked her which room her mother was in. 'Second floor, back, but she's dead. Oh, poor mum, she's dead, I know she's dead.'
>
> Roland gave me a full bucket of water and kept the stirrup pump himself. We soaked handkerchiefs, tied them over our nose and mouth and went up the

smoke-filled stairs on our hands and knees. He kicked open the bedroom door. The room was full of smoke but there was a red glow in one corner and he crawled towards this. I pumped and he directed the spray.

The incendiary had crashed through the roof and the bedroom ceiling, landing on the bed. All the smoke in the house was coming from the burning mattress and bedding. The bomb had long since burned itself out and the spray soon had the fire out. As the smoke cleared we could see an old lady in the bed. She was quite dead.

Once outside again we were grabbed by a little old man in a white muffler who begged us to put out some incendiaries lodged in his attic. We got these out fairly quickly but he then pointed to a ladder and an open skylight, saying that there were more on the roof. Somehow I found myself edging along the peak of the roof clutching a stirrup pump while Roland came behind with a bucket.

From up there we could see down into the street and away over the rooftops. It was an extraordinary sight: all around the horizon fires glowed, searchlights slowly raked the dark sky, anti-aircraft guns flashed silently, there being no apparent connection between them and the almost continuous noise of the guns. High above us shells burst like fireworks. But the most insistent noise came from the street immediately beneath us. It was the excited sound of many people shouting as they scurried in and out of their houses.

I started to spray the incendiary lodged by the chimney when I heard the sound of more bombs coming down and hugged the peak of the roof. Moments later a stick of small, 50-pound high-explosive bombs fell in a line across houses and street. [Almost certainly these were 110-pounder SC 50s, the smallest high-explosive bomb used in large numbers against Britain at this time.]

The bombers, earlier in the evening, had dropped nothing but hundreds of incendiaries. But this wave, a couple of hours later, came back with high-explosive bombs where the fires were brightest and most people were in the streets.

The explosions caused panic; people ran back into burning houses or threw themselves into basement areas. I heard screams above the explosions as I tried to dig myself into the slates of the roof.

The rain of bombs lasted only a few minutes but it was dawn before the fires were all out and the injured had been taken away. We sat in the kitchen of our house drinking cocoa with neighbours who had lived near each other for years but had never spoken. Now they were talking and gesticulating in a most un-English manner as they described the narrow escapes of the night.

As the New Year opened the Luftwaffe twin-engined bomber units deployed for the bombardment of Britain possessed a total of 1,291 aircraft, a number almost exactly equal to that available in September. The protracted operations from the ill-equipped forward airfields had taken their toll, however, and only 551 bombers were listed as serviceable in the returns for 4 January; this represented a fall in serviceability of one-quarter since September. At this time the third of the German beam navigation systems, the Y-Verfahren, came back into use. With the bugs now ironed out, it was considerably more reliable than before. The unit operating the system, III./KG 26, joined KGr 100 in the role of fire-raisers.

*A Heinkel 111 pathfinder of III./KG 26, with the extra aerial for the Y-Geraet mounted above the fuselage; a 2,200-pound bomb was mounted under the fuselage. Standing in front of the aircraft was Major Viktor von Lossberg, the commander of III./KG 26 during the attacks on Britain in 1941.* (Von Lossberg)

## NEW BRITISH RADAR, NEW BRITISH TACTICS

Also at the beginning of the New Year, Britain's night fighters began to increase in effectiveness. However, at first that improvement was barely discernible.

As we have observed, the most promising of the new devices to counter the night bomber was the Beaufighter with AI Mark IV radar. But if these were to realise their full potential, a medium-range precision radar on the ground was necessary so that the aircrew could be directed into position to intercept. The first of the new GCI radars already existed and, to reduce delays, it was decided to manufacture six more even before the prototype had completed its trials. The move was a gamble, because the set brought into use many new ideas, both technical and operational. But it paid off. By the beginning of 1941 six production GCI sets had been built and within a month they were all operational, sited to cover the main approach routes to London and the Midland targets.

One of the first operational interceptions bringing together the Beaufighter and GCI radar occurred on 12 January. The pilot was again Flight Lieutenant Cunningham, this time with the assistance of the prototype GCI station set up at Durrington near Shoreham. A steady stream of instructions from the ground controller took the Beaufighter into position behind the raider, then the AI operator, Sergeant Rawnsley, picked up a contact at extreme range, nearly 3 miles, slightly to port and below. Rawnsley guided his pilot to within visual range of the

*The early pattern GCI radar station at Sopley near Bournemouth, with the camouflaged operations hut to the right.*

bomber, which was recognised as a Heinkel 111, and Cunningham opened fire. After a few rounds, however, the fighter's armament failed due to a fault in the air-pressure system. Although damaged, the bomber was able to escape. After all that had been achieved, this last-minute and unusual failure was a bitter blow.

The 'all radar' interception was, however, a clear pointer to the future. It brought together the long-range low-precision Chain Home radar to provide early warning of the approach of raiders; medium-range medium-precision GCI radar to place the night fighter within AI range of the target; short-range high-precision AI radar on board the night fighter to enable the operator to direct the pilot to within visual range of the target; a well-knit aircrew directed from the ground by VHF radio; and last, but certainly not least, a fighter with the endurance to wait for, the performance to catch and the fire-power to cleave down the enemy bombers. At the beginning of 1941 each element of this defensive system was in service. It just remained to get all of them to work simultaneously.

*Inside the operations room at the Sopley GCI station. The man nearest the camera was a fighter controller, directing a night fighter from the tube in front of him; to his left sat a WAAF assistant. In the centre of the room sat a WAAF switchboard operator, and to her right a WAAF recorder. Standing on the dais was a WAAF plotter who marked up the positions of aircraft in the area on the local situation map.*

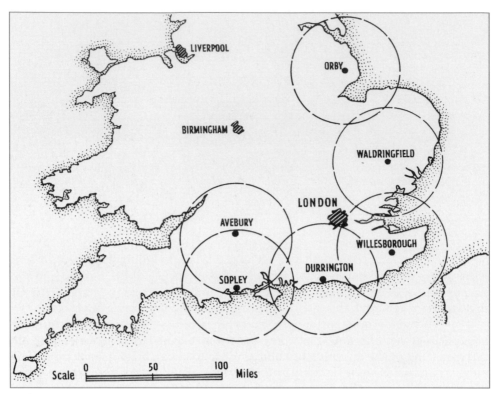

*Positions and approximate coverage of the first six Ground Controlled Interception radar stations, January 1941.*

By the middle of February there were two squadrons equipped with Beaufighters, and two more in the process of re-equipping.

## THE LONG AERIAL MINE

At the turn of the year the AI Beaufighter with GCI direction promised to be the most effective counter to the night raider. But it was not the only such airborne weapon under development in Britain. A less conventional solution to the problem was to lay out an 'aerial minefield' to trap the raiders: a curtain of slowly descending parachute bombs laid in front of enemy bombers approaching the coast. This scheme promised the advantage that high-performance aircraft were not necessary for its operation. Any machine that could carry 100 or so of the small parachute bombs to 20,000 feet was suitable. During 1940 ideas crystalised into considering using the obsolete Harrow bomber as 'mine-layer'; operating under orders from the ground, these aircraft were to release the mines in lines across the enemy bombers' flight path. The official name for the weapon was the Long Aerial Mine. Weighing 14 pounds at release, once clear of the aircraft it opened into a supporting parachute with a 1-pound bomb, beneath which dangled 2,000 feet of piano wire terminating in a second, furled, parachute. During the 'lay' the

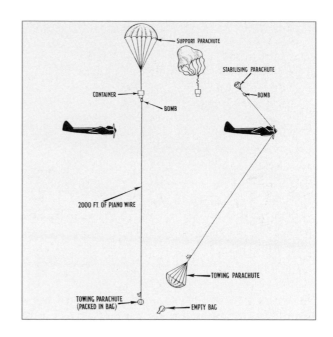

*The Long Aerial Mine. Released at 200-foot intervals at right angles to the German bombers track, the parachute mines unfurled to form a slowly descending curtain into which it was hoped their prey would fly. When an aircraft struck the wire the shock of impact released the upper parachute and at the same time unfurled the parachute at the bottom of the wire. The lower parachute, which rapidly took up a position behind the aircraft, pulled down the bomb which exploded on impact.*

mines were released at 200-foot intervals; the full Harrow complement of 120 was sufficient to produce a curtain some 4½ miles long and nearly half a mile deep. The mines descended at about 1,000 feet per minute. Thus, if released from 20,000 feet, they remained effective for about 10 minutes before they descended to below the level where they were likely to hit an enemy aircraft.

   When an aircraft struck the wire dangling beneath the bomb, the shock of impact was sufficient to break a weak link which released the upper parachute and at the same time unfurled the parachute at the bottom of the wire. The lower parachute took up a position behind the aircraft and pulled the bomb down on

*One of the oddest-looking bomber destroyers of all time: a shark-mouthed Harrow mine-layer of No. 93 Squadron. It was while flying this aircraft that Flight Lieutenant Hayley-Bell claimed an enemy aircraft probably destroyed on the night of 13 March 1941. (Hayley-Bell)*

*Long Aerial Mine containers in the bomb bay of a Harrow. The obsolescent bomber could carry up to 120 of these 14-pound weapons.*

the aircraft, where it exploded. The actual bomb, about the size of a half-pint tumbler and containing an 8-ounce charge of explosive, was large enough to inflict serious and probably lethal damage to an aircraft. If accurately laid, such a 'minefield' had a 1-in-20 chance of scoring a hit on each enemy bomber that flew through it. Since the small bombs carried no self-destruct mechanism, their use was permitted only over the sea.

During December 1940, No. 93 Squadron formed out of No. 420 Flight, which had carried out the trials with the Long Aerial Mine. Almost immediately the unit's old Harrows began flying sorties against the night bombers, the operation code-named 'Mutton'. The Harrow was the lowest-performance aerial 'bomber destroyer' to be used during the Second World War. It took more than 40 minutes to reach 20,000 feet and at that altitude its maximum speed was about 170 mph. On 22 December, 1940, however, Flight Lieutenant Burke released a string of mines from his Harrow in front of two enemy aircraft observed on ground radar approaching the coast. One was seen to fly into the 'minefield', its echo faded and it was believed destroyed. During the months that followed, the mines frequently served as the first of many lines of defence that the raiders had to penetrate to get to their targets.

## OPERATION LAYERS

With the radar-controlled Beaufighters and Harrows operating in the zones off the coast and in front of the targets, there was a clear need to keep the 'Catseye' fighters, the Hurricanes and Defiants operating at night without radar, out of these zones. The single-engined fighters cluttered up the radar screens as they wandered aimlessly, and their presence carried the ever-present risk that friendly twin-engined aircraft might be shot down in mistake for enemy bombers. Since the German attacks were invariably protracted affairs, however, there was plenty of time to concentrate the 'Catseye' fighters over the target. These tactics were formalised in an instruction issued to single-engined night-fighter squadrons on the final day of 1940, under the code-name Operation 'Layers'. Once the target was known, the Group headquarters responsible for the area was to order up between twelve and twenty single-engined fighters to patrol over it. Each fighter was given an altitude at which to patrol, to provide a separation of 500 or 1,000 feet between aircraft. The lowest altitude for the patrolling fighters was usually 14,000 feet, in which case the anti-aircraft gunners had orders to fuse their shells to explode at 12,000 feet or below. The areas in which 'Layers' operations could take place were all previously designated. In the case of Portsmouth, for example, it was the area within 10 miles of the city centre. While the 'Layers' operation was in progress, all other aircraft were prohibited from entering the zone within 20 miles of the city centre. The first 'Layers' operation was flown over Portsmouth on the night of 10 January and one enemy aircraft was claimed destroyed. On 21 February a second such operation was mounted over Swansea and again a raider was taken. At this time Fighter Command had 3½ squadrons of Defiants, 2 squadrons of Hurricanes and 2 squadrons equipped with both Hurricanes and Defiants, specialising in night fighting. In addition, normal day-fighting squadrons could also be called upon to take part in the 'Layers' operations. Throughout 1941, this form of target-defence operation was frequently used. In April 1941 Operation 'Layers' was renamed 'Fighter Nights' but continued much as before.

Yet another method of bringing discomfort to the raiders was to send aircraft to shoot up and bomb their bases. In December 1940, No. 23 Squadron, equipped with Blenheims, was withdrawn from defensive operations to take part in these intruder operations. After a short period of retraining, the unit mounted its first intruder operation on 21 December. Six aircraft carried out individual bombing attacks each on one airfield in northern France. The bombs appear to have caused little damage and although four enemy aircraft were seen, none could be engaged. Similar operations were mounted on 22 and 29 December, with similarly negative results. Yet, although it would prove more difficult to mount successful intruder operations than anticipated, the basic concept was sound. Aircraft just airborne or on the final approach for landing had little reserve speed for evasion and were virtual 'sitting ducks' – as their crews knew all too well. The intruders would never be able to destroy many enemy aircraft by direct action. Nevertheless, they were able to exert a powerful indirect pressure on enemy air operations. Aircrews returning from operations, some flying damaged aircraft perhaps with wounded on board, were forced to land on airfields where the lighting had been dimmed. Several aircraft were wrecked which would have landed normally had it not been for the actual or supposed presence of intruders. There could be no thought of 'going round again', no matter how bad the approach for landing, if intruders were suspected to be in the area.

## IMPROVEMENTS TO AA WEAPONRY

So much for the various facets of the British airborne defences. Early in 1941 far-reaching improvements were in train for the gun defences, also. The 3.7-inch and 3.5-inch guns were adequate against the German bombers then in service. The great

*The separate transmitter and receiver sets for the Mark II gunlaying radar. Although it was an extremely crude piece of equipment, the GL II brought about a marked improvement in the accuracy of British anti-aircraft fire at night. The receiver was particularly sensitive to siting, however, and to provide even conductivity of the surrounding ground the latter had to be covered with staked-down chicken wire out to a radius of 80 yards from the aerial.* (IWM)

problem was how to devise a system of fire-control to enable them to hit their targets. During the early months of 1941 the Mark II gunlaying radar came into service. This set had been designed for fire-control and was a considerable improvement over the Mark I. The ideal of continuous accurately predicted fire against aircraft, usual with visually aimed fire by day, was still some way off. With the new radar it was possible to follow only the approximate movements of the enemy aircraft and provide information for a box-barrage in that part of the sky. For technical reasons the gun-laying radar was particularly sensitive to siting. The surrounding ground had to be flat and of even electrical conductivity – in other words, the ideal site was one rarely to be found under operational conditions. After some experimentation that problem was overcome by covering the ground under the radar-receiver aerials with a mat of chicken wire out to a radius of about 80 yards. Of this modification General Pile wrote in his official dispatch: 'Experiments with a trial mat

were a complete success and the principle was adopted universally. What I had not realised was that the project would involve using *the whole of the country's stock of wire net* for the first 300 mats.' (Author's italics.)

To improve the efficiency of the searchlights, a new radar code-named 'Elsie' was introduced for fitting to the light projector itself. With a maximum detection range of about 8 miles on a twin-engined aircraft, this aligned the projector accurately on the aircraft before the light came on. Initial production of 'Elsie' was slow, however, and the device was available only in small numbers.

Also at the end of 1940 a more powerful searchlight, the 150-cm became available. This gave a beam of 510 million candle power, more than twice that of the earlier 90-cm type. Usually, one 150-cm light with radar control served as 'master light' for a section of three; the 'master' would expose first to illuminate the aircraft, then the other two lights would expose to 'cone' the target.

As has been said, the 3.7-inch and 4.5-inch guns had sufficient performance to knock down any German bomber active in the spring of 1941. These were expensive weapons, however. Production was slow and there were insufficient for all the many possible targets to receive the required density of guns. As a cheap and simple means of stiffening the defences, the 3-inch rocket

*'Elsie' radar, fitted to a 90-cm searchlight. This set enabled the operators to align their projector on the bomber, before they switched on the light. The left-hand upper aerial was used for transmission, the right-hand upper aerial for identification. The four lower aerials fed the receiver and the operator moved the projector until equal strength signals were picked up by each of these aerials. (IWM)*

was introduced for high-altitude defence. During 1940 a few had been deployed for low-altitude defence. Officially, it was known as the 'Unrotated Projectile', referring to its method of flight. In contrast to the spin of the ordinary shell, these fin-stabilised rockets were fired at high-flying raiders in salvoes of 128. Each battery comprised 64 double projectors. After launch the UP rocket accelerated rapidly to an all-burnt velocity of about 1,000 mph, achieved in 1½ seconds. Thereafter the missile coasted to its maximum engagement altitude of 19,000 feet. The rocket weighed 54 pounds at launch and was 6 feet 4 inches long. The warhead weighed 22 pounds and was fused to explode at a pre-set time after launch. Early in 1941 a battery of the so-called Z-guns was set up to defend Cardiff. From the start it was clear that the 3-inch rocket was a poor substitute for the more conventional forms of heavy anti-aircraft defence. It was considerably less accurate than a heavy anti-aircraft shell and, because of the time required to reload all the projectors, it was almost impossible to loose off more than one salvo before an aircraft passed out of range. The weapon was not widely deployed.

*The so-called Z gun in action, a twin projector for 3-in 54-pound rockets. A makeshift improvisation for defence against high-flying raiders, this weapon was considerably less effective than conventional anti-aircraft guns and was deployed in relatively small numbers.* (IWM)

## COUNTERMEASURES TO THE NAVIGATION SYSTEMS

While the development of these direct defensive measures proceeded apace, almost every possible means was exploited to counter the various beam systems. The 'Aspirin' and 'Bromide' transmitters, to jam Knickebein and X-Verfahren respectively, were being deployed in progressively greater numbers. The signals from the newly reintroduced Y-Verfahren had been identified by No. 80 Wing monitors in November 1940 and Dr Cockburn's section at Swanage received orders to build a transmitter to jam that system also. The prototype of the resultant jammer, code-named 'Domino', employed a receiver at Highgate and the BBC's dormant television transmitter at Alexandra Palace to the north of London. The receiver picked up the 'echo' signal from the German bomber and passed it to the transmitter. There the signal was 'doctored', and reradiated to the aircraft from the transmitter at Alexandra Palace. The German ground station heard only the aircraft's signals. But as these were being upset by the 'Domino' jamming, the ranging signal thus found had little relation to the aircraft's actual position. By the end of February two such 'Domino' sets were in operation.

Other counters to the German beam systems were rather more violent. There is an old adage in radio countermeasures that the best of all is a medium-sized bomb on the enemy device to be countered. The German beam transmitters were no exception, if they could be hit. If German bombers could use the beams to fly to targets in Britain, it seemed a simple matter for British bombers to fly down the beam in the reverse direction towards the source.

*The scene in front of the Bank of England and the Royal Exchange, after the attack on the night of 11 January 1941. A large bomb had penetrated the surface and exploded in the booking hall of the bank underground station. The roof caved in and the resultant crater was the largest caused during the Blitz on London. Blast travelled down the shaft to the platform, and killed thirty-eight people sheltering there.* (IWM)

As mentioned earlier in this chapter, during Operation 'Cold Water' on the night of the attack on Coventry on 14 November, two Whitley bombers attacked the Knickebein and X-Verfahren transmitters near Cherbourg. Such attacks were repeated at irregular intervals in the months to follow. However, these small pin-point targets were heavily defended by flak. In addition there were lines of barrage ballons on each side of the transmitter, where their cables would not interfere with the beam transmissions. The attackers' main problem was that, since they flew down a beam whose precise alignment was known in advance, there was little room for flexibility of attack or in the direction of approach. In February 1941 a special flight with four Wellingtons formed within No. 109 Squadron for the specific purpose of attacking the beam transmitters. So far as can be discovered, the raiders never scored a direct hit on a beam transmitter. But they did score several near misses, some of which caused embarrassment. On one occasion a bomb cut the power supply cable to a transmitter, putting it off the air for some days. By and large, however, direct attacks on the transmitters were considerably less effective than the No. 80 Wing jamming in neutralising the beam systems.

## 'STARFISH' DECOY SITES

No study of the methods of air defence employed to protect targets in Britain is complete without mentioning the decoy fire sites, code-named 'Starfish'. Sending aircraft to start fires at a target, to guide in the follow-up force of bombers delivering the main attack, had been shown to be a sound tactic. But if fire-fighters could extinguish sufficient of the fires, and if realistic decoy fires could be lit in the surrounding countryside in time, the latter might draw a large proportion of the bombs upon themselves.

Colonel J. Turner, one-time head of the RAF works department, received orders to set up an organisation to construct and operate 'Starfish' under the control of No. 80 Wing. The decoys had to look plausibly like cities under attack and the timing of the blaze was critical: it had to start just at the right time to catch the main attack and ideally the raiders should have to fly over it to reach their actual target.

The usual layout of a 'Starfish' was a cluster of fires in open countryside, about 3 or 4 miles from the target it was intended to protect. The fires were ignited electronically from a concrete control post about 600 yards away, the operator being in telephone contact with a command post at the target itself. The policy was to light the decoy fires as soon as the target came under attack, while fire-fighting units at the real target made every effort to extinguish the fires there. At the 'Starfish' it was essential to get a large blaze going quickly. The fastest-burning type of decoy comprised a building-shaped structure of steel and asbestos, covered in tared roofing felt. The felt burned rapidly and to keep the fire going additional rolls of felt were attached to the roof. As the fire burned through the strings holding the extra rolls in position, the latter unrolled at intervals to provide new supplies of combustible material. Because the 'building' was clad in asbestos sheeting, it could be used several times. Other, slower-burning types of decoy used coal, paraffin or creosote as their combustible materials, to provide variety in the size, colour and intensity of the resultant fires and their smoke. Each 'Starfish' comprised a number of decoy fires of many different types.

An ever-present problem was the selection of sites for the 'Starfish'. Naturally, nobody wanted one anywhere near his home. The area selected had to be at least 1 mile away from the nearest village, and the people living within 400 yards of the site had to be rehoused. To avoid wrangling and delays, the local Agricultural Officer had either to agree to the provision of the land requested for a decoy site, or had to provide a suitable alternative within 24 hours. By the beginning of March 1941, 108 'Starfish' sites were operating and from time to time they drew large numbers of bombs away from their intended targets.

To sum up, by the beginning of 1941 Britain's air defences comprised successive lines through which the night raiders had to pass to reach their targets. First there were the intruder aircraft patrolling over the German bases; next, in front of the British coast, there were descending curtains of Long Aerial Mines; from the coast to the target radar-directed and 'Catseye' night fighters hunted their prey. At the target itself barrage balloons deterred the raiders from attacking below 5,000 feet; from 5,000 feet up the anti-aircraft guns engaged the bombers. If a 'Layers' operation was in progress, a gunfire ceiling of 12,000 feet was imposed and above that the single-engined fighters searched for their enemy. The various forms of jamming made the German beam systems difficult to use; and 'Starfish' sites situated round the main targets endeavoured to attract as many bombs as possible. Yet for all their variety, the defences were still unable to destroy more than a minute proportion of the raiding bombers.

## HITLER'S NEW DIRECTIVE

On 6 February 1941, Hitler issued his War Directive No. 23, entitled 'Directions for Operations against the English War Economy'. This began with an assessment of the effect of the German naval and air operations so far:

(a) Contrary to our former view, the greatest effect of our operations against the English war economy has lain in the high losses in merchant shipping inflicted by our naval and air forces. This effect has been increased by the wrecking of port installations, the destruction of large quantities of supplies and by the diminished use of ships when they are compelled to sail in convoy.

(b) The effect of direct air attacks against the English armament industry is difficult to estimate. But the destruction of many factories and the consequent disorganisation of the armament industry must lead to a considerable fall in production.

(c) The least effect of all (so far as we can see) has been that upon the morale and the will to resist of the English people.

On points (a) and (c) the Fuehrer's assessment was accurate. On point (b) he was somewhat over-optimistic: although there had been severe disruption of production at individual factories, the efficiency of the damage-repair organisation was such that this rarely lasted for long.

By this time planning for the forthcoming invasion of Russia was well advanced and, Hitler continued, within the next two or three months a large part of the Luftwaffe would be withdrawn from operations against the British Isles. Therefore, the air attack was now to be concentrated on assisting the U-boats to sever Britain's sea communication, with an intensification of the attack on ports. Simultaneously, attacks would continue against targets associated with the aircraft industry. In an admission that the 'knock-out blow' had failed in its purpose, the Fuehrer pointed out 'No decisive success can be expected from terror attacks on residential areas . . .'. Until the regrouping of the forces for the attack on Russia, every effort was to be made to intensify the attack from the air and by sea. This would not only inflict the greatest possible damage to the British economy '. . . but also give the impression that an invasion on Britain is planned for this year'.

So far as the British people were concerned, the change in the German policy brought little noticeable change to their ordeal. The darkness, sometimes the weather, the British defences and in particular the jamming of the German radio beams all combined to prevent the bombers from making precision attacks. The pattern of diffused attacks continued, with bombs falling evenly over the industrial, port and residential sections of the cities under attack. During February the weather prevented large-scale attacks on many nights. Only Swansea came under sustained attack, with medium-scale raids on the nights of 19 and 20 February.

During March the weather improved and the Luftwaffe resumed its onslaught, with heavy assaults on London, Portsmouth and Birmingham, Liverpool, Glasgow and Sheffield, Bristol, Hull and Plymouth. Respresentative of these attacks, and of the working of the British defences to counter them, was the action fought on the night of 12 March.

## Target Liverpool

The objective for the night was a strike on Liverpool and shortly after dark the vanguard of the raiding force of 339 bombers began taking off from bases in France, Holland, Belgium and Norway. Pathfinder aircraft of KGr 100 and III./KG 26 were in the leading waves of the attack which, in conformity with the now-established German practice, approached the target from all directions between due south and north-east over a period of several hours. The fifteen He 111s of KGr 100 attacked from altitudes of about 12,000 feet. At that height the bombers were beyond the reach of the X-beams and the crews bombed visually. The fourteen He 111s of III./KG 26, attacked from altitudes of between 16,000 and 19,000 feet using their Y-beams. Both pathfinder units released large numbers of incendiary bombs in the target area. The moon was full and visibility good, and bomber crews could pick out their targets with relative ease.

Fighter Command put up 178 fighters to counter this attack. The first line of defence for the British city was positioned over the German bomber bases in France. As soon as it became clear that a large-scale assault was in the offing, No. 23 Squadron sent Blenheims to patrol the airfields at Caen, Rossiers, Amiens, Arras, Achiet, Cambrai, Lille and Norville. The intruders claimed no success. But from German records it is known that a Heinkel 111 of III./KG 26 crashed near the airfield at Amiens killing one of the crew. Possibly this crash was due, indirectly, to the fighters' visit.

Liverpool's second line of defence comprised No. 93 Squadron's aerial mine-layers. During the attack a single Harrow patrolled off the south coast of England for more than 3 hours, but was unable to get into position to release its mines in front of any bombers.

As the raiders crossed the coast, the GCI-directed night fighters went into action. No. 604 Squadron put up 7 Beaufighters and claimed 1 bomber shot down, 1 probably shot down and 2 damaged. The only confirmed kill by this method went to Flying Officer Keith Geddes, who was directed on to one of the bombers first by the Sopley GCI station and then by his radar operator, Aircraftsman Cannon. He followed their instructions then, as he later reported:

The operator reported 'It's above you.' I looked up and saw the enemy aircraft 1,000 feet above. I was still overtaking so I did 'S' turns and climbed and lost my visual after two minutes, reported to the operator and turned back on to 360 [degrees, due north]. The operator instructed 'Enemy aircraft 1,500 feet away, motor on and climb straight ahead, then a little right.' This lost speed and the enemy aircraft started to gain but after a minute I saw it again (the moon was behind in a light clear sky). Enemy aircraft was fully 440 yards away . . . I stalked it while gaining height, the speed of the enemy aircraft was 170. I got to within 100 yards, 100 feet below and identified it as a Ju 88. I closed the throttle slightly, eased the nose up and the enemy aircraft passed through my sights. I pushed the stick forward and opened fire; immediately there was an explosion inside the fuselage and the enemy aircraft then began burning all along the fuselage starting from the front port side. The enemy aircraft started to dive. I drew to port and then followed it down from 13 to 6,000 feet, still burning furiously. Here it did a steep diving turn to starboard, went down vertically and exploded on the ground near Warminster.

On this clear moonlit night 'Catseye' night fighters enjoyed some success. As the bombers streamed over England to and from their target, some passed through the Kenley Sector where the improvised fighter control system using gun-laying radar was employed with some effect. First a Defiant of No. 264 Squadron shot down a Heinkel 111 near Dorking. Then, shortly before midnight, Flying Officer Terence Welsh and his gunner Sergeant H. Hayden were patrolling in a Defiant of the same squadron near Kenley. Welsh afterwards wrote:

I was vectored after an enemy aircraft at buster [maximum speed] on vectors between 130 degrees and 160 degrees whilst the GL [radar] heights gradually became lower and lower and I crossed the coast on a 150° vector at 8,000 feet. I saw a spot outlined against the sea below me on which the moon was reflecting, but on diving to investigate I identified it as an aircraft, and continuing my dive I came up alongside it at about 40 yards range. My gunner and I immediately saw it to be a Heinkel 111. I was doing 260 mph indicated which was some 30 mph faster than the enemy aircraft which adopted no evasive action and which never returned my fire. I did a cross-over attack [i.e., curving round the nose of the bomber] from beneath and Sgt Hayden opened fire with two one-second bursts at 25 yards. The de Wilde ammunition could be seen bursting inside the cabin and the pilot was probably killed immediately as when I pulled into a steep turn to attack from the port side, I saw the enemy aircraft in a vertical dive. Smoke and sparks were coming from it and both Sgt Hayden and I saw the enemy aircraft plunge into the sea.

The Heinkel crashed about 15 miles south of Hastings.

Flying on patrol lines immediately to the east and south of Liverpool itself, the Hurricanes and Defiants of No. 96 Squadron made several contacts with the raiders. Two Defiants succeeded in getting into firing positions alongside bombers, only to suffer gun stoppages. The pilot of one Defiant was wounded by the bomber's return fire, but succeeded in making a normal landing. Sergeant McNair, flying a Hurricane of the same unit, was able to avenge his comrade's wounds. He found a Heinkel 111 and closed in to 75 yards before loosing off a 4-second burst. Immediately the fighter's windscreen was covered in oil and McNair noticed the bomber's port engine was trailing smoke and the undercarriage leg on that side was hanging down. He closed in and made two further attacks to finish off the raider, which crashed near Widnes.

Above 14,000 feet Liverpool was protected by a 'Layers' operation mounted by Hurricanes and Defiants of No. 96 Squadron. None of the fighters made contact with enemy bombers probably because, as we have seen, with the exception of the III./KG 26 pathfinders, almost all the bombers attacked at altitudes below 13,000 feet.

Protecting Liverpool and the immediate area from strikes below 5,000 feet were more than 100 balloons. Since no bombers appear to have attacked at altitudes below this level, the balloons can be said to have been successful in acting as a deterrent. The volume of sky over the target between 5,000 feet and 12,000 feet was covered by nearly 100 heavy anti-aircraft guns. Returning German crews reported the gunfire over Liverpool as 'strong and accurate'.

One bomber probably brought down by anti-aircraft fire at the target was the Junkers 88 flown by Feldwebel Guenther Unger; although his unit, III./KG 76, was in the process of converting to the new type, Unger had volunteered to fly this mission with the II. Gruppe. Unger approached the target from the south and ran in at 10,000 feet to attack shipping in the Mersey Estuary. During the bombing run his observer, Feldwebel 'Ast' Meier, sat next to him crouched over the eyepiece of his Lotfe bombsight. Meier's left hand rested on Unger's right foot on the rudder pedal, guiding the bomber up to the bomb-release point. Just as the bombs, four 550-pounders and ten 110-pounders, were being released in a long stick Unger noticed a reflection on his canopy. Then, he recalled:

> I looked round and saw a small but very bright glow on the cowling immediately behind the starboard engine. The metal was actually burning, which meant there must have been intense heat, probably from a fire inside the nacelle. At first the visible spot of fire was very small; but it grew rapidly and flames began to trail behind the aircraft. I could see there was no hope of our getting home so I ordered the crew to bale out. The flight engineer opened the escape hatch at the rear of the cabin and jumped, followed by the radio operator. As they left I turned the bomber until it was pointing out to sea, so that when it crashed there would be nothing for the enemy to find. As I left my seat the observer dropped out of the hatch. The Junkers was flying properly trimmed, flying straight and level on both engines. For a moment I considered trying to get home alone, but a further glance at the blaze made it clear that this would have been impossible; I clambered to the rear, and followed my crew out of the hatch.

All the crewmen parachuted to safety. The only one to have any serious difficulty was Unger himself. He came down in shallow water but took over an hour to wade ashore, having to take circuitous routes to avoid the many deep water channels that cut through the sand banks off the coast. He finally walked ashore at Wallasey, where he gave himself up to a member of the Home Guard.

The main weight of the attack fell on Birkenhead and Wallasey, to the west of the Mersey. Liverpool itself and Bootle, to the east of the estuary, suffered less heavily. An estimated 270 groups of incendiary bombs fell on the built-up area, starting more than 500 fires, of which 9 reached major proportions. About 350 high-explosive bombs and 60 parachute mines caused widespread damage. In the port area some machinery and dockside handling equipment were destroyed. Two ships and a large floating crane were sunk and three

*Gunther Unger (second from the left) and his crew, pictured a few hours before they took off for the attack on Liverpool on the night of 12 March, when they were shot down. (Unger)*

further ships suffered damage. Three flour mills were damaged, the Vacuum Oil Company's installation at Birkenhead was practically destroyed and both gas holders at Wallasey were burnt out. There was extensive damage to residential property and in this attack, and a smaller one on the following night, 631 people were killed and a similar number injured.

With so much death and destruction actually inflicted on Liverpool and the surrounding area what can the defences – the night fighters, the anti-aircraft guns, the radio jamming and the decoy sites – claim to have achieved? According to German records the bombers in the raiding force carried about 270 tons of high-explosive bombs and nearly 2,000 canisters of incendiary bombs. From a British bomb count made immediately after the attack it was estimated that 90 tons of high-explosive bombs were scattered over a built-up area of about 66 square miles (it was not possible to count individual incendiary canisters). From this it can be seen that the general harassment caused by the fighters and the guns, combined with the confusion from the radio jamming and the 'Starfish' sites, helped draw about two-thirds of the bombs away from the target area. Moreover, the weight of the attack was concentrated not on the narrow strip of dockland on either side of the Mersey, as the German planners had intended. Instead, the bombs that hit the built-up area were scattered widely over it.

Altogether, the fighters claimed four bombers destroyed, four probably destroyed and three damaged. The gunners claimed three destroyed, one probably destroyed and four damaged. From the incomplete German records surviving, it is known that at least seven aircraft failed to return and two more crashed in German-occupied territory. It was the heaviest loss yet suffered during a night attack on Britain.

In terms of aircraft shot down on the night of 12/13 March 1941, the defences had not achieved much. Even if all the claims for bombers shot down or probably shot down were correct, the loss amounted to less than 4 per cent of the force committed. However, the defences had been able to prevent a large group of German bombers from flattening Britain's most important port. And that, during the early months of 1941, was the best that could be expected.

On the following night, 13 March, Liverpool again came under attack, though by only 65 aircraft. A slightly larger number of bombers went for Hull, while the main attack of the evening, by 236 aircraft, was on Glasgow–Clydeside. During this action it is probable that the Long Aerial Mine achieved a rare success. At 1930 hours that evening Flight Lieutenant Hayley-Bell of No. 93 Squadron took off from Middle Wallop in a Harrow. He climbed to 17,000 feet then, directed by the GCI radar at Sopley, was positioned about 4 miles ahead and 3,000 feet above one of the incoming bombers. At 2050 hours, 12 miles off the coast near Swanage, Hayley-Bell released his mines at 200-foot intervals across the bomber's path; soon afterwards he observed a small explosion beneath him, followed by a much larger one. Hayley-Bell not only saw the second explosion, but felt the concussion in his aircraft. The radar operators on the ground observed that the aircraft originally intended for destruction had missed the minefield by about 2 miles. But three or four other bombers were in the area at that time and it was believed one of these had struck the mine. Hayley-Bell was credited with one enemy aircraft 'probably destroyed'.

## OPERATION 'SAVANNA'

Strong forces of German bombers attacked Glasgow and Sheffield on the night of 14 March, and London on the 15th. While the latter attack was in progress, a lone Whitley was flying to Brittany carrying five parachutists. Their aim: to hit the pathfinder unit Kampfgruppe 100 at its most vulnerable point – on the road between Vannes and the nearby airfield. The aircrews were billeted in the town of Vannes, and prior to each attack they were taken to the airfield in buses. The parachutists were to ambush these buses. Some months earlier, when the threat posed by KGr 100 had become clear to British Intelligence, the Special Operations Executive had been asked to prepare such an ambush. Planning began but the operation, code-named 'Savanna', nearly foundered at the very beginning due to objections from an unexpected source. When he heard of the plan, the Chief of the Air Staff, Air Chief Marshal Sir Charles Portal, wrote to Gladwyn Jebb, the Chief Executive Officer at SOE: 'I think that the dropping of men dressed in civilian clothes for the purpose of attempting to kill members of the opposing forces is not an operation with which the Royal Air Force should be associated. I think you will agree that there is a vast difference, in ethics, between the time-honoured operation of the dropping of a spy from the air and this entirely new scheme of dropping what one can only call assassins.' These objections were overruled at the highest level.

On the evening of 15 March the parachutists, all French regular soldiers, were dropped 8 miles to the east of Vannes with their equipment. To provide a diversion,

*Armourers loading 2,200-pound mines on to the external racks of a Heinkel 111. Fitted with impact fuses, these thin-cased weapons were dropped on land targets in Britain, where their blast was effective in demolishing houses. These weapons were slowed in their descent by a parachute, however, and when released from high altitude they were impossible to aim with any accuracy.*

a small force of bombers attacked the airfield. The men hid their equipment which included a specially designed 'road trap', and waited until the following day to carry out a reconnaissance of the area. They then found that crews of Kampfgruppe 100 no longer travelled to the airfield by bus but instead went in ones and twos by car. An effective ambush was no longer possible. Accordingly the attack was abandoned and the leader, Captain G. Berge, ordered his men to disperse and carry out a general reconnaissance of occupied France before their evacuation to Britain by submarine.

During the remainder of March raiding forces of more than 100 bombers attacked Bristol, Hull, London and Plymouth. In April there were no fewer than 14 major attacks on British cities: 5 on Plymouth, 2 on London, 2 on Birmingham and 1 each on Glasgow, Coventry, Newcastle, Bristol and Belfast.

## STARFISH SUCCESS

Portsmouth had a lucky escape on the night of 17 April, when a nearby 'Starfish' site took almost all the bombs from a raiding force of 249 aircraft. The weather conditions were ideal for the operation of decoys: over the area there was a mist just thick enough to obscure much of the coastline yet not thick enough to conceal fires on the ground. The 'Starfish' site at Sinah Common on Hayling Island was ignited as the first of the bombers arrived over the target, and almost immediately came under attack. Squadron Leader John Whitehead, the controller at No. 80 Wing Headquarters that night, later recalled: 'During the attack I rang the Starfish operator at Hayling Island and asked him how things were going. "Oh fine", he answered, and held out the receiver so that I could hear the crump-crump-crump of bombs going off. I said to him "Now, you look after yourself", to which he replied: "Oh, it's all right, I've got my tin hat on!".'

That night only eight bombs fell on Portsmouth. A total of 170 high-explosive bombs, 32 parachute mines and many thousands of incendiary bombs fell round the 'Starfish'. Even more dropped harmlessly into the sea between Portsmouth and Hayling Island. It was the greatest triumph of the 'Starfish' operations. On the debit side, however, this occasion was one of the very few in which casualties could be attributed to the use of a decoy. A hutted camp for anti-aircraft gunners 800 yards from the decoy was almost destroyed and many houses on Hayling Island suffered damage. In total, 8 people, most of them AA gunners, were killed and some 30 gunners and civilians were injured. Yet such losses, though regrettable in themselves, were only a minute proportion of those that would have been suffered had the raiders been able to hit their intended target.

## THE FINAL PUSH

During the first half of May the German bomber force mounted a series of heavy attacks to bring its bombing offensive against Britain to a climax, before the move against Russia. Liverpool was hit particularly hard, with raids on each of the first seven nights of the month. The attack on 2 May was the most dramatic, for it resulted in the explosion of the ammunition ship SS *Malakand*, lying in Huskisson Dock with 1,000 tons of bombs and shells aboard intended for the Middle East. The ship blew up with great violence. Afterwards parts of her plating were found more than 2 miles from her berth. Lesser explosions continued for the next three days and nights. Considering the force of the explosion, the death toll of only four was astonishingly low. Two of these were a married couple who had been driving home along the dock road when a large piece of steel plating fell on their car and killed them. In contrast, several of those close to the scene of the explosion had remarkable escapes. One dockyard employee had been picking his way through broken carboys of acid when the ship went up. The next thing he knew he was on his hands and knees beneath the side plate of the ship which, torn off and badly buckled, covered him and protected him from the raining debris. He escaped without injury.

The *Malakand* explosion was the most serious single incident on Merseyside during the war and it left an arc of destruction extending over several acres of dockland. But, cumulatively, other smaller incidents during the series of attacks proved more serious. Vast amounts of damage were done to buildings in the centre of the city and transport was disrupted over a wide area. The week's list of casualties amounted to some 1,900 people killed and 1,450 seriously injured. Nearly half the deaths were caused during the heaviest of the attacks, by nearly 300 bombers on the night of 3 May.

On the nights of 5 and 6 May the main bomber forces attacked Glasgow and Clydeside. On the 8th it was the turn of Sheffield, Hull, Derby and Nottingham. Of these, Derby and Nottingham got off almost scot-free as a result of successful jamming and 'Starfish' actions. A force of 23 bombers made for the Rolls Royce works at Derby, with the Heinkels of KGr 100 in the lead. The X-beams were well jammed by No. 80 Wing, however, and the bombs fell harmlessly on the moors to the north-east of the town. Simultaneously, ninety-five bombers were making for Nottingham; the leading raiders reached their target and started some fires. Immediately a 'Starfish' near the small hamlet of Cropwell Butler, to the south-east of Nottingham, was lit and soon afterwards the attack on the city ceased. But

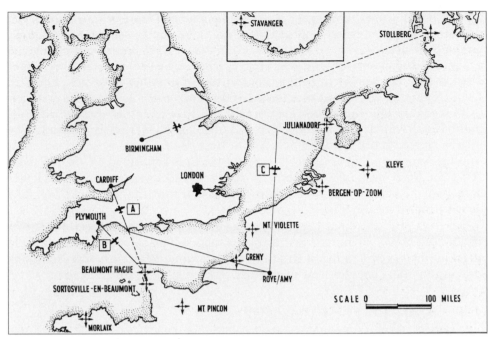

*Even after the jamming had rendered Knickebein ineffective for bombing, it was still useful for route navigation; the eleven beam stations used during the attacks on Britain are seen here. From a map kept by one German bomber pilot of his routes to targets in Britain, the reader can see how use was made of the beam stations during some of the attacks. During this period he was flying a Ju 88 with III./KG 1, from Roye/Amy near Compiegne. A: attacks on Cardiff on the nights of 1 and 3 March 1941, picking up the Beaumont-Hague beam at the coast and flying from there straight to the target. B: attacks on Plymouth on the nights of 21, 28 and 29 April 1941, picking up the Beaumont-Hague beam off the Cherbourg Peninsular and flying from there straight to the target. C: attack on Birmingham on the night of 16 May; he flew almost due north from his base to pick up the Kleve beam, then north-west towards the Humber until he met the Stollberg beam, then along the Stollberg beam to the target. During March and April, when the defences were still rather ineffectual, the bombers often used the same route for repeat attacks. By May, however, it was considered prudent to make a wide detour to avoid the defences in south-eastern England.*

although bombers were still in the area, the decoy was not attacked either. The weight of the attack fell on open countryside in the Vale of Belvoir. Almost certainly what had happened was that the Nottingham raiders had seen the Cropwell Butler decoy burning and, mistaking it for the expected fires at Derby, had used it as a fixing point. As a result they dropped their bombs on the Vale of Belvoir – the same distance and bearing from Cropwell Butler as Nottingham is from Derby. A total of 230 high-explosive bombs and several hundred incendiary bombs fell across the Vale, killing two cows and two chickens. On the next day, German news broadcasts spoke of successful attacks on both Derby and Nottingham.

The final large-scale attack on London of the series occurred on the night of 10 May, when the Luftwaffe put up a total of 541 bomber sorties against the capital. For this final fling, made at a time when several bomber units had begun the move eastwards, many bomber crews had to fly double sorties. For example, one Ju 88 of III./KG 1 took off to attack London at 2345 hours on the 10th and again at 0215 hours on the morning of the 11th; each sortie took about 2 hours and the crew spent half an hour on the ground between each. For each sortie the aircraft was loaded with three 1,100-pound bombs and one 550-pounder.

This raid caused the highest number of casualties of any of those during the night Blitz, with 1,436 people killed and about 1,800 seriously injured. The bombs started more than 2,000 separate fires, 9 of which were classified as 'conflagrations' and 20 as 'major'; together, the fires consumed an area of about 700 acres. More than 5,000 houses were destroyed and a similar number seriously damaged; 12,000 people were made homeless. From the attack 14 German bombers failed to return.

Six days after the final London attack, on 16 May, the Luftwaffe put in a smaller attack on Birmingham with 111 bombers. The sole significance of the attack to this account is that it was to be the last mounted against Britain in such strength for more than one and a half years. The great night Blitz was over.

## THE NIGHT BLITZ SUMMED UP

During the day and night bombing offensive against the British Isles, in the ten-month period from the beginning of August 1940 to the end of May 1941, more than 43,000 civilians were killed, about 51,000 seriously and 88,000 slightly injured. These figures, although bad enough, fell far below the 600,000 killed and 1,200,000 wounded predicted before the war for the first 6 months of a sustained bombing offensive. German records show that during the major attacks on London the bombers carried about 18,000 tons of bombs which, British records show, caused about 90,000 fatal or serious casualties. Thus, the average casualty rate was 5 per ton of bombs. The pre-war figure of 50 per ton had been exaggerated by a factor of 10. Later, Mr Churchill wrote of this discrepancy: 'Before the war we were greatly misled by the pictures they painted of the destruction that would be wrought by Air Raids. This is illustrated by the fact that 750,000 beds were actually provided for air raid casualties, never more than 6,000 being required.' Moreover, just as the casualties likely to be suffered during an aerial bombardment had been greatly overestimated before the war, the resilience of civilian morale in the face of such an attack had been seriously underestimated. In 1940 and 1941 there was no general weakening of national morale.

Of course, the pre-war predictions on the effect of air attacks had been made on the assumption that the Luftwaffe would mount a series of accurate daylight attacks on London and other major cities using its available bomber strength. In fact, for the reasons already discussed, the Germans never did that. London was the only major centre of population to be attacked in force by day: on only 3 occasions were more than 200 bombers involved and on 2 others the attacking force numbered about 100. On no daylight attack was more than a third of the serviceable twin-engined bomber strength of the Luftwaffe committed. The night

*The morning after: men and women picking their way through fire hoses at the corner of Farringdon Street and Shoe Lane on their way to work on 11 May 1941, after the heaviest attack of all on the capital.* (IWM)

attacks on the capital and other cities in Britain were far more numerous and involved greater numbers of bombers. But the accuracy of the night bombing was generally poor and damage was scattered over wide areas.

After the Blitz the Commander-in-Chief Fighter Command, Air Chief Marshal Sir Sholto Douglas, wrote 'We were confident that if the enemy had not chosen that moment to pull out, we should soon have been inflicting such casualties on his night bombers that the continuance of his night offensive on a similar scale would have been impossible.' While the British night defences would certainly reach such a position later in the war, there is little evidence to show that they were nearing it in the late spring of 1941. The heaviest loss suffered by a German raiding force was during the final attack on London on 10 May, when fourteen bombers failed to return. This represented a loss rate of less than 3 per cent of the sorties put up against the capital that night, a figure lower than necessary to deter the Luftwaffe from repeating such attacks. The defences had indeed made great progress since the beginning of the night offensive. But there was still a long way to go before they could deter the night bomber as effectively as they deterred its daylight counterpart.

*This Heinkel 111, from 11./KG 27, was closing in to deliver a low-altitude attack on Yeovil when it struck a mist-covered hill near Lulworth Cove in May 1941. The fender attachment fitted in front of the wings and fuselage was intended to ward off barrage-balloon cables.*

One further aspect of the campaign needs to be examined at this point. As mentioned earlier in this chapter, since the late spring of 1940 the Luftwaffe signals service had been busily extending its network of landline communications to link operational airfields in the occupied western territories with their headquarters. As each airfield was connected into the network, it ceased using wireless to send and receive messages in high-grade ciphers. Thus, by the spring of 1941, as the British cipher-breakers went from strength to strength to produce a flood of invaluable information on German military activities in other theatres, they were able to produce little on Luftwaffe operations against Britain. This would remain the case for the rest of the war. From Luftwaffe units in the west the main sources of signals intelligence would come from breaking the low-grade ciphers used in air-to-ground communications, and a careful analysis of voice radio traffic.

In the next chapter we shall follow the course of the air attacks on Britain that followed on from the night Blitz, and the continuing moves to strengthen the defences.

# CHAPTER 6

# Fairly Quiet on the Western Front, June 1941–December 1942

I have often thought that their fierce hostility to me was more on account of the sleep I made them lose than the number we killed and captured.

*John Mosby*, War Reminiscences, *1887*

Shortly before dawn on the morning of 22 June 1941, without a formal declaration of war, German forces opened their offensive against Russia. Supported by more than half the Luftwaffe, during the weeks that followed the German Army advanced rapidly eastwards. By the late autumn it had reached the gates of Moscow and invested Leningrad. In a series of great encircling actions it captured 2½ million men, 9,000 tanks and 16,000 guns. To many it seemed that further Russian resistance could be measured only in weeks. With Russia safely out of the war, Hitler could again concentrate his forces against Britain.

With a suddenness that seemed almost unreal, the pressure on Britain eased. Gone, for the moment at least, were the dangers of imminent invasion and the devastating attacks on the cities. To support the new-found ally in the East, Mr Churchill ordered British forces to move to the offensive where they could. Everything possible had to be done to draw and hold German forces away from the eastern front. Only the Royal Air Force could go over to the offensive immediately, however, and initially its efforts would be limited to shallow-penetration daylight operations over northern France, and weak night attacks on targets in Germany. As the expansion of RAF Bomber Command got into its stride the attacks on German targets would become more powerful, and it could be expected that the Luftwaffe would retaliate against targets in Britain. But such retaliatory attacks could be made only by withdrawing bomber units from the East, which was the intention of the British policy.

While these operations were in progress, the British air defences continued to strengthen as units took delivery of equipment that had been demanded with such urgency during the previous months. By the middle of July 1941 seventeen GCI radar stations were operational. There were now six squadrons of AI-equipped Beaufighters and two more were converting to the type.

At least as important as the deployment of the new radars and the new fighter type in greater quantity was the fact that aircrews, operating crews and maintenance personnel had been gaining in familiarity and experience with these systems. Thus a higher proportion of the new equipment was now serviceable, and being used more effectively than before.

Although the large-scale attacks on Britain's cities had come to an end, the steadily reducing German bomber force in the West would continue to mount medium-scale attacks for some time to come. In June there were two such attacks, on Birmingham and Southampton, each involving about eighty aircraft. In July and August raiding forces in similar strength struck at Birmingham twice and London once. That summer the few Luftwaffe bomber units operating against Britain faced insurmountable problems. Not only were the defenders becoming better equipped and better trained by the month, but the nights were short and the raiding forces were too small to achieve saturation of the defences. As a result, individual units recorded heavy cumulative losses. Kampfgruppe 100 was particularly hard hit. On 14 June the Gruppe possessed 34 operational crews and 35 aircraft (17 serviceable). During the next 5 disastrous weeks it lost 13 aircraft and 11 crews in action.

KGr 100 lost one of its bombers during the small hours of 9 July, and it was lucky not to lose the entire crew as well. Oberleutnant Hansgeorg Baetcher cruised over Somerset at 11,500 feet as he headed for the target near Birmingham. Unknown to him, operators at the GCI radar station at Huntspill near Weston-super-Mare were tracking the Heinkel and directing a Beaufighter into position to intercept. Flying Officer R. Woodward and radar operator Sergeant A. Lipscombe of No. 600 Squadron accelerated to maximum speed to close on the bomber. Lipscombe picked up the enemy aircraft on radar just over 2 miles ahead, but the rate of closure was too great to make a successful interception. Woodward throttled back, but as the Beaufighter lost speed the bomber opened the range until it disappeared off the AI radar screens. Woodward had to ask the ground controller for further help. Ignorant of the drama taking place behind him, Baetcher continued towards his target. By now the two planes were to the north of Cardiff, heading north-east. Later Woodward reported:

> After further vectors ending with 040° [AI radar], contact was regained. Bandit [enemy aircraft] was then at 11,500 feet so I dived to 10,500 feet keeping the Bandit in contact dead ahead. Our speed then about 160 mph. A visual of exhausts was obtained about 1,000 feet above and ahead. Having identified the aircraft as Hostile I closed in, climbing slowly to 300 feet and fired a three-second burst. No return fire was experienced. There was a blinding flash and explosion, and bits were seen to fly back. I gave another short burst before the enemy aircraft dived sharply to port with flames and smoke coming from its starboard side.

Hansgeorg Baetcher's recollection of the engagement links closely with Woodward's report. The first warning the German crew had of the presence of the enemy fighter was when the ventral gunner suddenly shouted 'Night fighter' and the aircraft shuddered under the impact of exploding cannon shells. Baetcher jettisoned the bombs and hurled the aircraft into a diving turn, making for a cloud bank far below. Lipscombe watched the bomber dive steeply with one engine on fire, then disappear into cloud.

Fortunately for Baetcher, the speed of the dive extinguished the flames before they took hold. Once in the cloud's enveloping folds he levelled out the bomber and took stock of the situation. The Heinkel was in serious trouble. The ventral gunner was dead and the radio operator seriously wounded. The port engine was stopped and Baetcher feathered its windmilling propeller. The starboard engine had also suffered damage and developed less than its full power. A large section of the rudder had been shot away and, with the 'live' engine trying to push the Heinkel into a turn to the left, the pilot was unable to hold a straight heading. Nor, on the available power, was it possible to maintain altitude. To add to the catalogue of woes, one fuel tank had been punctured and was losing fuel fast. Also, the bomber's main compass system no longer worked.

The navigator tuned the radio compass to a beacon near Cherbourg to provide a heading reference. After some experimenting Baetcher discovered a novel method of getting the crippled bomber to progress in that general direction, albeit in a slow descent. He held the plane on an approximate southerly heading for as long as possible then, when he could no longer hold it straight, he reversed the rudder and turned the plane left through 300°. As it neared the required heading he rolled out of the turn and held it in the required direction for as long as possible, then repeated the process. Using this 'three steps forward, one step back' technique and flying close to its stalling speed, the Heinkel headed for France.

As more fuel was consumed, the aircraft became progressively lighter. Gradually, the rate of sink decreased, until Baetcher could maintain altitude at 1,200 feet. At the same time the bomber became progressively easier to handle. The straight runs between the turns became increasingly longer, until Baetcher could maintain the bomber on the desired heading. Shortly after reaching the coast near Cherbourg, he set down the battered Heinkel in a crash landing on an airstrip near the port. It had been a superb demonstration of flying skill, in the most trying of circumstances.

Woodward claimed to have destroyed the Heinkel, but as no wreck was found he was credited with only a 'probably destroyed'. However, from Luftwaffe records we know the Heinkel was damaged beyond repair. So Woodward's original claim, for an enemy plane destroyed, had been correct.

Apart from a raid on Manchester by some forty bombers on the night of 12 October, there was no attack of any consequence on an inland target for the remainder of 1941. The ordeal of the coastal towns would continue for a little longer, however: North and South Shields, Newcastle and Hull all suffered one or more sharp assaults during this period.

The reduced scale of German air activity over Britain during the summer and autumn of 1941 meant that when they did come, raiders suffered almost continual harassment from the defences. Against this background, No. 80 Wing's Meacon stations were able to secure some notable successes.

Early on the morning of 24 July, a Junkers 88 of I./KG 30 had been returning from an attack on Birkenhead when it was forced off course to avoid a night fighter. The threat passed and, as the pilot turned back on to his original heading,

*Early on the morning of 12 October 1941 the RAF secured its first example of the new Dornier 217 bomber, when an aircraft of KG 2 became lost after a shipping reconnaissance sortie over the Atlantic and, following a successful Meacon action, crash-landed in Kent.* (IWM)

the bomber's radio operator tuned his radio compass to the radio beacon at St Paoul near their home airfield at Brest. Unknown to the crewman, however, the St Paoul beacon was covered by the Meacon at Lympsham near Weston-super-Mare. It was the latter that gave such a firm indication on the pointer of the radio compass. As the bomber neared the Meacon, the crew observed a balloon barrage looking reassuringly like that covering the port of Brest (in fact, it covered Bristol). The Junkers made a perfect landing at Broadfield Down airfield near Weston-super-Mare, and was captured intact. The crew of another Ju 88 of the same unit got lost under similar circumstances that night. It made a belly landing near Bembridge on the Isle of Wight.

There was a similar success, two and a half months later, early on the morning of 12 October. A Dornier 217, a type which had become operational in the Luftwaffe only a short time before, crash-landed in Kent after being misled by Meacons.

While such incidents punctuated the relative calm, Britain's night air defences underwent some fundamental changes. At the close of 1941 there were twenty-eight GCI stations in operation, serving ten squadrons of AI-equipped Beaufighters and seven of Defiants. In addition, there were several squadrons of Hurricanes that could be diverted to night operations if required.

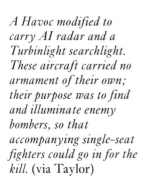

*A Havoc modified to carry AI radar and a Turbinlight searchlight. These aircraft carried no armament of their own; their purpose was to find and illuminate enemy bombers, so that accompanying single-seat fighters could go in for the kill.* (via Taylor)

## THE TURBINLIGHT

To enable the single-engined fighters to operate with greater effect at night, especially if there was no moon, a specially developed airborne searchlight was now put into service. The light, known as the 'Turbinlight', was the brainchild of Wing Commander W. Helmore. It fitted into the nose of modified Havoc aircraft, which also carried AI radar. Directed on to its target by GCI radar or by searchlights on the ground, the Turbinlight aircraft was accompanied into action by a Hurricane fighter. The searchlight Havoc carried no armament. Its sole function was to find and illuminate the enemy aircraft, so the Hurricane could make the kill.

By the beginning of October 1941, five flights of Turbinlight aircraft had formed, with a total of twenty modified Havocs. The initial training sorties soon revealed the difficulties of such operations. One of the greatest problems was for the fighter to maintain formation at night on the searchlight aircraft. If the fighter pilot took his eyes off the latter even for a short time, for example to look inside his cockpit, he was liable to lose contact. Moreover, once the target had been illuminated and began taking evasive action, if the searchlight aircraft tried to follow it could easily get in the way of the attacking aircraft. Nevertheless, at the time there was considerable enthusiasm in Fighter Command for the Turbinlight. The Commander-in-Chief, Air Chief Marshal Sir Sholto Douglas, went so far as to proclaim its development '. . . the most promising aid to night fighting since the introduction of AI'. He decreed that it was not to be used in action yet, however. It was to be held in reserve until the Luftwaffe resumed larger-scale attacks on Britain.

As the Turbinlight came in, the Long Aerial Mine went out. During 1941 No. 93 Squadron had given up its lumbering Harrows in favour of faster Havocs, but even with these aircraft it had proved extremely difficult to lay the curtains of mines accurately across the flight paths of German bombers. The mine-laying scheme was considerably less efficient than normal forms of fighter operation,

*At the end of 1941 a few Defiants were issued to Nos 96 and 264 Squadrons equipped with AI Mark VI radar. There was no room in the turret for the radar indicator so the latter, fitted with a semi-automatic control system, was fitted in the cockpit and operated by the pilot. Technically the radar was a success but the performance of the Defiant was inferior to that of the German bombers that attacked Britain in 1942, and the new set achieved little.*

and in October 1941 it was finally abandoned. One RAF commander wrote a fitting epitaph to the weapon when he commented, 'The LAM has today received last rites of burial and may henceforth be regarded as frozen meat.'

Early in 1942 a new night fighter entered service in Fighter Command: the Mosquito, which had a performance considerably better than the Beaufighter. Carrying an armament of four 20-mm cannon and four .303-inch machine-guns, the Mosquito II could reach 370 mph at 12,000 feet. The early Mosquitos carried the new AI Mark V radar, a set broadly similar to the earlier Mark IV but with indicators for the pilot as well as the radar operator. No. 157 Squadron received its first fully equipped Mosquitos early in April and began operations at the end of the month. Like the Beaufighter before it, however, the Mosquito and its new radar experienced teething troubles and did not enjoy immediate success.

## IMPORTANT NEW RADAR

All developments in airborne radar at this time were transcended by the introduction into service of the first experimental 'centimetric' radar, the AI Mark VII. The essential difference of this set was that it worked on a wavelength considerably shorter that those that preceded it. The earlier AI radars had all worked on a wavelength of 1½ metres. The new Mark VII, on the other hand, worked on a wavelength of only 10 cm – hence the title 'centimetric' radar. The use of the shorter wavelength brought several technical advantages. Instead of using aerials 75 cms long for the transmission and the reception of signals, the new set used an aerial only 5 cms long. A reflector dish behind the aerial focused the signals into a fine beam 12 degrees wide, which could be made to scan over a cone 90 degrees wide in front of the aircraft. A clever electronic switch made it possible for the same aerial to alternate rapidly between transmission and reception (lacking this refinement, the Mark IV radar had separate sets of aerials for the transmission and reception of signals).

With the technical advantages of centimetric radar came important operational advantages. The narrower beam was less liable to pick up unwanted reflections from the ground, so targets flying at low altitude could be tracked far more easily than was possible on the earlier sets. Moreover, the scanning beam gave a more precise indication of the whereabouts and movements of the target, with less risk of ambiguities.

Early in 1942 the first hand-built AI Mark VII sets underwent operational trials, fitted into Beaufighters. On 5 April the new radar secured its first operational success, when it guided a pilot of the Fighter Interception Unit into a firing position on a low-flying Dornier 217 which was promptly shot down. The AI Mark VII went into limited production. It was to be followed, at the highest priority, by the fully engineered mass-produced Mark VIII later in the year.

## THE SMACK SYSTEM

With the changes in equipment there came a fundamental change in night-fighting tactics. GCI radar was acknowledged to be the most efficient means of bringing night fighters into contact with enemy bombers. Yet, because the early GCI stations could direct only one fighter at a time and an interception took about 10 minutes, this system could easily be saturated. A ground station could control only about six interceptions an hour. So all the raiders flying through the area at that time, except for the unfortunate six, were safe from this form of attack. To enable more night fighters to go into action against massed raiding forces, should the Luftwaffe resume large-scale attacks, at the close of 1941 Sir Sholto Douglas introduced a new system using searchlights to assist fighters to intercept enemy aircraft. Code-named 'Smack', this system was to operate in parallel with the GCI system.

With the introduction of 'Smack', there was an extensive redeployment of searchlights to assist night fighters. Previously these had been set out in clusters of three at intervals of 10,400 yards. These clusters had not been close enough to provide continuous illumination of targets, however, and because there were insufficient lights the density could not be increased. Now, to expand the area covered, the searchlights were deployed singly. Many lights had radar control, the rest were to receive it as soon as the necessary equipment was available. Almost the whole of southern England and the Midlands was divided into a series of 'Fighter Boxes', arranged whenever possible in front of the gun-defended main targets. The size of individual boxes varied according to the area available in front of the target, but the ideal was about 32 miles deep and 14 miles wide. The first 12 miles of the searchlight belt was termed the Indicator Zone. Here low-powered 90-cm lights were set out singly at 10,000-yard intervals, to point out but not necessarily illuminate incoming raiders. In the middle of the Fighter Box a vertically pointing searchlight served as a beacon, round which the fighter orbited while waiting for his enemy to come to him.

When an enemy aircraft entered the Indicator Zone the fighter pilot received the order to attack. Simultaneously, the searchlight that had served as his orbit beacon depressed to an angle of 20 degrees, pointing towards the raider. As the

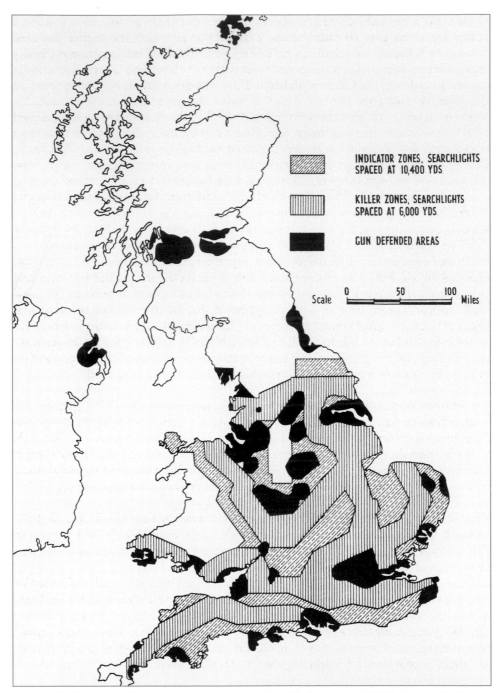

INDICATOR ZONES, SEARCHLIGHTS
SPACED AT 10,400 YDS.

KILLER ZONES, SEARCHLIGHTS
SPACED AT 6,000 YDS.

GUN DEFENDED AREAS

Scale    0        50        100    Miles

*Late in 1941 the searchlights were repositioned to form 'Indicator' and 'Killer' zones for the
night fighters, through which the raiders had to fly to reach inland targets. For the remainder of
the war the system of searchlight control worked in parallel with that of GCI radar control to
bring night fighters into contact with their prey.*

fighter pilot moved out to engage his prey, the latter entered the so-called Killer Zone: the rear 20 miles of the Fighter Box in which the higher-powered 150-cm searchlights were laid out at 6,000-yard intervals. This searchlight density was sufficient to provide continuous illumination of the enemy aircraft, so attacks could be made by the 'Catseye' fighters. If, on the other hand, the fighter carried AI radar and had good contact with the raider, the pilot could broadcast a code-word and the searchlights would douse. Provided the fighter possessed a speed advantage over the bomber of 20 per cent or greater, there was a good chance of completing the interception before the raider reached the rear of the Killer Zone. Since the latter often coincided with the outer part of the gun-defended area, unless action was imminent the fighter pilot had to break off his interception.

The basic pattern of GCI and 'Smack' night-interception tactics was established by the beginning of 1942, and remained in use for the rest of the war. Where improvements were made, these were geared towards giving the night fighter greater freedom to change from one direction to another, depending on circumstances.

At the beginning of 1942 Britain's heavy gun defences comprised 935 static and 465 mobile 3.7-inch guns, 416 of the heavier 4.5-inch guns and 144 obsolescent 3-inch guns. These weapons now operated with a crude form of radar control and night-firing accuracy, which, while far short of that possible by day using optical fire control, was a great improvement over that during the dark days of 1940.

With the ending of the massed bomber attacks on Britain, there was pressure on General Pile to give up able-bodied men for service in the field forces. Pile later wrote of a conversation he had on this matter with Mr Churchill:

> I told him that I would not agree to leaving guns out of action. If he gave me the guns I would find some means of manning them, whether it was with whole-time soldiers, ATS [servicewomen] or Home Guard. This greatly appealed to Churchill, and he said that could it be achieved it would be at least as valuable as a major victory. The Prime Minister had rapidly added up in his mind the figures involved. 'Forty thousand men saved,' he said, 'equals a major victory for this country.'

The 40,000 men represented about one-sixth of Pile's manpower. But in spite of this and later demands for men, and the influx of untrained men and women to fill the gaps in the ranks, there was ample time to train the newcomers before large-scale attacks resumed.

During the first quarter of 1942, the British air defences had little opportunity to come to grips with the enemy. The Luftwaffe contented itself with tip-and-run attacks carried out by Messerschmitt 109 fighter bombers by day, and small-scale attacks by night, almost all of them limited to coastal targets. These raids caused little damage and few casualties. During March 1942, for example, not more than a score of people were killed during the air attacks on Britain.

## THE BAEDEKER RAIDS

The uneasy calm came to an end in April, following a heavy RAF attack on Luebeck which razed large sections of the city. This development enraged Hitler,

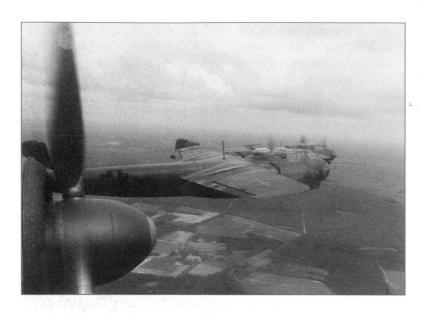

*Night-camouflaged Dornier 217Es of Kampfgeschwader 2, one of the units that took part in the Baedekker attacks on Britain in the spring of 1942.*

who ordered his air force to retaliate. On 14 April a top-secret signal from the Fuehrer's headquarters to the operation headquarters of the Luftwaffe stated:

> The Fuehrer has ordered that the air war against England is to be given a more aggressive stamp. Accordingly, when targets are being selected, preference is to be given to those where attacks are likely to have the greatest possible effect on civilian life. Besides raids on ports and industry, terror attacks of a retaliatory nature are to be carried out against towns other than London. Minelaying is to be scaled down in favour of these attacks.

The opening attack in the new series came just over a week later. On the night of 23 April some forty aircraft, Do 217s of KG 2, Ju 88s of Kampfgruppe 106 and a few He 111s of I./KG 100 (Kampfgruppe 100 had been redesignated I. Gruppe of Kampfgeschwader 100, in January 1942), made for Exeter. The sky was overcast and the bombs fell over a wide area. Only one aircraft bombed Exeter and its stick of 4 1,100-pound bombs killed 5 people and injured 8, causing damage to some 200 houses. A Beaufighter of No. 604 Squadron shot down a Do 217 near the target.

On the following night the Luftwaffe returned to Exeter, with an attack in two waves each comprising some twenty-five bombers; many crews flew in both waves. This time visibility was good and, unhampered by any balloon barrage, some bombers descended below 5,000 feet to release their bombs accurately. This double attack caused considerably more damage than the previous one, and 73 people were killed and 54 injured. Fighter Command put up 127 sorties against the raider and claimed 3 destroyed; a fourth was claimed by anti-aircraft gunners near Portland.

During the following night the target was Bath. For this attack the Luftwaffe mustered almost every available twin-engined bomber in the West, even using aircraft and instructors from training units. With almost all aircraft flying double sorties, the attackers put in two concentrated raids each lasting about half an hour. A total of 151 bomber sorties were flown and 4 bombers failed to return. On the following night the raiders returned to Bath. The 2 attacks caused severe damage to the city and resulted in the death of some 380 people and injuries to a similar number.

Gradually, the pattern of the new series of attacks, which came to be known on both sides as the 'Baedeker Raids', became clear. Launched against the smaller, less-well-defended cities, the attacks were made by concentrated forces on moonlit nights. Most raids lasted about half an hour, with double attacks on the same target a frequent occurrence. That was in contrast to the long drawn-out attacks of the previous year. Because the targets had been chosen for the weakness of their defences the bombers were able to attack from comparatively low altitudes, often between 5,000 and 10,000 feet. The greater part of the raiding force was made up of Junkers 88s and Dornier 217s, the fastest bombers

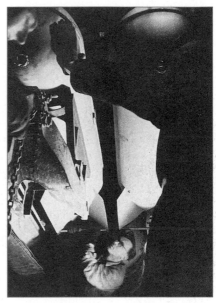

*Armourers loading ABB 500 incendiary bomb containers into the bomb bay of a Do 217 of KG 2.*

then available to the Luftwaffe. The Heinkel 111, which had made up the bulk of the bomber force the previous year, now constituted only a small proportion.

For the 'Baedeker' assaults some bombers carried a new type of incendiary bomb canister, the ABB 500, which contained 140 of the 2.2-pound stick incendiary bombs. After release the canister dropped to a previously set altitude, where a barometric switch opened it and the incendiary bombs fell away. Set to open at low altitude, the canisters produced unprecedentedly high concentrations of incendiary bombs on the ground. During one attack on Bath, for example, 96 incendiary bombs landed within an area of only 30 square yards; 20 of these passed through the roof of one house. Such overwhelming concentrations gave the local fire services serious problems.

Following the two attacks on Bath the raiders visited Norwich on 27 April and York on the 28th. During the latter attack, Turbinlight went into action for the first time. One pair of aircraft, a Havoc of No. 1459 Flight and a satellite Hurricane of No. 253 Squadron, made contact with a Dornier 217. The Havoc led its fighter up to the enemy aircraft, which the fighter pilot saw before the searchlight was switched on. As the Hurricane moved forwards to engage, its pilot asked the Havoc to leave the light off. This request was not heard, however, and the Turbinlight came on. The enemy aircraft was held in the beam for about 10 seconds, during which time it took violent evasive action. The Hurricane pilot saw the bomber clearly but was unable to get into a firing position, because he was too close to the Havoc and had to cross through the beam to get at the bomber. The enemy aircraft escaped.

Two nights later, the bomber was not so lucky. Early on the morning of 1 May, Flight Lieutenant C. Winn in a Havoc of No. 1459 Flight and Flight Lieutenant D. Yapp in a Hurricane of No. 253 Squadron took off from Hibaldstow near Scunthorpe. The two aircraft headed northwards under control of the GCI station at Patrington near Spurn Head. The ground station directed the pair on to a suspected enemy bomber, until it was within range of the Havoc's AI radar. The Turbinlight aircraft and its satellite closed in and, as on the previous occasion, the Hurricane pilot caught sight of the enemy before the light was switched on. This time the light remained off and Yapp closed to about 100 yards. He was just about to open fire when the bomber went into a violent diving turn to starboard. Yapp followed the spiralling bomber, which he recognised as Heinkel 111, firing several bursts which he saw striking the engines and the fuselage. After a fairly long burst the Heinkel entered cloud but shortly after that a large glow lit up the cloud for about 2 minutes. Almost certainly this was from the wreckage of the German bomber burning on the sea some 20 miles off Flamborough Head. For the first time a single-seat fighter had been successfully led by another aircraft into a firing position although, it should be noted, the Turbinlight made no contribution to the destruction of the Heinkel.

This was to prove one of the very few successes for the Turbinlight. Working together, No. 253 Squadron and No. 1459 Flight claimed one bomber probably shot down and two more damaged during the months that followed. No other fighter squadron working with Turbinlight claimed anything at all. As a method of countering the short, sharp, shallow-penetration attacks now being mounted by the Luftwaffe, the system was too cumbersome.

On the night of 3 May Exeter suffered its third and heaviest attack. On the following night raiders bombed Cowes and on the 8th Norwich was the target. Throughout the 'Baedeker' assaults bombers had tried to make use of the X- and Y-beam systems, operating on many different frequencies to make jamming difficult. Meanwhile, No. 80 Wing had been busily engaged in jamming these and controlling the various 'Starfish' decoy sites. The reader can get a clear idea of the build-up of one such night's operations from the Wing's records for 8/9 May, when bombers tried to attack Norwich.

Shortly after 2200 hours the first beam signals had been heard by No. 80 Wing listening stations; by 2252 hours four X-beams and one Y-beam were being radiated. No aircraft had yet been seen on radar, however, and the jammers, though tuned in and warmed up ready to transmit, were silent. The Wing's operations logbook noted:

*2323*  First plots of enemy aircraft on table – two aircraft 30 miles south of Dunkirk. Controller orders Benjamin jammers (to counter the Y-beam) to radiate on 42.8 megacycles. Still no sign of Y-beam range signal. Controller orders Bromide jammers to radiate on 70.0 and 70.5 megacycles (X-beam frequencies).

*2325*  Cherbourg X-beam on 52.5 megacycles and Boulogne X-beams on 68.75 and 74.0 megacylces now active; jamming cover being arranged.

*2330*   Four enemy aircraft now plotted.

*2334*   Signals from Y-beam range station at Cassel heard on 42.4 megacycles. Domino station (to jam Y-beam range system) ordered to stand by.

*2345*   Raiders now heading north from the Frisian Islands. Starfish sites on the east coast alerted.

*2358*   Present jamming position:
         X-beams from Cherbourg: 70.0, 70.5 and 73.5 megacycles, all jammed.
         X-beams from Boulogne: 68.75 megacycles, being jammed; 74 and 74.5 megacycles, jamming ready.
         Y-beam Cherbourg: 42.8 megacycles beam signals, jammed.
         42.5 megacycles ranging signal, Domino standing by.
         Listening station confirms that no Y-beam aircraft have yet been heard. X-beams are laid on the Norfolk area.

*0002*   Y-beam on 43.0 megacycles coming from Cassel; jamming ordered.

*0005*   Bromide jamming ordered on 74.0 megacycles.

*0018*   Four enemy aircraft observed flying NW as far as the latitude of Norwich, then turned west.

*0020*   X-beam signals from Boulogne heard on 67.25 megacycles. Jamming ordered on this frequency and also on 74.5 megacycles. Analysis of the beam signals indicates that the beams are laid on Norwich.

*0030*   Three enemy aircraft coming in towards Norwich.

*0040*   First enemy aircraft crossed the Norfolk coast. All jammers radiating.

*0043*   Report from Norwich that flares and high explosive bombs have been dropped to the south of city, close to the Bramerton Starfish site.

*0057*   Bramerton Starfish ordered to ignite. About eight enemy aircraft now approaching from the east.

*0102*   Bramerton Starfish ignited.

*0106*   Flares and bombs dropped south of Norwich.

*0110*   There are now approximately 16 enemy aircraft approaching Norwich from the east and north east.

*0118*   There are now 10 enemy aircraft over Norwich and nine more coming in.

*0120*   Monitoring aircraft report jamming effective.

*0140*   Report that nine high explosive bombs have landed within 800 yards of the Bramerton decoy. About 30 bombs have fallen in the vicinity of Norwich, mostly round the outskirts. Enemy aircraft appear to be between Norwich and the coast but are wandering.

*0148*   There are still seven enemy aircraft near Norwich. The remainder have gone home.

*0155*   There are now three enemy aircraft crossing the coast on their way home. There appear to have been some 30 enemy aircraft involved in tonight's raid.

*0200*   Table now clear.

That night the weather at the target was good, with only two-tenths cloud at 4,000 feet. There was no moon, but bright starlight. Yet only two bombs hit the built-up part of Norwich and there were no casualties on the ground. Most raiders approached the target at low level, posing a difficult problem for the night fighters. One Junkers 88 struck a balloon cable and crashed to the south of Norwich.

The 'Baedeker' attacks continued, with raids on Hull, Poole, Grimsby and Canterbury in May. During June Ipswich, Poole and Canterbury, Southampton, Norwich and Weston-super-Mare were all hit. Also, for the first time in the new series, there was a small raid on Birmingham, three more on Middlesbrough and a single raid on Hull.

By the end of July 1942 three squadrons of Mosquito night fighters were operational and the type was beginning to amass a reasonable number of kills. An action on the last day of the month illustrates how searchlights could assist fighters to engage bombers flying outside the range of GCI radar. Early on the morning of 31 July the commander of No. 264 Squadron, Squadron Leader C. Cook, was airborne in one of the unit's new Mosquitos. The 'Longload' GCI station near Yeovil passed details of an unidentified aircraft moving northwards 8 miles in front of them. Cook turned to follow and opened his throttles. But his radar operator, Pilot Officer McPherson, had not made contact with the aircraft before it passed outside the range of 'Longload'. However, 6 miles in front of the Mosquito, Cook observed a 'cone' of searchlights tracking something. He followed the 'cone' and shortly afterwards McPherson picked up a contact on AI.

One by one the searchlights went out as the aircraft passed out of their range, until none were on. But by then McPherson had firm contact on radar and the Mosquito was closing in fast. He guided Cook to within 150 yards of the aircraft and the latter was observed ahead. It was a dark moonless night, however, and the two crewmen had difficulty in identifying the vague silhouette. Finally, Cook decided it was a Dornier 217 and loosed off fifty-three rounds of 20-mm in three short bursts. The bomber – in fact a Junkers 88 of Kampfgruppe 106 making for Birmingham – caught fire in the port wing, began to break up and crashed near Malvern. The crew baled out and all, with the exception of the pilot who suffered a broken rib, reached the ground safely.

During the summer of 1942 the strength of the units involved in 'Baedeker' raids eroded steadily, as the defences took their toll. Yet there was still pressure on the Luftwaffe to step up attacks on Britain by all possible means. Since the Luebeck assault in March the RAF attacks on Germany had become progressively heavier, culminating in the 'Thousand Bomber' raid on Cologne at the end of May. During June there were two attacks of similar strength, on Essen and Bremen. The German leaders dearly wished that they could retaliate in kind but, with the bulk of their air force locked in the bitter struggle in Russia, few bombers could be diverted for attacks on the enemy in the West.

## RAIDS FROM THE STRATOSPHERE

At this time, however, the Luftwaffe received a few examples of a new type of high-altitude bomber, the Junkers 86R. Based on the old Ju 86 bomber that had been obsolescent at the beginning of the war, the R version had been redesigned for very high-altitude bombing operations. The latter had a pointed wing with a span of 104 feet, an increase of some 30 feet over that of the original aircraft. The gun positions were faired over and the two-man crew was housed in a fully pressurised cabin (this was the first bomber to enter service fitted with this refinement). Like earlier versions the Ju 86R was fitted with two-stroke compression ignition diesel engines, but power at high altitude was boosted by exhaust-driven turbo-superchargers and nitrous-oxide injection equipment. The Junkers 86R was not particularly fast – it cruised at a true airspeed of 180 mph – nor did it carry any armament. For its survival it relied solely on its outstanding altitude performance: it could cruise at heights above 40,000 feet. For attacks from such altitudes, however, its offensive load was limited to a single 550-pound bomb.

*Leutnant Erich Sommer, the commander of the experimental Junkers 86 unit that carried out the high-altitude attacks on southern England during the summer of 1942. (Sommer)*

During July 1942, two Junkers 86Rs were issued to the Luftwaffe High Command's high-altitude trials unit, Hoehenkampfkommando der Versuchsstelle fuer Hoehenfluege. Tests began at the research establishment at Oranienburg. One of the two pilots involved in the trials was Horst Goetz, now a feldwebel, who had previously operated over Britain with Kampfgruppe 100. Trials proved the feasibility of bombing operations from altitudes over 40,000 feet. In mid-August the two bombers moved to Beauvais in northern France. Under the command of Leutnant Erich Sommer, the Ju 86Rs were to mount a series of experimental

*A Ju 86R about to taxy out from its dispersal point at Beauvais for an attack. (Goetz)*

*A Junkers 86R coming in to land at Beauvais, showing its long pointed wing. This high-altitude bomber had a wing span greater than that of the British Lancaster, though the latter weighed two-and-a-half times more.* (Goetz)

high-altitude attacks on England. Since there seemed little to fear from the defences, the raids were to be flown by day.

On the morning of 24 August all was ready and Goetz, with Sommer as his observer, took off from Beauvais for the first attack. Remaining over France they climbed for about an hour then, at an altitude of 39,000 feet, headed north towards England. They crossed the coast near Selsey Bill, dropped their bomb on Camberley, and left via Brighton having spent 35 minutes over Britain without any interference from the defences. Shortly afterwards, the other Ju 86R attacked Southampton. Fighter Command put up fifteen fighters in attempts to intercept the raiders, but without success.

On the following day, 25 August, Goetz and Sommer were over England again. This time, confident of their immunity from interception, they flew a meandering course that took them over Southampton, Swindon, round the north of London to Stanstead where they released their bomb. They continued down the eastern side of the capital and they left the coast near Shoreham. The Ju 86R spent more than an hour over England, the intention being to sound as many sirens as possible and cause maximum disruption and loss of production. The defenders refused to play this time, however. Unless there was evidence to the contrary, single intruders were treated as reconnaissance aircraft not carrying bombs. The sirens remained silent. Nine Spitfires took off to engage but none was able to get within 2,000 feet of the bomber.

On the morning of 28 August a Ju 86R attacked Bristol. Six Spitfires attempted to intercept but found the raider, identified variously as a 'Dornier 217' or a 'Heinkel 177', too high for them. By now the two German crews had become accustomed to watching as interested spectators, while fighters several thousand feet below tumbled out of the sky in their efforts to reach the bombers. The policy of not sounding the sirens for individual raiders was a calculated risk, justifiable in wartime, but on this occasion the citizens of Bristol had to pay the penalty. The bomb landed on Broad Weir, almost in the centre of the city. Without warning it exploded close to three buses, wrecking them all and killing most of those on board. It was the worst single bomb incident suffered by Bristol during the war and resulted in 48 people killed, 26 seriously injured and 30 slightly wounded.

During the ten days that followed the bombers carried out eight further attacks on southern England. The nearest either Ju 86R came to being intercepted was on 6 September, when Goetz and his observer watched a Lightning fighter (of the USAAF 94th Squadron) get uncomfortably close before it stalled and fell away.

Meanwhile, however, Fighter Command was taking more positive steps to counter the new menace. Early in September a special high-altitude unit, the 'Special Service Flight', was formed at Northolt under the operational control of No. 11 Group to engage the high-flying raiders. Two Mark IX Spitfires were modified for the role and delivered to the Flight. Lighter wooden propellers were substituted for the normal metal ones. All armour was removed as were the four machine-guns, leaving the aircraft with an armament of two 20-mm cannon. The aircraft were painted with a special lightweight finish and all equipment not strictly necessary for high-altitude fighting was removed. As a result of this pruning, the Spitfires weighed 450 pounds less than the standard model.

As well as special aircraft to deal with the high-altitude bombers, a new form of ground control was necessary if the fighters were to reach a firing position on their elusive quarry. The system instituted by No. 11 Group under the code-name 'Windgap' employed GCI radar stations in the Group's area to feed plots on the high-altitude bomber and the intercepting fighter, to a special Area Control Room. From the information on the plotting table in front of him, the area controller directed the interception. This form of precise but centralised control covering a large area was necessary. Even the modified Spitfire required about half an hour to reach the raider's altitude, so an interception covered an area far greater than that observed from a single GCI station.

The 'Windgap' procedure was tried for the first time on 11 September. But although the Spitfire succeeded in getting to 45,000 feet, an estimated 2,000 feet higher than the Ju 86R, radio failure prevented an interception.

On the morning of 12 September Goetz and Sommer again took off to attack Bristol. At 0853 hours, 28 minutes after take-off, the still-climbing bomber was first observed, at a range of 120 miles, by the Chain Home radar stations on the south coast of England. During the minutes that followed the counters on the plotting tables indicated an aircraft climbing higher. Yet another high-altitude raid was in the offing.

Now, for a second time, the 'Windgap' procedure went into operation. At 0927 hours, soon after the Junkers crossed the north coast of France, Pilot Officer Prince Emanuel Galitzine of the Special Service Flight, a white-Russian émigré who had come to Britain in 1919, received the order to scramble from Northolt. The Spitfire orbited over base climbing rapidly then, as it passed 15,000 feet, it was ordered on to a south-westerly course. Galitzine's Spitfire was not the only one that had been scrambled to intercept the raider: a pair of fighters of No. 421 Squadron attempted to catch the Junkers near the Isle of Wight, but

*Pilot Officer Prince Emanuel Galitzine flew the modified Spitfire that, on 12 September, intercepted Goetz and Sommer over the New Forest. It was the highest operational fighter interception ever made over Britain, and almost certainly the highest during the Second World War. (Galitzine)*

could get nowhere near their foe cruising serenely at 42,000 feet. Shortly after 0950 hours Goetz and Sommer crossed the coast near Southampton and continued towards their target.

As the Ju 86 neared Salisbury the calm on board was rudely shattered. Goetz later recalled:

> Suddenly Erich, sitting to my right, said that there was a fighter closing on us from his side. I thought there was nothing remarkable about that: almost every time we had been over England in the Ju 86, fighters had tried to intercept us. Then, he said, the fighter was climbing very fast and was nearly at our altitude; the next thing it was above us. I thought Erich's eyes must have been playing him tricks, so I leaned over to his side of the cabin to see for myself. To my horror I saw the Spitfire, a little above us and still climbing.

Goetz acted fast. He jettisoned the bomb, switched in extra nitrous oxide to increase engine power then, after his and Sommer's oxygen masks were clamped on, depressurised the cabin so that there would be no risk of an explosive decompression if it was hit. Then he tried to out-climb his assailant.

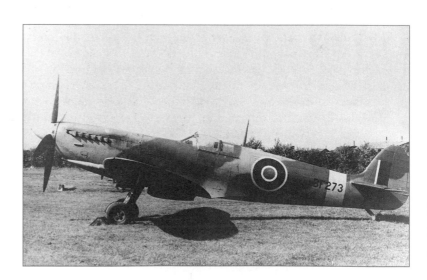

*The Mark IX Spitfire flown by Galitzine during the action on 12 September, photographed shortly before it was stripped down for high-altitude work. (via Hooton)*

*The port wing of the Junkers 86 after it had returned to Beauvais following the action on 12 September. Galitzine's 20-mm armour-piercing round had passed clean through the structure from the rear, without striking anything vital.* (Sommer)

The area controller had directed Galitzine neatly in behind the Junkers. The Spitfire pilot watched the bomb fall away and the bomber begin its climb, but found little difficulty in overhauling his foe in the race for altitude. Galitzine climbed to a position 300 feet up-sun of his quarry, then dived to attack. He closed to 200 yards astern and opened fire with his cannon. One round struck the port wing of the Junkers and went clean through from rear to front without striking anything vital. Almost immediately afterwards, the Spitfires' port cannon jammed. The starboard weapon continued firing but its recoil force was so great that the fighter slewed round and began to fall out of the sky. Then, as the Spitfire passed through the bomber's wake, its cockpit canopy misted over.

The Spitfire's canopy took some time to clear, and when Galitzine next saw the Junkers it was heading south out to sea. Again he climbed above the bomber then dived to attack it from out of the sun. But Goetz demonstrated a skill born of years of flying experience: at the last moment he spun the Junkers round and out of the Spitfire's gunsight. Galitzine curved after him, but as he opened fire with his remaining cannon the Spitfire again slewed and he had to break off the assault. Twice more Galitzine attacked his elusive quarry, and each time the story was the same.

Goetz struggled to shake off his tormentor. So far luck had been on his side, but suddenly it seemed to desert him. The diesel engines had been working on their limit for too long; now one of them lost power and began to trail unburnt oil. Goetz thought his last moment had come. His only defence had been the ability to stay at high altitude and outmanoeuvre his adversary. Now he could no longer do either. There seemed only one slim chance for survival: he pushed down the nose of the Junkers into a steep dive, hoping to convince his enemy that the bomber had been hit and was falling out of control.

As his windscreen cleared, Galitzine saw the bomber going into a patch of mist. But he could also see the north coast of France getting disconcertingly close. Reluctantly he broke away and turned northwards for home. So ended the highest air battle ever fought over Britain, and almost certainly the highest fought during the Second World War.

Goetz, suspecting that his fragile aircraft had been hit, landed at Caen. On the ground, a quick inspection revealed the single hole through the wing. Satisfied that nothing vital had been damaged, he took off again and returned to Beauvais. The unique interception caused a ripple of excitement through the Luftwaffe High Command. Goetz later commented: 'Several senior officers came to visit us at Beauvais to talk about it. Some even expressed doubts that we could possibly have been attacked by a British fighter at such a high altitude. "Well", I told them, "we did not make that hole in the wing ourselves!"' The upshot of this incident was that the high-altitude bombing attacks on Britain ceased. With the aircraft able to carry only a single 550-pound bomb on each sortie, they had been of value only so long as they could be made without loss. Now, it was clear, it would be only a matter of time before a Ju 86R was shot down.

The bombing ended, but the Junkers 86R made one final appearance over Britain. With Fliegerstabsingenieur Altrogge at the control, Sommer flew in an unladen bomber with reduced fuel over southern England on 2 October, to test the defences. The Ju 86R crossed the coast at nearly 48,000 feet and penetrated as far as Tunbridge Wells before turning back. Six Spitfires took off to intercept, including one from the Special Service Flight, but none could get close to this highest flying of all intruders.

So ended the remarkable series of high-altitude raids on Britain. Technically, they are of great interest, for not until well into the jet age would bombing attacks from such altitudes be possible as a matter of course. Militarily, however, they achieved little. Altogether the two Ju 86Rs had dropped a total of fourteen bombs on Britain. Only one of these, during the attack on Bristol, had caused serious damage or loss of life.

While the high-altitude daylight attacks were in progress, the night raids continued though with a steadily reducing number of bombers. During August night-raiding forces of less than twenty aircraft attacked Norwich, Swansea, Colchester and Ipswich. During the following month Sunderland and King's Lynn were visited in similar strength. The Luftwaffe crew training organisation was unable to supply new bomber crews as fast as they were being lost over Britain and on the eastern and southern fronts. As a result, the fighting strengths of the bomber units drained away. Kampfgeschwader 2, for example, began 1942 with eighty-eight crews, but had only twenty-three crews remaining by September.

In its efforts to find an Achilles' Heel of the British defences, the Luftwaffe tried almost every possible stratagem. Sheer height had not been enough to render attacking aircraft immune to interception, nor was the cover of darkness. On the other hand, raids by fighter bombers on targets on or close to the coast were known to be difficult to counter. Hitherto these had been made with small forces, rarely more than a dozen aircraft. But in October, following a particularly heavy attack by the RAF on Düsseldorf, the German tactics changed.

Late on the afternoon of 31 October a force of thirty Focke Wulf 190 fighter bombers drawn from Jagdgeschwader 2, Jagdgeschwader 26 and Zerstoerergeschwader 2 made a low-level attack on Canterbury. A similar number of fighters flew as close escort and thirty more as rear support. One of the fighter-bomber pilots who took part in the operation, Feldwebel Adolf Dilg of ZG 2, later recalled:

> On our way in we hugged the surface of the sea, to keep beneath the prying beams of the British radar. The visibility low down was good but above us at 2,000 feet there was an almost continuous blanket of cloud; almost ideal weather for our purpose. Keeping out to sea we skirted round the Dover flak defences, then turned due west to cross the coast just to the north of Deal. I think we achieved complete surprise; at the coast a few guns opened up an inaccurate fire against us, but we soon left them behind. Flying at maximum speed we took only about three minutes to reach Canterbury. We made for a point just to the north west of the city, then turned port through a semi-circle and ran in to attack. Each Focke Wulf carried a single delayed-action 1,100 bomb, fused to explode when the last attacker had got clear. At the target the defences were fully alert and they opened up with everything they had. Particularly disconcerting were the rockets, which left dense trails of smoke as they climbed in front of us on parallel paths; it looked as though they were trying to erect some sort of wire net in the sky to trap us and I banked steeply

*A Dornier 217K of KG 2 about to take off for a night attack on Britain.*

to avoid the smoke. [In fact there was no 'net'. The smoke trails had been caused by rockets from a 'Z' battery at Canterbury.] Still keeping low, we made our escape along a route similar to that we had used going in. From start to finish we had been over England less than six minutes.

Fighter Command put up sixty-three fighters to meet the incursion and there were several combats with the German escorts. Of the raiding force 3 aircraft were destroyed by fighters or anti-aircraft fire. A total of 28 bombs landed in and around Canterbury, causing scattered damage; 30 people were killed and 48 suffered injuries. That night there was a follow-up attack by twin-engined bombers. This was far less accurate, however, and caused little damage and only 9 casualties.

The Canterbury attack was the last mounted by the Luftwaffe on even a moderate scale in 1942. For the remainder of the year the pressure was maintained against the coastal towns by small forces of fighter bombers and twin-engined bombers operating in ones and twos. Although they sometimes proved discomforting for those on the receiving end, such attacks could have little military effect.

During 1942, 3,236 people were killed and 4,148 suffered serious injuries as a result of the bombing attacks on Britain. These figures were rather less than one-fifth of those for the previous year. In the course of 1942 the British air defences had continued to grow stronger. They had demonstrated they could inflict punishing losses on small raiding forces penetrating far inland, whether by day or by night. Short penetrations at low level enjoyed a measure of immunity from interception, but those made high in the stratosphere had been shown to be vulnerable. Although the German air attacks on Britain caused relatively little damage and few casualties, in one respect they were extremely successful. The Luftwaffe had resumed its offensive with only about 200 conventional bombers and a few fighter bombers. Yet these tied down more than 1,400 British fighters, including the latest types, at a time when such planes were desperately needed in other war theatres and might have made a decisive impact there. The diversion of effort did not end there. There were some 2,000 medium and heavy anti-aircraft guns, and about double that number of lighter weapons, deployed around the country. Also a large scientific and production effort was devoted to developing and building new types of radar to defeat the night bomber. The Luftwaffe attacks during this phase of the campaign need to be judged not only on their physical effects, but also on what they prevented their enemy from achieving.

Throughout 1942 the Luftwaffe bomber force in the West had been a declining asset, starved of resources. Now that was about to change, as reinforcements were earmarked and plans laid for a resumption of large-scale attacks on Britain early in the new year. In the next chapter we shall see how the revitalised bomber force fared against the much-improved air-defence system.

## CHAPTER 7

# In Fits and Starts, January–December 1943

Force and fraud are in war the two cardinal virtues
*attributed to Niccolo Machiavelli*

From several points of view the beginning of 1943 could be said to mark the turning point of the Second World War. In Russia the German forces had reached the limit of their advance and would shortly suffer a crushing defeat at Stalingrad. In North Africa the Afrika Korps was falling back after the battle at El Alamein and had been expelled from Egypt and most of Libya; in the West, Allied forces had landed in Morocco and Algeria. And in the Pacific the Japanese forces were being contained and thrown on the defensive.

Over Germany itself, the Royal Air Force was mounting regular night attacks with forces of more than 200 bombers. So far these raids, made over distances far greater than those of the Luftwaffe against Britain, had lacked both accuracy and concentration and had had little effect on war production. This was soon to change, however, as Bomber Command began to receive the electronic equipment to enable its bombers to find their targets. And as this transition got under way,

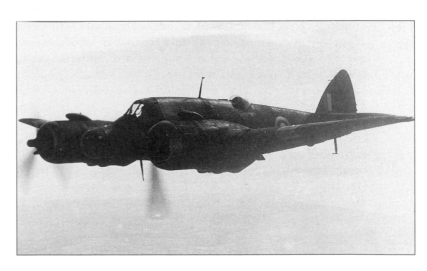

*A Beaufighter fitted with AI Mark VIII 'centimetric' radar, which became operational at the beginning of 1943.* (via Oughton)

*Close up of the scanning dish of the AI Mark VIII, which was housed inside the streamlined nose radome of the Beaufighter.* (IWM)

there would be demands for retaliatory attacks by the Luftwaffe against major cities in Britain. The period of tranquillity over the British capital was soon to end.

At the beginning of 1943 the night defences of Britain comprised twelve squadrons of Beaufighters, some of them equipped with the new AI Mark VIII 'centimetric' radar, and six squadrons of Mosquitos. These operated a total of some 400 aircraft, of which about 300 were serviceable at any one time. In addition there were two intruder squadrons operating Boston Mark IIIs (a type similar to the Havoc, but with a slightly improved performance). The Turbinlight Havocs were no longer considered effective, and the units were on the point of disbanding. Although larger and better equipped than ever before, the night-fighter force had to be spread thinly to cover the entire country. With the snap attacks being mounted by the Luftwaffe, there was no time for night fighters based far from the raiders' route to get into action.

For the close defence of targets, Anti-Aircraft Command now operated 288 heavy gun batteries with 2,075 radar-controlled guns. The 157 light batteries possessed 1,453 40-mm Bofors guns and 105 20-mm cannon converted for ground use. In addition, 344 Bofors guns and 837 cannon were deployed at the coast to counter the German tip-and-run attacks.

## London Attacked

Following a period of reinforcement, by mid-January the force of twin-engined bombers available to Luftflotte 3 for the attacks on Britain comprised some sixty Dornier 217s of Kampfgeschwader 2 and a similar number of Junkers 88s of Kampfgeschwader 6. At this time KG 2 was receiving the latest K and M versions of the Do 217. With engines of increased power and redesigned more streamlined nose section, these had a maximum speed 20 mph greater than the E model they replaced. KG 6 operated the latest A-14 version of the Junkers 88,

*A Dornier 217K of Kampfgeschwader 2. Fitted with a more streamlined nose and more powerful engines, this version, which began operating over Britain during the winter of 1942, was about 20mph faster than the earlier 'E' version.* (via Seeley)

which carried additional armour protection for the crew and other improvements over earlier models.

Thus revitalised, the night-bomber force began the year on the night of 17 January with 118 bomber sorties on London itself – the first against the capital on a large scale since May 1941. The bulk of the raiding force came from KG 6 and the attack was delivered in two waves with most crews flying double sorties. The main targets were the Millwall and Woolwich dock areas.

This was the first occasion on which the radar-laid searchlights round the capital had a chance to prove themselves and they did so in no uncertain terms. Four of the five successful interceptions by night fighters were a result of searchlight illumination of the bomber or the direction to it. The fifth aircraft lost, a Ju 88 of I./KG 6, was shot down by an intruder shortly after it had taken off from Beauvais. The raiders caused sporadic damage round the target and started nearly sixty fires, none of which reached major proportions. The only serious incident occurred at Greenwich, where a power station was badly damaged.

On 20 January, German fighter bombers made their most ambitious attack since 1940. A force of 28 Focke Wulf 190s carried out a low-level attack against the capital by day. The aircraft were plotted as they crossed the coast between Rye and Beachy Head, shortly after midday. From then on, however, the raiders' path was smoothed by a series of coincidences which allowed them a clear run to the target. As luck would have it the raiders' track took them along the boundary separating the Maidstone and Horsham Observer Corps areas. Soon after they crossed the coast the force of swiftly moving fighter bombers split into two, the main attacking force moving towards London and the diversionary attack against Maidstone. Both the Horsham and the Maidstone Observer Corps Centres thought that they were tracking a single attack, however, and the Focke Wulfs all received the same track designation, Raid 411, on the plotting tables. As succeeding plots came in on the raiders' track, it appeared on the plotting table at Fighter Command Headquarters like a zigzag heading in the general direction of Maidstone. This impression was strengthened when, due to an equipment failure, two plots on the London raid failed to reach the Fighter Command operations room.

The misconception lasted only 6 minutes, but this was long enough for the fighter bombers to cover nearly 30 miles – most of the distance between the coast and their target. In London itself the balloon barrage had been hauled down so essential calibration work could take place on the gun-laying radars (due to the confusion of echoes, calibration could not take place if balloons were flying above 500 feet within 8 miles of the radar site).

The Focke Wulfs dropped 8 bombs on Lewisham, 2 on Poplar and 12 on Deptford, Bermondsey and Greenwich. The worst casualties were in Lewisham, where a bomb struck a school before the children could take shelter. Although the defenders had been slow in reacting to the attack, they were able to demonstrate that a raiding force could not penetrate that far by day and escape scot-free. During the withdrawal phase of the action three fighter bombers and six covering fighters were shot down. Following this attack there was a thorough investigation into the system of raid reporting, and changes were made to reduce the likelihood of a recurrence.

## Tragic Accident

There was a pause for over a month then, on the night of 3 March, the Luftwaffe returned to London with over a hundred aircraft. The bombs caused little damage, though they were indirectly responsible for a massive loss of life. As the sirens sounded a large number of people began descending the dimly lit staircase at the new Underground station at Bethnal Green. The latter was almost complete except for the railway lines and had been converted into an air-raid shelter. As the raiders approached, a Z battery in nearby Victoria Park fired a salvo of rockets. The unexpected noise startled those moving to take cover and caused a general stampede. The crowd was rushing down the stairs when a woman near the bottom, encumbered by a small child and a bundle, stumbled and blocked the way for an instant. Miraculously she survived, but those who tripped over her were less fortunate. In the words of the magistrate who investigated the accident, the stairs were 'converted from a corridor into a charnel-house in from ten to fifteen seconds'. When the mass of bodies was finally cleared, several hours later, the magnitude of the disaster became clear: 178 people had been killed, most by suffocation, and 60 more suffered serious injuries. Following this incident the entrances to the stations used as shelters were altered to prevent a repetition.

On 7 March the fighter bombers raided Eastbourne, on the 11th they went for Hastings and on the 12th they attempted to repeat their January success against London. The attack on the capital proved a failure, however. Although sixteen bombs fell in and around Ilford and Barking, they caused little damage and few

*Oberst Dietrich Peltz, second from left, was appointed Angriffsfuerhrer England in March 1943. He held this position until 1944.* (Peltz)

casualties. Thereafter the fighter-bomber units confined their daylight attacks almost entirely to coastal targets.

## ANGRIFFSFUEHRER ENGLAND

During March Oberst Dietrich Peltz was appointed Angriffsfuehrer England, and charged with the task of directing the air war against Britain. Peltz had made his name as a dive-bombing expert earlier in the war and at the end of 1942 was created Inspector of Bombers. Peltz worked hard to improve the effectiveness of the bomber arm in the West but, in the absence of stronger forces, better equipment and better-trained crews there was little he could do. Of the attacks on England he has told the author: 'It was a question of duty. The British and the Americans were destroying German cities one after another and the German people looked to the Luftwaffe to strike back. We in the bomber force had our orders, and we had to do the best we could with the limited resources available. What alternative was there?'

Like many others in Germany at this time, Peltz realised that total victory no longer lay within his nation's grasp. For him the moment of truth had come when he operated against the mass of Allied shipping during the invasion of Algeria. The clear Allied *matériel* superiority made a deep impression on him. But he did not see total defeat as the sole alternative to total victory. A negotiated peace still seemed possible in which case the air attacks on Britain, even if they were ineffective in the military sense, might still prove politically useful. One of Peltz's first moves was to push the formation of a new pathfinder unit, the First Gruppe of Kampfgeschwader 66, to mark targets for the other bombers as KGr 100 had done during 1940 and 1941. It would be some months before the new unit began to appear over Britain, however.

Following the attack on the capital on the 3rd, March saw night attacks on Southampton, Newcastle and Norwich by raiding forces averaging about forty

*A Focke Wulf 190 of Schnellkampfgeschwader 10, a fighter-bomber unit that was active over southern England during the first half of 1943.* (Wenk)

aircraft. In spite of this low rate of effort, losses were heavy. In these attacks and mine-laying operations off the coast, Kampfgeschwader 2 lost twenty-six complete crews during the month.

## FIGHTER-BOMBER ATTACKS BY NIGHT

April was quiet until the night of the 14th, when ninety-one bombers launched a rather inaccurate attack on Chelmsford. Two nights later, on the 16th, there was an interesting new development. The Second Gruppe of Schnellkampfgeschwader 10 sent twenty-eight Fw 190 fighter bombers against the capital in an experimental high-level night assault. Crossing the coast with RAF bombers returning after attacking Pilsen and Mannheim–Ludwigshafen, the raiders reached London but caused little damage and no casualties. During the attack some fighter-bomber pilots were assisted by ground direction-finding stations in France, though with remarkably little success. Two raiding pilots mistook the lights at the RAF airfield at West Malling for those at their base in France and landed there. A third simply got lost and set down at the airfield. A fourth crashed nearby and two others failed to return, making six Focke Wulfs lost in all. One of the more remarkable aspects of this fiasco was that it came about without any assistance from No. 80 Wing. On the nights of 18 and 20 April there were repeat attacks on London by the Fw 190s of SKG 10; during these operations losses were low but so, too, were successes.

Initially the night-flying Focke Wulfs suffered little interference from the defences. Some even believed that the high performance of this aircraft would render them immune to attack from conventional night fighters. This particular notion was soon laid to rest, however.

The Fw 190, although a formidable fighter, was considerably less fast and manoeuvrable when loaded with two 66-gallon drop tanks and a 550- or 1,100-pound bomb. On the night of 16 May No. 85 Squadron demonstrated that the Focke Wulfs could be dealt with in the same way as normal raiders, when the unit's Mosquitos destroyed two fighter bombers and caused serious damage to two others.

*Mark XII Spitfires of No. 41 Squadron. This version was built specially to counter the Fw 190 at low altitude and No. 41 Squadron was the first to receive it, in February 1943.* (IWM)

No. 80 Wing played no part in countering the initial fighter-bomber attacks at night. As might be expected, however, it was not long before the unit introduced its own brand of harassment for the raiders. The transmitter at Alexandra Palace was modified to cover the frequencies used to control the Focke Wulfs; the new countermeasure received the code-name 'Cigarette'. By June this jammer was fully operational and other transmitters were hastily modified to cover this part of the frequency spectrum. In the face of 'Cigarette' jamming, the use of radio to assist the fighter bombers waned rapidly. The psychological effect of the jamming

*The Mosquito XII, fitted with the latest Mark VIII AI radar, proved a match for the Fw 190 fighter bomber attacking by night.* (IWM)

*The cockpit of the Mosquito XII, showing the radar operator's position to the right. Compare the compactness of the AI Mark VIII indicator with that of the earlier AI Mark III (page 46).* (IWM)

on lone pilots outweighed any advantage that might be gained from the rather poor system of ground control.

During 1943, No. 80 Wing improved its ability to deal with new German navigational systems as they were identified. By this time, largely as a result of the unit's activities, the X-Verfahren had passed out of favour. The Y-Verfahren, though known to be vulnerable to jamming, was still used from time to time. During the year Knickebein gained a new lease of life with the introduction of a new receiver able to receive signals on thirty-four different frequencies instead of the original three. This move greatly increased the jamming problem. No. 80 Wing's 'Aspirin' jammers were hastily modified to cover the new frequencies, however, and the threat was contained. Although the new Knickebein was used from time to time during attacks on Britain, it proved no more successful than its predecessors in guiding bombers to inland targets.

## COASTAL ATTACKS BY FIGHTER BOMBERS

During the spring of 1943, Schnellkampfgeschwader 10 began a series of attacks on coastal targets. In April there was one, against Eastbourne on the 3rd. In May there were ten assaults, each involving eighteen or more fighter bombers. June began in the same vein, with five attacks during the first six days. The one mounted against Eastbourne on 6 April was representative of these 'tip-and-run' raids. The sixteen Focke Wulfs of II./SKG 10 approached their target from almost due south. Leutnant Helmut Wenk recalled:

> As we neared the target we shifted from our cruising formation, line abreast by *Schwaerme*, into our attack formation, line astern. At the same time we opened up to full power, flying about 10 metres above the sea to avoid the British radar.

Just before we crossed the coast the leader pulled up to about 300 metres and we followed, turning in to attack. Plunging down through the flak we released our bombs in a *Steckrubenwurf* [turnip-lob] shallow dive attack, then got back to low level and curved round to port to escape round Beachy Head and out to sea.

One Focke Wulf was shot down by anti-aircraft fire. Seven people were killed during the attack with forty-three injured. It was to prove the last daylight fighter-bomber raid mounted against Britain in such strength, for during the following week SKG 10 received orders to move two of its three Gruppen to the Mediterranean area. The assaults on the coastal towns continued for the rest of the year, but now with only one or two fighter bombers involved each time.

Also during May there were

*The SD-2 anti-personnel bomb, which became known in Britain as the 'Butterfly Bomb'. Usually it was carried in the AB 250 container, which held 108. The containers were released from the bomber and, at a previously set altitude, opened to allow the SD-2 bomblets to fall separately. Once it was clear of the container the SD-2's casing opened to form a 'wing' and the weapon fluttered to earth. Sometimes fitted with anti-handling fuses, these bombs were liable to cause casualties long after the raiding force had passed.*

night attacks by twin-engined bombers on Norwich, Cardiff, Chelmsford and Sunderland. In the following month Plymouth, Hull and Grimsby suffered fairly concentrated bombing.

## BUTTERFLY BOMBS

One conspicuous feature of the attack on Grimsby on 13 June was the use of large numbers of the 4.4-pound SD-2 anti-personnel bombs (known in Britain as 'Butterfly bombs'). These small cylindrical weapons, 3 inch in diameter and 3½ inch long, were carried in the aircraft in special containers of various sizes; typical of those released over Britain was the AB 250 container, which housed 108 of the small bombs. After release the container broke open at a predetermined altitude, to scatter the bombs over a wide area. As they fell clear of the container the casings of the SD-2s sprang open to form a pair of wings. The individual bombs spun earthwards like sycamore seeds. Prior to their loading into the container, the SD-2s were set to explode on impact, after a delay of up to half an hour, or if they were disturbed. The last two types of fusing were intended to enhance the nuisance value of the weapon. As a result of the attack on Grimsby

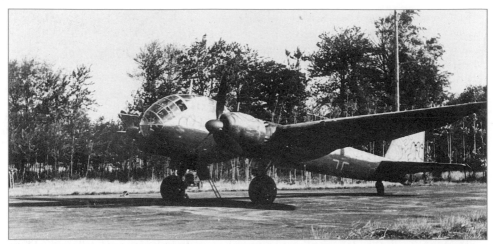

*Junkers 188s belonging to the pathfinder unit I./KG 66, based at Montdidier in France.*

there were 163 casualties, the majority of which occurred after the 'all-clear' had been sounded and people were emerging from their shelters and returning home. Many were killed when they disturbed bombs that had fallen on or near their homes. Some idea of the problem caused by these small bombs can be gained by the fact that the search for these in and around Grimsby occupied some 10,000 working hours.

## ATTACK ON PORTSMOUTH

During July and the first half of August there were further raids on Grimsby, Hull and Plymouth. Then, on the night of 15 August, ninety-one bombers set out to attack Portsmouth. To observe the pattern of the German assaults by the summer of 1943 and the working of the British defences, we shall examine this action in detail.

The raiding force approached the target at low level, to stay below the cover of radar for as long as possible. The plan was to fly to a point 24 miles south of Brighton, then commence a climb at full power to take the bombers to 15,000 feet for their bombing runs on Portsmouth.

During previous months RAF Bomber Command had finely honed its pathfinder technique during the attacks on Germany. Now, I./KG 66 was to perform a similar function during the raids on Britain. First over the target was the Zielfinder, the target finder, who was to release flares, while minutes later the Zielmarkierer, target marker, aircraft arrived to drop incendiary bombs to mark the target illuminated by the flares. Then 2 minutes later still a pair of Beleuchter, illuminator, aircraft were to release further flares over the target after which the main force was to attack.

*Major Helmut Schmidt, the commander of I./KG 66.*

In conformity with the usual Fighter Command procedure, when there was no enemy activity, a few fully armed night fighters were sent off for training sorties, practising GCI and searchlight interceptions on each other. These aircraft were, therefore, airborne and available for immediate action when the vanguard of the attacking force was observed on radar climbing towards Portsmouth. Flying a Mosquito XII, Wing Commander Geoffrey Park, the commander of No. 256 Squadron, received orders from the Durrington GCI station to break off his exercise and head southwards to investigate. As he closed on the climbing bombers his radar operator, Flight Lieutenant Cooke, made contact with a Do 217, which was promptly shot down. Then, as Park afterwards reported:

During this combat another contact was obtained on the tube. We were informed by GCI that another aircraft was about. We now turned immediately starboard to a south-westerly direction and obtained another contact, hard over to port, range 8,000 feet. We turned in after the second contact which was taking regular evasive action. Closed in rapidly and obtained a visual on a Do 217 at 2,000 feet range. We closed in with the moon on the other side of the enemy aircraft. When about at 500 feet range we gave the enemy aircraft a 2 second burst with 4 cannon. Enemy aircraft's port engine burst into flames which rapidly spread and we watched the enemy aircraft crash into the sea. No return fire was experienced . . . We turned south to watch the enemy aircraft hit the sea and looking at the reflection of the moon on the sea I had a fleeting glimpse of what appeared to be another aircraft, range about 8,000 feet and below. We turned towards it and although visual was lost [AI] contact was obtained at 7,000 feet, below and to starboard. We lost height and obtained another visual. Closing in, identified this aircraft as a Do 217 from about 2,000 feet. Closed in further and when about 1,500 feet away enemy aircraft opened fire and started extremely violent evasive action. We gave a 2 second burst with cannon from 800 feet. No results seen. A running fight ensued, in which we managed to keep the enemy aircraft up the moon path on the sea going south, both aircraft firing several bursts the whole time. The enemy aircraft was losing height rapidly, still kinking violently. At one point the visual was lost, but regained with AI. Our second burst resulted in an explosion in the belly of the enemy aircraft, but no fire resulted. The last burst from the enemy aircraft put 2 shells through the scanner and the armour plating of the Mosquito. Flt Lt Cooke sustained a splinter wound in the palm of his hand. Our perspex nose was holed which later disintegrated. Large pieces were driven into both our radiators. We again turned on to the enemy aircraft but with our speed now dropping and the port engine starting to burn. Gave the enemy aircraft a final long burst range about 800 feet which resulted in a second big explosion. Visual was lost almost immediately and no further results observed. Finally fight broken off approximately 55 miles south of base [Ford]. Height now about 2,500 feet. We turned north for base as our port engine appeared to be on fire. Feathered port prop. and fire ceased at once. Maintained northerly course asking for fixes and homing. We maintained height, speed about 180 mph. After some 4/5 minutes our aircraft appeared to become less manoeuvrable. This was probably due to further disintegration of the nose. As vibration was also noticed we suspected we might have to ditch. We decided to try the port engine again. Port prop. unfeathered, engine again caught fire so prop. again feathered and fire extinguisher used. Two vectors given from Durrington. We managed to gain 500 feet and crossed the coast at 3,000 feet. Over Littlehampton Bofors opened up but luckily very inaccurate. Landed on the starboard engine only.

A third Dornier had the bad luck to be spotted by the crew of a Mosquito from No. 410 Squadron RCAF, which was returning from an intruder operation over France. Following a brief exchange of fire the Dornier crashed into the sea. A second Mosquito of No. 256 Squadron fought inconclusive engagements with two further Dorniers.

The attack on Portsmouth began shortly before midnight and lasted about an hour, causing light damage. The defending heavy gun and rocket batteries engaged the raiders and claimed two shot down and one damaged. Smoke generators were ignited to conceal the dock area. From German records it is known that four Dornier 217s of KG 2 failed to return from the night's operations and a fifth was wrecked on landing. The commander of III./KG 2, Hauptmann Scharweiss, had one of his engines shot out and his undercarriage damaged by anti-aircraft fire but made a belly-landing without injuries to his crew or further damage to the aircraft.

Two nights after the Portsmouth assault, on 17 August, the Luftwaffe sent eighty-eight bombers to attack Lincoln. Harassed by both night fighters and guns, the raid went well astray – no bombs hit the city and eleven bombers failed to return. September was one of the quietest months since the beginning of the aerial bombardment of Britain, with only five people killed and eleven injured.

## IMPROVED AA GUNS AND RADARS

During the first three years of the war the 3.7-inch and 4.5-inch anti-aircraft guns demonstrated they had the performance to engage the great majority of German bombers. With improved predictors, their engagement ceilings were now 32,000 feet and 34,000 feet respectively. A massed attack from very high altitude was always a possibility, however, and early in the war the Army General Staff issued a requirement for a new type of gun able to fire at targets flying at altitudes of up to 50,000 feet. Two weapons were placed in production to meet this requirement: the 5.25-inch naval gun, fitted to a special land anti-aircraft mounting, which fired a shell weighing 80 pounds. And the so-called 3.7-inch Mark 6, which was in fact a 4.5-inch gun with a special barrel firing 3.7-inch shells but using a 4.5-inch charge to provide a one-third greater muzzle velocity. Both weapons entered service in 1943. In the event neither gun was effective above 43,000 feet, but this performance was good enough to engage any bomber operating against Britain during the latter half of the war.

Simultaneously, there was an improvement in gunnery accuracy brought about by the introduction of the Mark III gunlaying radar, designed and built in Canada, which worked on a centimetric wavelength. Once the new device had overcome its teething troubles and the gunners became familiar with its use, their fire was about twice as accurate as that directed by the earlier GL Mark II during the first half of 1942. And this, it should be noted, in spite of the fact that German bombers now flew much faster and higher than before. During 1942 the most common speed for bombers over Britain was 225 mph and the most common height was 7,000 feet; by the latter half of 1943 these figures had risen to 310 mph and 21,000 feet respectively, posing a more difficult engagement problem for the gunners.

## INTRODUCTION OF 'WINDOW' AND 'DUEPPEL'

Since the spring of 1942 it had been clear that the metric wavelength precision radars used by the British air defences, GL, AI and GCI, were vulnerable to jamming by 'Window': strips of metal foil (known in the USA as 'chaff') released by aircraft to produce spurious echoes. RAF Bomber Command had wished to use 'Window' to protect its bombers from the German defences almost as soon as the countermeasure had been discovered. But its use was withheld until the British air defences had precision radar equipment that was less vulnerable to its effects, in case the Luftwaffe retaliated in kind. By the summer of 1943 two radars were in production for Fighter Command that promised to be less vulnerable to 'Window' than their predecessors: the Type 21 GCI radar and the American Mark X AI set. Both worked on centimetric wavelengths and employed special circuitry to enable operators to track aircraft through moderate 'Window' jamming. The Mark III gunlaying radar, too, promised to be less vulnerable than its predecessors to this form of countermeasure.

With the new radars in their final stages of development, RAF Bomber Command finally received permission to use 'Window' during its attacks on Germany. Using this countermeasure, Bomber Command launched a series of devastating attacks on Hamburg at the end of July 1943 with minimal losses. From that moment on, use of the countermeasure to protect German bombers operating over Britain was only a matter of time. Early in October, the blow fell.

On the night of 7 October a force of seventy-five bombers launched a twin attack on Norwich and London. Some idea of the problems caused by the metal strips can be gained from the report on the night's action from the GCI radar at Neatishead and the CHL radar at Happisburgh, both north-east of Norwich.

At Neatishead at 2028 hours, indications were observed on the PPI tube of aircraft travelling west corresponding to filter room tracks of some friendly bombers. At 2026 hours the number of echoes increased rapidly and by 2050 hours a considerable area of the tube blanked out. Accurate control of fighter aircraft became practically impossible, IFF [indications] could not be seen, and the height/range tubes were swamped. It was not observed for some time that the mass of echoes was stationary. At Happisburgh CHL station, too, an area raid of 80 aircraft was seen on the tube, covering about 150 square miles and travelling at a speed of 180 miles per hour on course 280°. Individual aircraft were noticed at the southern leading edge of the area raid, at about five miles south of the main mass and travelling on a course of 340°. At approximately 2043 hours the raid had increased to about 200 echoes and split

*Armourers loading an SC 1000 2,200-pound bomb on to the external carrier of a Junkers 188.*

into two main parts, a northerly and a southerly mass with a gap of six miles between them. Fighter aircraft were difficult to control because their IFF was not visible through the interference on the cathode ray tube.

The German code-name for the metal strips was 'Dueppel'. Measuring 80 cms long and 1.9 cms wide, they had a powerful effect on the older types of British radar; the newer types were still in short supply and none was available for use against this initial attack. That night, fighter crews found themselves chasing contacts on which they appeared to be closing head-on; when they turned on to a reciprocal heading to engage from the other direction, however, they still seemed to be meeting the contacts from head-on until finally the latter faded from their screens. The air picture was further complicated by the presence of large numbers of RAF bombers returning from an attack on Stuttgart; again and again the Mosquitos and Beaufighters found themselves chasing friendly bombers.

The only night-fighter crew to achieve a kill under these conditions was from No. 68 Squadron. In their Beaufighter Pilot Officer Serhant and his radar operator Flight Sergeant Necas worked their way through several spurious echoes after one contact on which they closed far slower than the others. As they headed out to sea the German bomber crew seemed to think themselves safe and ceased

*The Messerschmitt 410, a small high-performance fighter bomber, which began operating in the latter part of 1943.*

dropping the 'Dueppel' strips and it proved their undoing. After a chase lasting about 25 minutes Serhant was able to close in and recognised the bomber as a Dornier 217. He fired a long burst from short range and the raider exploded and crashed into the sea.

It was the sole loss during an attack aimed at Norwich by some thirty-five bombers. The raiders failed to press their advantage, however, and no bombs hit the city. An attack by a similar number of bombers on London, without the protection of 'Dueppel', resulted in the loss of four raiders.

From now on 'Dueppel' would play an important role whenever the Luftwaffe visited Britain in force. For the time being, however, there was a downturn in bomber activity. At the close of October there were light attacks on London and Yarmouth. November saw moderately heavy raids on Ipswich and Plymouth while December was a quiet month, with only ten people killed and forty-one injured during air raids.

Although the bombing attacks in 1943 started out being heavier than any of those of the previous year, the lower standard of training of the German bomber crews coupled with improvements in the defences resulted in fewer casualties: a total of 2,372 people were killed and 3,450 seriously injured, about a quarter less than in 1942. Commenting on the attacks on Britain in 1943, Lord Cherwell wrote to Mr Churchill early in the new year:

(1.) The total tonnage dropped was 2,320 (the RAF dropped 136,000 on Germany in 1943 and 2,480 on Berlin last Tuesday). [This was a reference to the attack on 15 February 1944.]

(2.) There were only 20 raids when more than ten tons were dropped on any one town.

(3.) No town except London more than 20 miles from the coast received more than ten tons in any one raid.

(4.) On a rough average the German bombers deployed one sortie every 18 days (ours made one sortie every 6 or 7 days). Also only four-fifths of those crossing the coast bombed. One in 11 of those crossing the coast was destroyed. A German plane on the average dropped one ton of bombs. One ton on the average killed one person. Two members of the German Air Force were lost for every five British killed. For every fire caused by the German Air Force, about 30 resulted from normal human causes.

Clearly the Luftwaffe bomber force in the West was at a low ebb. Yet the devastation inflicted on city after city in Germany during 1943 had to be answered. As the year drew to its close, the Luftwaffe once more gathered its forces for a full-scale bomber offensive against Britain. This will be described in the next chapter.

# CHAPTER 8

# 'Steinbock' and After, December 1943–March 1945

On the Fuehrer's instructions, Goering has now gone to the west to prepare the reprisal attacks against England. For this we need about two hundred heavy four-engined aircraft, which in one night will each fly to England twice and deliver a massive blow against the capital. Of course, we cannot carry out an attack like this often enough; but it should serve as a reminder to the English that we are still around. I myself think that it will have a deep psychological effect.

*Dr Goebbels's Diary, 7 December 1943*

The year 1943 had been hard for the German fighting forces, with much ground lost on all fronts. Yet in each case the battle lines had been stabilised and there was hope for the future. At sea the U–boat arm had been roughly handled by Allied aircraft and escort ships in the Atlantic. But it was now recovering and with new equipment it was planned to reopen the onslaught against convoys in the latter half of 1944. In the South the German forces had

*Junkers 88 of KG 76 crossing the Alps on its way to Germany in January 1944, to join the force being assembled in preparation for Operation 'Steinbock'.*

been pushed out of southern Italy, but the invaders' advance had stalled in that country's difficult terrain. In the East the German forces had been forced to withdraw, and in some places up to 400 miles, before the massive Russian thrusts had been fought to a standstill. Over Germany itself the Allied heavy bombers had caused grievous damage to several of the larger cities. Yet the German day and night defences had got the measure of the attack and were taking a steady toll of the raiders.

Over Britain, the relatively small German bomber force had suffered heavy losses during 1943. Now however, by bringing in bomber units from other fronts and deploying the latest equipment, it was hoped once again to be able to administer a bitter medicine to the British people.

On the morning of 28 November 1943 Dietrich Peltz, now a Generalmajor, was summoned to a top-level conference at Neuenhagen near Berlin. Reichsmarschall Goering was in the chair and after cautioning those present on the need for absolute secrecy he told them the purpose of the meeting. They were to plan a new series of retaliatory attacks against Britain, with London as the primary target. The code-name for the operation was 'Steinbock' (Ibex).

Goering, under strong pressure to get the operation under way as rapidly as possible, informed the assembled officers: 'I have told the Fuehrer that we shall be ready in fourteen days . . . It is absolutely necessary that we should have 300 aircraft ready for the first operation. If I can have about 100 in the second attack and early in the morning about 150, that will come to between 550 and 600 sorties; that is what we must aim at.' Peltz assured the Reichsmarschall that his bombers would be able to make two sorties against London during one night, but three was asking too much. After some discussion, Goering accepted this.

For the 'Steinbock' operation two Gruppen of the new Heinkel 177 four-engined bombers would be available. It was the first time these heavy bombers were to operate over Britain and Goering was keen that whenever possible each aircraft should carry a couple of 5,500-pound bombs, the heaviest available to the Luftwaffe. To enhance the effectiveness of these already powerful bombs, he ordered those used during 'Steinbock' to be filled with the so-called 'England mixture' comprising Trialen and Hexogen explosives.

The 5,500-pound super-heavy bombs were to be used until stocks ran out. But even when they did, there would still be plenty of 4,000- and 2,200-pounders to keep the offensive going. For concentrated incendiary attacks, the bombers were to carry the AB 1000, a new type of container which held up to 620 of the 2.2-pound stick incendiary bombs.

As well as the new types of bombs, there were new navigational aids to assist the crews of I./KG 66 to find their targets. Of these the most important was the highly accurate Egon system, which worked on a principle similar to the British 'Oboe'. Egon employed a pair of Freya radar stations situated about 100 miles apart. One Freya tracked the aircraft as it flew round the circumference of a circle, whose radius was the distance between the radar station and the bomb-release point. If the pilot of the bomber deviated from the line of the circumference, he received correction instructions by radio. The second Freya also tracked the aircraft and when the latter's range corresponded to the bomb-release point, the crew received the order to release the bombs. When functioning properly, Egon was accurate to within approximately .3 degrees in bearing and 220 yards in range, out to a distance of about 170 miles from the furthest ground transmitter.

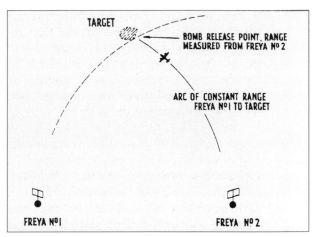

A further innovation was Truhe, a special airborne receiver that enabled German bomber crews to find their position by using transmissions from the British GEE navigational system. The 'pirating' of these transmissions was a closely guarded secret: once the defenders learned what was happening, the GEE transmissions would be changed so it would be impossible for the enemy to use them. Because of this constraint, the use of Truhe was restricted to a few pathfinder aircraft of I./KG 66.

To provide fixing points off the coast for bombers before they entered the zone where the British jamming was effective, and also to camouflage the newer systems, there was to be a large-scale use of the older Y Verfahren and Knickebein systems during the 'Steinbock' operation.

*Method of operation of the Egon blind bombing system, used by German pathfinder aircraft during 'Steinbock'. Egon, like the similar British system 'Oboe', exploited the fact that a radar set can measure the range of an object to within very fine limits (though it is considerably less accurate in measuring bearing). One Freya radar tracked the aircraft and controlled it as it flew along an arc of constant distance from the ground station; if the aircraft deviated from this path, the pilot received correction signals by radio. A second Freya also tracked the aircraft, on a different radio channel. When this station observed the aircraft's range to correspond with that of the bomb-release point, the pilot received the order to drop his bombs. To extend the range of the system, the aircraft carried a two-channel repeater, which amplified the Frey signals before re-transmitting them.*

Peltz himself was under no illusions regarding the likely effectiveness of his force. He knew that to start self-sustaining fires, such as those caused by the RAF in German cities, would require a far greater weight of bombs than his bombers could deliver. In any case, from what he had seen in the German cities, Peltz knew that the time needed to recover from even heavy attacks was remarkably short. He later commented: 'The attacks on the cities were like a few drops of water on a hot stone: a bit of commotion for a short time, then the whole thing was forgotten and people carried on much as before.' Had he had the choice, Peltz would have preferred to send his best crews against power stations in Britain, in low-level precision attacks at night or during bad weather. He felt that in this way, his limited force would have the greatest effect on the British economy. The power stations were small targets and difficult to hit; if they were properly defended by light anti-aircraft guns, the attacking bombers would suffer heavy losses. On this point, Peltz commented: 'Of course there would have been losses if we had tried to attack the power stations. But it was clear that however I employed my force against England, in 1944, there would have been serious losses. The important

*The Heinkel 177 heavy bomber operated over Britain for the first time during the 'Steinbock'
attacks early in 1944. Although it had the appearance of a twin-engined aircraft, it was in fact
powered by four engines in two pairs with each pair coupled together and driving a common
airscrew. In service this arrangement gave considerable trouble. The example depicted belonged
to I./KG 100. (Seeley)*

thing was to have something to show for it at the end.' But Peltz's political
directive had come from Hitler via Goering, calling for attacks on London and
other cities. There could be no arguing with such a directive.

Despite the urgency of the 'Steinbock' operation and the priority afforded it,
the starting date began to slip back. Originally planned to open during the full-
moon period in December, it was delayed first until the end of the month and
then until mid-January 1944. (Goering's operational order for Steinbock, dated
3 December, is included as Appendix E. Appendix F gives the strengths of the
units committed to the operation.)

*Groundcrewmen preparing a Ju 88 of I./KG 76 at Varrelbusch, for one of the early 'Steinbock' attacks. The weapon is an AB 1000 container, which could hold up to 620 small incendiary bombs. At previously set times during its fall, the layers of incendiary bombs were released at intervals, to give an even spread over a large area.* (KG 76 Archive)

Meanwhile, the British air defences had continued to improve with the entry into service of the new types of AI, GCI and gun-laying radar designed to operate in the face of 'Window' jamming. By the third week in 1944 No. 11 Group of Fighter Command, which would have the task of defending London against the new series of attacks, possessed 5 squadrons of night fighters with a total of 97 Mosquitos, 15 of which were fitted with the latest AI Mark X radar.

A step that would greatly increase the effectiveness of heavy anti-aircraft fire during the battle to follow was the introduction into service of a new type of predictor, the American-built BTL. Designed to exploit the advantages of the latest types of radar, the BTL soon demonstrated its superiority over the earlier types. Using the combination of GL Mark III radar and BTL predictor, AA fire was five times more accurate than with GL Mark II radar and earlier types of predictor. Radar-laid fire was still not as accurate as optically aimed fire, but the gap between the two had closed markedly.

## FINAL PREPARATIONS FOR 'STEINBOCK'

The RAF received its first inkling that a new operation was afoot in December, in a decrypt of a signal to Luftwaffe bomber units based in northern Italy. The message stated that a move was imminent and listed a series of elaborate measures, including deceptive radio messages, intended to keep the move secret. By 10 January other decrypts made it clear that all six bomber Gruppen in Italy had been withdrawn to Germany, and another bomber Gruppe had moved from Germany to an airfield near Brussels.

During the third week in January the bomber units allocated to 'Steinbock' began moving to forward airfields in France, Belgium, Holland and northern Germany. There the planes were carefully camouflaged, to prevent their being seen by Allied reconnaissance aircraft. On the afternoon of 21 January there was a flurry of activity at the more important German bases as the bombers started to concentrate and refuelling and rearming began.

At dusk the crews learned for the first time that they were to take part in a large-scale attack on London that very night. During the briefings the need for strict attention to routing and time was impressed upon all. After the briefing crews began boarding their aircraft and soon after 1930 hours the first bombers began taking off. Once off the ground the leaders orbited near their airfields until their comrades were airborne, then all moved off towards their target.

## ATTACK ON LONDON

Soon after 2030 hours the vanguard of the attackers began to appear on the British radar screens. The strength of the raiding force appeared to increase rapidly, as the incoming bombers released vast quantities of 'Dueppel' foil. A total of 227 bombers set out for the assault on London, the main body of which crossed the coast on a relatively narrow front between Hastings and Folkestone and headed straight for their target.

That night the concentrations of 'Dueppel' were so dense that controllers using the older metric-wavelength GCI radars had considerable difficulty directing their fighters. Those with the newer centimetric types were able to conduct interceptions, but there were far more raiders than they could cope with. As a result, the majority of the night fighters had to rely on searchlights to put them on targets. Representative of the latter was the Mosquito XIII of No. 96 Squadron piloted by Flight Lieutenant N. Head with Flying Officer A. Andrews as radar operator, which had taken off from West Malling at 2010 hours. The crew received permission to carry out a freelance hunt for raiders coming in over Kent, making what use they could of the searchlights. Afterwards Head reported:

> Several searchlight intersections were investigated without result and height was reduced to 15,000 feet. An intersection was seen with an aircraft illuminated and the observer obtained contact at about 6,000 feet range. The aircraft was identified as a Ju 88 and was taking evasive action in searchlights and opened fire on the Mosquito at about 1,000 feet range. The evasive action of the enemy aircraft became much more violent and each time the Mosquito attempted to get its sights on, the enemy aircraft turned in to the attack. Finally, I got in a good burst at 4/600 feet range, strikes being seen on the fuselage and the port wing root, height of combat 12,000/15,000 feet. Enemy aircraft turned to port, Mosquito overshot and enemy aircraft went on to its back with the port engine well alight, and as aircraft was falling away it partially recovered and then went on to its back again and disappeared from sight . . . Several minutes later another searchlight intersection was investigated and a visual was obtained of an aircraft identified as a Ju 88 at about 12,000 feet height, taking violent evasive action, seemingly to get out of the cone. The enemy aircraft opened fire first with an inaccurate burst at about 1,000 feet range. Mosquito fired several deflection shots without result, and finally a burst at 4/500 feet resulted in strikes on the starboard engine; and as the Mosquito passed over the top the starboard engine was seen to be alight and the aircraft fell away rapidly. Mosquito orbited and saw a fire below as though an aircraft had crashed. Two Ju 88s claimed as probably destroyed.

*A close shave for the crew of a Heinkel 177 of I./KG 100. A hit has blown out one of the fuel tanks in the starboard wing, fortunately for them without setting fire to the aircraft.*

South of London, Ju 88s and Ju 188s of I./KG 66 put down a line of white flares pointing towards the city. The target area, Waterloo station, was marked using white and green flares. After releasing their bombs, the raiders turned starboard and withdrew eastwards along the Thames Estuary. On returning to their bases, those bombers serviceable were quickly refuelled and rearmed, and shortly after 0400 hours 220 took off for a repeat attack on London.

To meet the two attacks, Fighter Command put up a total of ninety-six sorties, which claimed sixteen enemy bombers destroyed or probably destroyed. According to German records twenty-five aircraft were lost to enemy action during the two attacks, indicating that the remaining nine probably fell to anti-aircraft fire. The London defences had indeed come a long way since the bleak autumn of 1940, when raiders could flaunt themselves over the capital with impunity. In addition, eighteen bombers were lost for reasons other than enemy action, mainly due to crews getting lost or crashing on their return to the dimly lit bases. This loss rate amounted to just under 10 per cent of the sorties dispatched or 8 per cent of Peltz's force. The General could not afford a recurrence of losses on such a scale, if he was to keep his force intact. As a result there were no further double attacks.

Considering the number of bomber sorties and the losses suffered, the double attack caused remarkably little damage. Of the 245 incidents reported that night 201 were outside the London defence area, of which 110 were in Kent, 53 in Sussex and 18 in Essex.

*A close shave for the crew of a Mosquito of No. 85 Squadron. On the night of 24 March Flying Officer E. Hedgecoe and his navigator Flying Officer N. Bamford attacked a Junkers 188 on its way to bomb London. Hedgecoe had closed in to 100 yards to deliver a lethal burst, whereupon the bomber blew up in front of him. The Mosquito was covered by burning petrol and oil and was enveloped in flames as it flew through the debris. Hedgecoe succeeded in making a normal landing at West Malling. (IWM)*

Following a week of poor weather the Luftwaffe mounted its next raid on London on the night of 29 January, with 285 bombers attacking in a single wave. This was more successful than the previous one and caused 343 fires of various sizes in the capital, including a large one at the Surrey Commercial Docks. Some fourteen bombers were lost, to all causes. Together, the two January attacks on London resulted in about 100 deaths with double that number injured.

## LUFTWAFFE PROBLEMS

The main reasons for the bombers' lack of success had been the poor training of their crews and the strength and technical superiority of the defences. On the German side there were many failures in equipment, also. The aircraft used were either obsolescent or, in a few cases, so new that teething troubles had not yet been overcome. Particularly disappointing was the new four-engined bomber, the Heinkel 177. This aircraft was in the same weight category as the British Lancaster or the American B–17 Fortress. But it differed from both of them in having its four engines coupled together in pairs, with each pair driving a single aircrew via a gearbox and common shaft. Thus, although the type had four engines, it had the external appearance of a twin-engined aircraft. The coupled-engine arrangement reduced drag and therefore increased performance; in service it gave continual trouble, however. The engines were difficult to keep serviceable and were prone to overheating, which sometimes resulted in fires. Following the first 'Steinbock' attack, Hitler had scathing words for the Heinkel's serviceability record. Discussing the attack with Generaloberst Guenter Korten, Chief of Staff of the Luftwaffe, the Fuehrer pungently remarked on 28 January: 'One gets the impression that once again the Heinkel 177 has suffered 50 per cent breakdowns. They can't even get that far [London]. This heap of crap [*Drekmaschine*] is obviously the biggest load of rubbish that has ever been built. It is the flying *Panther*; and the *Panther* is a crawling Heinkel!' [The *Panther* at that time was a particularly unreliable tank.]

Nor were these Peltz's only problems. On the same day 'Steinbock' opened, the Allies made a further landing in Italy, at Anzio. Almost immediately he received orders to release four Gruppen of bombers, three with Ju 88s and one with He 177s, for operations in the Mediterranean area. This loss represented about 100 aircraft, a drastic cut in Peltz's already inadequate force.

## THE ATTACK RESUMES

During the first two weeks in February the Luftwaffe visited London on five nights, causing little damage on any of them. On the night of the 18th, however, the force mounted the sharpest attack on the capital since May 1941. Crews were becoming more familiar with their target and the defences covering it, and the 200 bombers involved put down three-quarters of their loads, about 140 tons of bombs, in the London area. Similarly concentrated attacks were mounted on the nights of 20, 22, 23 and 24 February. The Operational Order for I./KG 2 for the attack on 23 February is included in Appendix G.

*'Das Ziel ist London . . .'.*
*Hauptmann Kurt Seyfarth briefing*
*crews of Kampfgeschwader 2 for the*
*attack on London on the night of*
*23 Febraury 1944.*

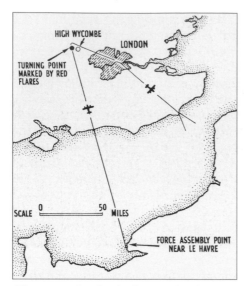

*The route taken by the German bombers during the attack on London on the night of 24 February 1944. The bombers flew at high level to their turning point near High Wycombe, which was marked by red flares; they then turned starboard and headed for their target, the Westminster area of London. After bombing the raiders headed south-eastwards in a high-speed descending withdrawal.*

Representative of these attacks was the last of them on 24 February, when the target was Westminster. The main body of the 170 raiders took off at about 2030 hours and concentrated from all directions on Le Havre, then headed north-north-westwards in a tight stream flying at high altitude to their turning point near High Wycombe, marked by red flares. As they passed the turning point the bombers curved on to a south-easterly heading for their target, which was marked by red and white flares. One pilot of the pathfinder unit I./KG 66, Leutnant Hans Altrogge flying a Junkers 88S, released eighteen 110-pounder red markers on Westminster from 29,000 feet. After releasing their loads the bombers turned on to a south-easterly heading for Dungeness, descending at high speed. This descending withdrawal was a feature of several 'Steinbock' attacks and greatly complicated the work of the defences. Nevertheless, the night fighters claimed to have shot down thirteen of the raiders, six of which fell on land.

One successful crew that night was that of Flight Lieutenant P. Hall and Flying Officer R. Marriott, flying a Mosquito of No. 488 Squadron. Since they were based at Bradwell Bay in Essex, their Sector was outside the area over which the bombers were flying. The crew received permission to cross the Thames Estuary, however, to carry out a freelance hunting patrol over Kent with the aid of searchlights. By the time the Mosquito was in position the bombers were streaming to the south-east descending at high speed. The crew spotted a Do 217 moving at about 300 mph coned by searchlights. Hall succeeded in closing to 200 yards and opened fire. He observed hits on the port engine and the fuselage; the bomber began to trail smoke. As Hall curved round to administer the *coupe de grâce*, however, the Dornier went into a descending turn and managed to shake him off. He saw no more of it. Still with ammunition left, the crew went after another searchlight intersection and found what they thought to be a Junkers 188 held in the beams. Hall moved into a firing position and as he reached it he asked the lights to douse, which they did. He loosed off three short bursts and the bomber dived away burning, to crash near Tonbridge. Subsequent examination of the wreckage revealed it to be a Heinkel 177 of I./KG 100.

The February attacks caused considerable damage to parts of London and the use of larger bombs during 'Steinbock' was immediately apparent. Wing Commander E. Hodsoll, the Inspector General of Air Raid Precautions, recorded:

*Major Schoenberger, the commander of I./KG 2, briefing crews before the attack.*

A greater proportion of high calibre bombs was noted in these raids and there was a very appreciable increase in the blast effect they produced. There was also a closer pattern of bombs on the ground and the percentage of unexploded bombs was higher. Apart from this there was very little that was unusual or unexpected in the attack but certain probalems arose from the increased radius of damage, a good example of which was shown in Battersea where a stick of four bombs caused devasation over an area of 24 acres and damaged more than 3,000 houses.

*This Junkers 88 of KG 54 suffered damage from AA fire over London, which put one engine out of action, the compass system and other instruments. The crew headed in the direction of what they thought was Holland and when they saw airfield lights they made a forced landing. The airfield turned out to be the RAF airfield at Bradwell Bay in Essex.*

*A Junkers 88S of the pathfinder unit I./KG 66. Fitted with nitrous-oxide boosting for the engines, these aircraft frequently operated over Britain at night at altitudes of over 33,000 feet. (Altrogge)*

The effect of the 'Steinbock' attacks on the population was greater than previous experience had led the authorities to expect. Hodsoll also noted:

> The population are more jittery than they were in the old days due probably to a lot of contributory factors such as belief that we had air superiority and therefore no more attacks to fear; war-weariness; lack of stamina, and so on. There were no signs of any panic, but the people seemed more helpless and more dependent on the Civil Defence services than they were in the old days. Everyone flocked to the wardens' posts now with their troubles after the raid and wanted a good deal of helping. The effect of the handling of the homeless, and so on, by the Civil Defence services was most marked and quickly helped to get their tails up again, but they found a good deal of apathy.

Air-raid casualties during February amounted to 961 killed and 1,712 seriously injured, the great majority in the London area. In achieving this, the Luftwaffe lost 72 bombers.

March saw four attacks on London, followed by unsuccessful raids on Hull and Bristol. The first two weeks in April were quiet. Then, on the 18th, there was the final manned bomber attack against the capital. This was followed by assaults on Hull and Bristol then, for four consecutive nights, the bombers concentrated on shipping in Portsmouth.

## GUIDED MISSILE ATTACK ON PLYMOUTH

The last attack during April, on the early morning of the 30th, involved 101 aircraft and was directed against Plymouth. The raid achieved no great success but is of technical interest because for the first and only time, radio-guided bombs were used against a target in Britain. About a dozen bombers, Dornier 217s of III./KG 100, carried the Fritz-X, a 3,100-pound armour-piercing weapon that was released from high level and whose trajectory could be

*The Fritz-X radio-controlled bomb, the first type of guided missile to be aimed at a target in Britain. On the night of 30 April, during the attack on warships in Plymouth harbour, about a dozen Do 217s of III./KG 100 carried these 3,100-pound weapons. The Plymouth smoke-screen worked effectively, however, and none of these guided bombs hit their target.*

corrected during its fall. During the Plymouth attack, however, the bomb aimers of missile-carrying aircraft were unable to find their primary target, the battleship *King George V*, due to 'mist' in the area. In fact there was no mist, but the Plymouth harbour smokescreen had been ignited. No serious damage was caused and the defences claimed three raiders, two from III./KG 100.

Early in February No. 80 Wing listening station picked up signals from the Egon system used to direct German pathfinder aircraft on to their targets. Because of the similarity of the signals to those of the British Oboe system, Egon's method of operation was immediately clear. Almost at once No. 80 Wing initiated jamming of the system, concentrating against the radio channels over which the pathfinder crews received their instruction. This proved reasonably effective, but the Germans replied by radiating the instructions on several different wavelengths simultaneously. To counter this move No. 80 Wing shifted its attack to the ranging system of Egon using a specially developed ground jammer, code-

*The rearwards-firing guns of a Junkers 188. The upper turret housed a power-operated 20-mm cannon, the lower position a hand-held 13-mm machine-gun.*

*Gefreiter Rudi Prasse of II./KG 2, whose account of the attack on Bristol on the night of 14 May appears below.* (Prasse)

named 'Briar H'. By the end of April three stations with the jammer were operational, at Portland, Brighton and Ramsgate.

## ATTACK ON BRISTOL

May was quiet until the 14th, when ninety-one bombers took off to attack Bristol. The deadly harassment faced by the German crews during the 'Steinbock' attacks is illustrated by the experiences of Gefreiter Rudi Prasse, who flew during the raid as an observer with III./KG 2. His Junkers 188 took off from Vannes at 0030 hours, laden with two 2,200-pound and two 110-pound bombs. Once airborne the bombers funnelled together over Guernsey, marked by a cone of four searchlights, then headed due north towards their target. By 0110 hours Prasse's Ju 188 was nearing the coast of England. Afterwards he wrote:

20,000 feet. Now we climb at 600 feet per minute, with the airspeed steady at 310 mph. In front of us there emerges a dark outline: the English coast. There is nothing of the defences to be seen, the long arms of the searchlight beams do not yet grope out for us. But we know that now, ten minutes before the English coast, the enemy is getting ready for us. Now the first sirens are sounding in the coastal towns and on the airfields the first night fighters are already taking off. Hans begins to jink the aircraft – turning, climbing, diving – for nothing is more dangerous than holding a straight course for too long.

As we cross the coast the first searchlight beams flash on: two, four, five beams finger the sky, searching. Behind us are many more, certainly about 50: this is the famous English coastal searchlight belt. Then we are through it and it is dark again. Before us lies Bristol, our target.

We arrive at the outskirts at 23,000 feet. Suddenly two great tentacles of light swing across the sky to flood the cabin with dazzling blue light, forcing us to screw up our blinded eyes. We are being coned by two searchlights, which now follow us . . . I hold my map against the nose so that the pilot can see his instruments. We dive through a thousand feet turning steeply to the left, then fly straight ahead. The two searchlights, which have been joined by a further two, hunt the sky for us but we are once more in darkness. 'Heavy flak coming up' calls Erich [the ventral gunner] and Hans [Unteroffizier Hans Engelke, the pilot] immediately changes course. There, above us at 26,000 feet, the first eight shells burst.

More searchlights cut across the sky and the flak bursts multiply. The dance has begun! The pilot flies uncommonly well, improvising an aerobatic programme before our eyes.

To the left and below us a flaming red torch goes down. I note in my log: 'Aircraft shot down at 0142 hours, south-west of Bristol.'

0145 hours! The first flares blossom in rows over the city, lighting the target with their bright white glow. Over them hang the row of green sky markers, which float down slowly. On the ground, the flak gunners concentrate their fire on the markers, in an attempt to shoot them out. But it is too late. On the city heavy bombs are now bursting, and dark red fires rise into the sky.

One short glance at the map – that must be the target there. I nudge Hans and point to the right: 'We will attack.'

Bomb-doors open, switches on!

There is a small jerk as our bombs fall away.

Bomb-doors close!

Our *Dora*, lighter by more than two tons, obeys its pilot and sweeps round in a steep left turn, on to a south-easterly course away from the target. Soon we are clear.

The Junkers landed at Vannes at 0305 hours without further incident.

From British records it is clear that the attack was not as successful as it appeared to Prasse. Of the 83 tons of bombs recorded as having fallen on British soil that night, only 3 tons fell on Bristol itself. Six bombers were shot down during the raid.

During the rest of May there were attacks on the ports where forces were concentrating for the forthcoming invasion of France: Portsmouth, Weymouth, Torquay and Falmouth. These proved to be the Parthian shots of the 'Steinbock' operation, which did not continue into June.

As the German leaders had hoped, Operation 'Steinbock' administered a nasty shock to the citizens of those areas of London that had been hit hard. But the limited force available to Peltz meant that only relatively small tonnages of bombs could be carried. Moreover, the poor training of many bomber crews, coupled with the massive harassment from the defences, usually resulted in scattered attacks and few areas were severely damaged. Only about two-fifths of the bombs intended for London actually landed on the sprawling area within its civil defence boundaries. During the first five months of 1944 air-raid casualties in Britain totalled 1,556 killed and 2,916 seriously wounded. More than half of these resulted from the five concentrated attacks on the capital during the week beginning 18 February.

During 'Steinbock' the German bomber force came close to smashing itself against the British defences. Losses amounted to more than 300 aircraft. The German aircraft industry could make good the losses in bombers relatively easily. The crews, however, would prove much more difficult to replace. During 'Steinbock' the Luftwaffe lost approximately one bomber and four trained crewmen for every five British civilians killed by the bombing. The defenders had demonstrated that if the German bomber force was to inflict casualties on the British people, it would suffer almost equally heavily itself.

The conclusion of 'Steinbock' brought with it the virtual end of the German manned-bomber attacks on Britain itself. Yet for London the ordeal was far from

*A V1 flying bomb mounted under the starboard wing of a specially modified Heinkel 111. (Selinger)*

over, for the Germans still had two new bombardment weapons available, which were being hastened into service with the utmost speed.

On 6 June 1944, Allied forces launched their long-expected invasion of France, a move that did more than anything else to bring to an end the conventional manned-bomber attacks on Britain. During the desperate battle that followed, German bomber units suffered further swingeing losses as they attempted to strike at the lodgement area and shipping off the coast.

## AIR-LAUNCHED V1 FLYING BOMBS

Early on the morning of 13 June, London came under attack from a new type of weapon: the Fieseler 103 flying bomb, alias Vergeltungswaffe 1 or V1 (Revenge Weapon No. 1). This form of attack was delivered by an unmanned aircraft, and bombardment by ground-launched missiles falls outside the purview of this account. However, a small but growing proportion of the missiles were launched from aircraft and this part of the operation is examined here.

The flying bomb resembled a small aeroplane with a wingspan of 17 feet 6 inches and a length of 25 feet 11 inches. The missile carried a thin-cased warhead weighing nearly 2,000 pounds, of which 1,870 pounds was powerful Trialen explosive. At launch the missile weighed 4,858 pounds; it was powered by

*A V1 falling away from its He 111 launching aircraft, during a firing trial.*

a simple 600-pound-thrust pulse-jet engine, which gave it a cruising speed of between 300 and 420 mph.

From the first week in July 1944, specially modified Heinkel 111 bombers of III./KG 3 based at Venlo and Gilze Rijen in Holland joined in the bombardment. When carried by an aircraft the flying bomb was attached to a rack fitted to the starboard wing between the engine and the fuselage, with sprung arms holding the missile's wings steady. The carriage of the flying bomb by the Heinkel presented no special problems. Reduction in speed amounted to no more than about 12 mph and the slight asymmetric drag was easily corrected on the rudder trim. The main problem was that of reaching the designated firing point with the necessary accuracy. The course of the flying bomb after release, and the distance it flew, had both to be set into the missile before the Heinkel took off. Thus there was no room for flexibility of approach and unless the bomber crew launched the missile from exactly the right place there was little chance of hitting the target.

An objective the size of London, whose built-up area extended 6 miles or more from the centre, might seem almost impossible to miss. But to hit it the Heinkels had to navigate to an accuracy of 6 miles over an unmarked spot in the North Sea on moonless nights at low level, and without radio aids that might betray their position to the enemy.

The usual tactic was to approach the firing area, about 100 miles from the target, flying at about 170 mph at altitudes below 300 feet. As the Heinkel neared the firing point the pilot pulled up to the release altitude of 1,600 feet, where he levelled the aircraft and accelerated to the missile's flying speed of 200 mph. Just 10 seconds before release the flying bomb's motor was started, belching flame that lit up the sky for miles around. When all was ready the flight engineer released the missile, which fell for about 300 feet before beginning its climb to its cruising altitude of about 3,000 feet. Once the missile was clear the bomber crew descended to low level and returned to base.

At first the air-launched V1s were not recognised as such by the defenders: they did not seem any different from their ground-launched counterparts. Gradually, however, evidence began to pile up indicating that the Germans were employing this form of attack. Although some flying bombs had been observed approaching London from the general direction of Belgium and the Dutch Islands, no ground-launching sites had been located in these areas. They were, in any case, some way beyond the 130-mile flying range of the unexploded V1s that had been examined in England. Moreover, unlike the flying bombs from France, which came over both by day and by night, those from the East came only by night. This was interpreted as meaning that the Germans might have something to conceal about the launch method.

On 31 July, new information served to confirm that flying bombs were indeed being launched from the air. As is the normal practice in wartime, the movements of friendly bombers had to be made known to the air-defence authorities. On the night of 30/31 July, Luftwaffe defensive units in Holland and Belgium were advised that nine Heinkel 111s would cross the Belgian coast near Blankenberge at 2125 hours and return at 2150 hours. At 0055 hours eight Heinkel 111s were to cross the coast at the same point and return at 0115 hours at an altitude of 700 feet; and also at 0055 hours three Heinkel 111s were to cross the Dutch coast at Walcheren, returning over Schouwen at 0130 hours. This signal was decyphered and read by the British Intelligence Service, to whom it provided some valuable clues. In the first place the time spent over the sea, between 20 and 35 minutes, was insufficient to allow the aircraft to reach England; nor was any conventional bomber activity reported that seemed to match their movements. However, between 2135 hours and 2215 ten flying bombs had been reported coming in from the direction of Ostende, followed between 0124 and 0150 hours by a further twelve from the general direction of the Dutch Islands.

Although the source of some V1s was now known, they constituted so small a proportion of those aimed at London that at first little effort was devoted to countering them: up to the end of August about 8,600 flying bombs were launched against London and Southampton from ground ramps in northern France. During this same period III./KG 3 had aimed about 300 bombs at London, 90 at Southampton and a score at Gloucester. The last two were too small to be profitable targets for the V1, and none hit Gloucester. In the case of Southampton the attack was so scattered and inaccurate that the British Intelligence Service believed the intended target was Portsmouth.

During the latter part of August the V1 ground-launching sites in France were engulfed by the rapidly advancing Allied forces and on the afternoon of 1 September the last flying bomb from that area reached England.

Now the defences were redeployed to counter the air-launched missiles coming from the East. Since the latter came only by night, the main fighter effort fell to the Mosquito squadrons. In addition a squadron of Tempests, No. 501, also engaged in night operations. The Tempest was the fastest fighter at low level available in any numbers. It carried no radar, but pilots were able to pursue their prey by following the bright flame emitted by the flying bomb's motor. On a clear night the flames could be seen up to 15 miles away. To overcome the problem of ranging as the fighter closed in, the distinguished scientist Sir Thomas Merton devised a simple optical range-finder.

Representative of the V1 attacks on London was that before dawn on 16 September, when fifteen launching aircraft were involved. Only nine flying bombs got under way and of these two were destroyed by Royal Navy warships and one by a Mosquito before reaching the coast. Two more fell to Flying Officer B. Miller of No. 501 Squadron in his Tempest. Afterwards he reported:

I was scrambled under Trimley control from Bradwell Bay for Diver [flying bomb] reported coming in on a course of 285 degrees at 2,500 feet and 340 mph. I dived down on it and closed in from 500 yards astern and opened fire. I saw strikes on the tail unit. Control told me to break off the engagement and I did so. I saw the Diver losing height and crash and explode on the ground near RAF Castle Camps 30 seconds after my attack at 0606 hours.

I saw a second one at 0608 hours heading over Bradwell Bay on a course of 250 degrees and 340 mph. I closed in astern and opened fire from 500 yards, closing in to 50 yards. Diver blew up in mid-air.

*Tempest V fighters of No. 501 Squadron, a unit that operated with success against flying bombs coming in by night.* (Charles E. Brown)

Of the remaining four bombs, two fell in open countryside and two reached the Greater London area, one exploding on Barking and the other on Woolwich. But even this unimpressive total – two bombs out of sixteen hitting the target – was above the average for this form of attack.

## COUNTERING THE V1 LAUNCHING AIRCRAFT

The low-flying Heinkels were extremely difficult targets for British night fighters. The launching aircraft spent only about 5 minutes within the view of the British ground-radar stations when running in to release their bombs. Immediately the bomb was clear they would drop below the radar horizon. When

*During August 1944 the V1 was not the only type of flying bomb to fall on England. During the period immediately after the invasion of France part of the special attack unit IV./KG 101 operated from St Dizier against the bridgehead area using the Mistel: an unmanned Junkers 88 with a 8,300-pound shaped-charge explosive warhead fitted in the nose, above which was mounted a Messerschmitt 109 fighter. The fighter pilot flew the combination to the target area, aimed both aircraft at the target, locked the bomber's controls and then fired the explosive bolts which released the fighter from the bomber underneath. The bomber continued on until it hit the target and exploded; the fighter returned to its base. Although the weapon was intended primarily as an anti-shipping device, one Mistel Ju 88 crashed in England on the night of 10 August, at Flade Bottom Farm near Andover. As might be expected from the explosion of such a large highly directional shaped charge warhead, the blast played strange tricks: at the point of impact there was virtually no crater, but a man more than 3 miles away was blown over. The reasons for the Mistel crash near Andover were far from clear, but probably the target was Portsmouth.*

attacked, the German crews made use of cloud cover or tried to shake off their pursuers by making evasive turns close to the sea. Some Mosquitos were lost when they stalled and crashed while trying to press home attacks on the low-flying missile carriers.

The reader may gain an impression of the difficulty of engaging the Heinkels from the report submitted by Wing Commander L. Mitchell, commander of No. 25 Squadron, following his sortie in a Mosquito on 25 September. Mitchell and radar operator Flight Lieutenant D. Cox had been directed by ground radar to a position about 50 miles east of Great Yarmouth, where a suspicious contact had been observed. He closed in, then:

> . . . I saw a flying bomb leaving the Bogey [unidentified aircraft] and this was also observed on the AI, control immediately afterwards giving the Bogey as a Bandit [hostile aircraft]. I followed for about 15 minutes at 220 mph (indicated) in thick cumulus cloud but without obtaining a visual although on three occasions the range was closed on AI to about 400 feet. The enemy aircraft then dived away to port and contact was lost.
>
> I was then vectored on to a second Bogey, given almost immediately as a Bandit as again a flying bomb was seen launched in a westerly direction. AI contact was obtained at four miles range on a 'jinking' target. Range was closed on AI to 850 feet in thick cloud, and at 400 to 500 feet range a visual was

*A dramatic photograph showing the final moments of the life of a V1 flying bomb. The missile's track through the sky can be seen as a white line from left to right, with anti-aircraft shells flying up from the right to meet it. The missile was hit and exploded, throwing a circle of white light on the clouds above. (IWM)*

obtained in a break in the cloud. As the enemy aircraft turned to starboard both my navigator and I recognised it as an He 111. A long burst from 800 feet range produced strikes on the starboard wing root and as it disappeared into cloud was seen, with the aid of night glasses by Flt Lt Cox, to turn hard starboard and go down. The combat took place at 1,000 feet and it is considered unlikely that the enemy aircraft could have pulled out from the dive before hitting the water. Greyfriars control states that only one aircraft emerged from the combat.

Mitchell could claim only one Heinkel probably destroyed, but without doubt the night saw the first loss of one of the launching aircraft to enemy action. About an hour after the combat a Mosquito of No. 409 Squadron, on patrol over southern Holland, shot down a Heinkel on its way home.

Four nights later, on the morning of 29 September, Mitchell and Cox were vectored into a wave of Heinkels coming in to launch flying bombs at the capital. Within a space of less than half an hour they shot down two missile carriers.

In September the worsening military situation forced III./KG 3 to leave Holland and pull back to Germany. During the following month the unit was redesignated I. Gruppe of Kampfgeschwader 53 and soon afterwards the II. and III. Gruppen of this Geschwader re-formed and began preparing for the missile-launching role.

While the fighters endeavoured to cut down the flying bombs and launching aircraft over the sea, anti-aircraft guns were repositioned to cover the eastern flank of the capital. By the middle of October more than 1,100 light and heavy weapons had moved to new sites in East Anglia. The dry summer had given way to a wet and cold autumn, however, which produced appalling conditions at many improvised sites. The Speaker of the House of Commons paid a visit to one of the batteries and afterwards wrote:

As the whole site had been hurriedly arranged within the previous fourteen days, and as it had been raining on and off for a longer period, the ground was in a very soggy state, and mud up to the knees everywhere. It reminded me of Flanders in the last war . . . Just as we were finishing our evening meal news came through that Heinkels were on the way. Off we went in the cars to the battery, but had not quite got there before the shooting started; we jumped out of the cars (I jumped into a pool of water) and at once spotted a 'Doodle-bug' coming in surrounded by tracer shells; time and again, it seemed to be hit, but still it went on; however, suddenly the light went out and it came down with a big bang. Simultaneously, we saw another farther south; this one appeared to have got through the barrage and was sailing on towards London, lit up by searchlights as far as we could see . . .

As the attack continued it became clear that semi-permanent all-weather sites were necessary if the guns were to perform effectively. Under a crash programme, sites were converted as the battle raged round them. It proved to be a mammoth operation, involving the laying of some 60 miles of roadway and the provision of 150,000 tons of rubble and hardcore for the foundations of the gun platforms and prefabricated huts for the crews.

In spite of the initial problems, when they had settled in the guns proved the most effective means of dealing with the flying bombs. Using the latest equipment, the American SCR 584 gun-laying radar, together with shells fitted with the recently developed radio proximity fuse, on average only 156 heavy anti-aircraft shells were fired for each V1 destroyed. It was an incredibly low figure, which showed that by this stage of the war radar-laid fire was as accurate as any laid visually. Of Anti-Aircraft Command's work against the flying bomb, General Pile later commented: 'More was learnt abut the potentialities of anti-aircraft work in 80 days than had been learned in the previous 30 years.'

During November the re-formed Kampfgeschwader 53 began to mount V1-launching operations with as many as sixty aircraft on selected nights. This increase in activity was to be short-lived. In the following month shortage of fuel in the Luftwaffe imposed a brake on operations. By conserving stocks a few large-scale operations could still be mounted, however.

In the early morning darkness of Christmas Eve, some fifty Heinkels set out to attack Manchester, outflanking the defences by releasing their bombs off the east coast between Skegness and Bridlington. There were 30 bombs observed crossing the coast. Only 1 crashed within Manchester's boundaries; 5 more impacted within 6 miles of the city centre and a further 5 within 15 miles; 37 people were killed and 67 seriously injured.

The attack by air-launched V1s continued intermittently into the first month of 1945, ending on the morning of 14 January when the last such flying bomb crashed near Hornsey.

From beginning to end the Heinkels launched about 1,700 flying bombs against targets in England, all but about 150 of them against London. The units involved lost seventy-seven aircraft, sixteen to night fighters and the rest in accidents due mainly to the hazards of low-level operations at night.

Not until September 1944, when the ground-launching sites in France were overrun, was it possible to observe the effect of the air-launched weapons in isolation. From then until the end of the attack an estimated 1,300 flying bombs

*During the final months of the war, the only German manned aircraft to fly regularly over Britain were the Arado 234 jet reconnaissance aircraft of Kommando Sperling, later re-designated I./Aufklaerungsgruppe 123. The Arado is seen being prepared for a sortie (right), and groundcrew removing the film magazine from the camera of an Arado 234 (below). (Goetz)*

were launched from the air at London. Of these just over 600 reached the coast or were otherwise seen by the defences; 321 flying bombs were brought down by anti-aircraft guns on land and 10 more fell to those of warships off the coast, 71 fell to fighters and 1 was shared by guns and fighters. A total of 66 flying bombs, 1 in 20 of those launched, impacted in the London Civil Defence Area. It is estimated that the air-launched V1s killed about 500 people and caused serious injuries to some 1,500 others.

## GERMAN JETS OVER BRITAIN

From the middle of 1944 activity over Britain by German manned aircraft had been minimal. Most of it comprised reconnaissance sorties, flown by the new Arado 234 jet aircraft – the only type in service wth the Luftwaffe with the range to reach Britain and the speed to overfly it with impunity. Once again Erich Sommer and Horst Goetz enter the story, for from early August they had flown the Arado during reconnaissance missions over the Normandy invasion area from Juvincourt in France. Also in August, Sommer made the first jet-reconnaissance sortie over Britain when he photographed airfields in the south.

After the withdrawal from France Goetz, now an oberleutnant commanding the Arado 234 reconnaissance unit Kommando Sperling, flew several jet-reconnaissance sorties over Britain from Rheine. On 5 October, for example, he flew a 2-hour mission during which he photographed shipping in the Wash area and airfields in East Anglia and Lincolnshire. On the following day he operated over south-eastern England. For the remainder of the war Goetz's unit, redesignated the 1. Staffel of Aufklaerungsgruppe 123 early in 1945, flew infrequent reconnaissance missions over Britain. These aircraft flew at speeds of about 450 mph at 33,000 feet and suffered no interference from the defences.

*Battered but defiant: the area around St Paul's cathedral in London, at the end of the war.* (IWM)

By March 1945 the Third Reich was nearing its end, with Allied forces poised on all sides for the final thrust into the heartland. There was still life in the Luftwaffe, however. Early on the morning of 4 March, as some 500 aircraft of RAF Bomber Command returned from attacks on Kamen and Ladbergen, over 100 German night fighters followed them back to their bases. The raiders attacked 27 airfields in Norfolk, Suffolk, Lincolnshire and Yorkshire, bombing and strafing. A total of 48 RAF aircraft came under attack, of which 22 were shot down and 8 damaged. The defenders claimed 6 German aircraft shot down. Two weeks later, on the night of 17 March, 18 Ju 88s took off from airfields in Holland for a repeat attack on the RAF bases. No bomber operations were planned for this night, however, and the intruders were able to shoot down only one aircraft on a training flight. It was to be the final offensive action over the country during the Second World War: the Blitz on Britain was over.

## THE RECKONING

During the Second World War about 52,000 people were killed and 63,000 seriously injured during the attack on Britain by bombers and air-launched flying bombs. A further 8,500 people were killed and just over 23,000 seriously injured by other forms of bombardment: the ground-launched V1 flying bombs, V2 rockets and long-range guns firing across the Channel. In terms of casualties, the worst time was during the final four months of 1940, when the Luftwaffe was able to launch powerful night attacks on targets in Britain with minimal interference from the defences: in this period more than 22,000 people were killed and 28,000 seriously injured – about one-third of the wartime totals for all forms of bombardment.

These figures, though representing an immense sum of human tragedy, were not of such an order as to come close to bringing a major nation to its knees. The chances of a British citizen being killed as a result of an attack on his country during the Second World War were just under 1-in-800 and those of serious injury were just over 1-in-500. Of course, the odds were shorter for those in the cities: in the London Civil Defence Area there was a 1-in-200 chance of being killed and a 1-in-160 chance of suffering serious injury. Such risks, spread over a period of nearly five years, were not high enough to bring about the breakdown in civilian morale that had been feared before the war. The home front had stood firm; the Blitz on Britain had failed in its intended purpose.

# Bibliography

Aders, Gebhard. *History of the German Night Fighter Force 1917–1945*, Janes, London, 1978
Balke, Ulf. *Kampfgeschwader 100 Wiking*, Motorbuch Verlag, Stuttgart, 1981
Bekker, Cajus. *The Luftwaffe War Diaries*, Macdonald, London, 1966
Caldwell, Donald. *JG 26*, Ballantine Books, New York, 1991
Collier, Basil. *The Defence of the United Kingdom*, HMSO, London, 1957
Dierich, Wolfgang. *Die Verbände der Luftwaffe*, Motorbuch Verlag, Stuttgart, 1976
——. *Kampfgeschwader 'Edelweiss'*, Ian Allan, Shepperton, 1975
——. *Kampfgeschwader 55*, Motorbuch Verlag, Stuttgart, 1975
Ethell, Jeffrey and Price, Alfred. *World War II Combat Jets*, Airlife, Shrewsbury, 1994
Galland, Adolf. *The First and the Last*, Methuen and Co. Ltd, London, 1955
Green, William. *Warplanes of the Third Reich*, Macdonald, London, 1970
Gundelach, Karl. *Kampfgeschwader 'General Wever' 4*, Motorbuch Verlag, Stuttgart, 1978
Hinsley, F.H. *British Intelligence in the Second World War Volumes I, II, III*, HMSO, London, 1979 to 1988
Irving, David. *The Rise and Fall of the Luftwaffe: The Life of Erhard Milch*, Weidenfeld & Nicolson, London, 1973
Kiehl, Heinz. *Kampfgeschwader 'Legion Condor' 53*, Motorbuch Verlag, Stuttgart, 1983
Priller, Josef. *Geschichte Eines Jagdgeschwaders*, Kurt Wowinckel Verlag, Neckargemuend, 1969
Ramsey, Winston, et al. *The Battle of Britain Then and Now*, After The Battle Publications, London, 1980; fifth edition 1989
——. *The Blitz, Then and Now, Volumes 1, 2 and 3*, After The Battle Publications, London, 1987
Ring, Hans and Girbig, Werner. *Jagdgeschwader 27*, Motorbuch Verlag, Stuttgart, 1971
Sarkar, Dilip. *Angriff Westland*, Ramrod Publications, Malvern, Worcs, 1992
Sharp, C. Martin and Bowyer, Michael. *Mosquito*, Faber & Faber, London, 1967
Smith, Peter. *Stuka Squadron*, Patrick Stephens Ltd, Wellingborough, 1990
Trenkle, Fritz. *Die deutsche Funkmessverfahren bis 1945*, Motorbuch Verlag, Stuttgart, 1979
——. *Die deutschen Funk-Navigations und Funk*, Motorbuch Verlag, Stuttgart, 1979
——. *Fuehrungsverfahren bis 1945*, Motorbuch Verlag, Stuttgart, 1979
Wakefield, Kenneth. *Luftwaffe Encore*, William Kimber, London, 1979
——. *The First Pathfinders*, William Kimber, London, 1981
Wood, Derek and Dempster, Derek. *The Narrow Margin*, Arrow Books, 1969
Young, Richard. *The Flying Bomb*, Ian Allan, Shepperton, 1978

Official British Air Ministry limited circulation publications
Previously classified documents, copies now held in the Public Record Office, Kew
*Air Ministry Weekly Intelligence Summaries* (various issues)
Royal Air Force Signals History:
    Vol. III *Aircraft Radio*
    Vol. IV *Radar in Raid Reporting*
    Vol. V *Fighter Control and Interception*
    Vol. VII *Radio Counter-Measures*
*The Air Defence of Great Britain*
*The Rise and Fall of the German Air Force 1933 to 1945*

# Appendices

## APPENDIX A
## RAF AND LUFTWAFFE UNITS

*Royal Air Force*

The basic fighter unit in the RAF was the squadron, comprising sixteen, later eighteen to twenty, aircraft. A wing usually comprised between two and five squadrons and a group comprised all the fighter squadrons within a set geographical area, sometimes thirty or more.

*Luftwaffe*

The basic unit in the Luftwaffe was the Gruppe, comprising three or four Staffeln each with nine aircraft, and a Stab (headquarters) unit with three.

The Geschwader, initially comprising three Gruppen and a Stab unit with four aircraft, was the largest German flying unit to have a fixed nominal strength. Later in the war a fourth, Ergaenzungs Gruppe was added to each bomber Geschwader to provide operational training for crews before they moved to the front-line Gruppen.

Within a Geschwader the aircraft were usually assigned to a single role, for example Jagdgeschwader (abbreviated to JG), fighters; Zerstoerer- (ZG), twin-engined fighters; Kampf- (KG), bombers and Sturzkampfgeschwader (StG), dive bombers.

Reconnaissance units were usually independent Gruppen, Aufklaerungsgruppen (Aufkl. Gr.). Other independent Gruppen were formed from time to time for specific tasks, for example Kampfgruppe 100 (KGr 100), a specialist precision attack unit.

All Geschwader and independent Gruppen were numbered with Arabic numerals, for example Kampfgeschwader 2, Aufklaerungsgruppe 123.

Usually, however, a Gruppe formed part of a Geschwader and was numbered in Roman numerals before the Geschwader designation. Thus the Third Gruppe of ZG 76 was written as III./ZG 76. The Staffeln within a Geschwader were numbered consecutively, using Arabic numerals. Thus in a simple unit comprising three Gruppen each of three Staffeln, the 1st, 2nd and 3rd Staffeln comprised the I. Gruppe, the 4th, 5th and 6th Staffeln comprised the II. Gruppe and the 7th, 8th and 9th Staffeln comprised the III. Gruppe. The third Staffel of Stukageschwader 3 was therefore abbreviated as 3./StG 3 and was part of I./StG 3.

## APPENDIX B
## COMPARATIVE RANKS

| Luftwaffe | Royal Air Force |
|---|---|
| *Commissioned* | |
| Generalfeldmarschall | Marshal of the Royal Air Force |
| Generaloberst | Air Chief Marshal |
| General | Air Marshal |
| Generalleutnant | Air Vice-Marshal |
| Generalmajor | Air Commodore |
| Oberst | Group Captain |
| Oberstleutnant | Wing Commander |

| | |
|---|---|
| Major | Squadron Leader |
| Hauptmann | Flight Lieutenant |
| Oberleutnant | Flying Officer |
| Leutnant | Pilot Officer |

*Non-commissioned*

| | |
|---|---|
| Oberfaehnrich | Officer Cadet |
| Feldwebel | Sergeant |
| Unteroffizier | Corporal |
| Gefreiter | Leading Aircraftsman |
| Flieger | Airman |

# APPENDIX C

# FIGHTER COMMAND TACTICAL MEMORANDUM NO. 8, JUNE 1940

The document produced verbatim below, Fighter Command Tactical Memorandum No. 8, was issued in June 1940 and gave the recommended tactics for use against escorted bomber formations. This memorandum remained in force throughout the Battle of Britain until November 1940, when revised instructions were issued (*author's comments are in italics*).

### SECRET FIGHTER COMMAND TACTICAL MEMORANDUM NO. 8
### AIR FIGHTING FIGHTERS V. ESCORTED BOMBERS

(1) Further to these Headquarters' letter FC/S.18507/Ops 1 dated 16 May 1940, which gave general notes on air fighting, the following memorandum is issued in amplification, and has been prepared from a careful study of all combat reports to date and from personal contact with Squadrons which have been in action in France and off the French and Belgian coasts.

### INTRODUCTION

(2) German tactics during the present phase have shown that, in large scale attacks, bombers are invariably escorted by formations of fighters, whose duty it is to protect them from our fighters.

(3) The German Air Force has now established bases in Norway, Holland, Belgium and Northern France; Southern and South-Eastern England are now within the effective range of the Me 109, and the Me 110 can cover the whole of England and Scotland.

(4) Our fighters have been taking a heavy toll of both these types under the more difficult conditions of the past few weeks, and results have shown that the Hurricane and Spitfire are more than a match for either the Me 109 or the Me 110. Under conditions of Home Defence, where a highly organised system exists, the task of our Air Force should be simplified. Already we have established a very definite moral ascendancy over the enemy, who are unwilling to stay and fight unless in superior numbers. [*This last sentence would certainly not be borne out during the initial phase of the Battle of Britain.*]

### THE AIM

(5) It may here be clearly stated that our ability to continue the war rests to a very large extent on the success of our fighters, in conjunction with the Fixed Defences, in the protection of our vital centres, and especially those concerned with aircraft.

(6) It must, therefore, be constantly borne in mind that our aim is THE DESTRUCTION OF ENEMY BOMBERS, and that action against fighters is only a means to this end.

(7) A study of enemy tactics which will probably be employed is therefore necessary so that the best means of achieving this aim can be put into effect.

### GERMAN TACTICS

(8) Bombers usually approach their objectives in sub-formations in line astern, each sub-formation consisting of three, five, or seven aircraft in 'Vic', so disposed that they are mutually supporting. Large formations in several columns, staggered laterally and vertically have also been encountered and other formations may be developed.

(9) The escorting fighters are normally between two and four thousand feet above and usually in the rear of the formation. Where two or more escorting Squadrons are employed they are normally in Squadron formation, with Squadrons stepped up to the rear and echeloned to one side or the other.

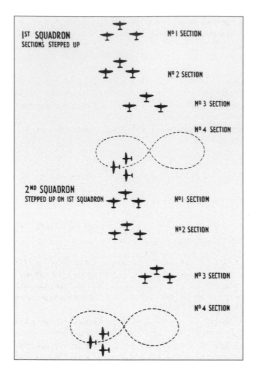

1ST SQUADRON
SECTIONS STEPPED UP

№ 1 SECTION

№ 2 SECTION

№ 3 SECTION

№ 4 SECTION

2ND SQUADRON
STEPPED UP ON 1ST SQUADRON

№ 1 SECTION

№ 2 SECTION

№ 3 SECTION

№ 4 SECTION

(10) These fighters frequently remain in position until our fighters attempt to attack the bombers. They then attack in a dive when our fighters' attention is taken up with their targets. This form of attack consists of a straight dive by individual fighters, the dive being continued well below. They then return, if numerically superior, and continue the same tactics.

(11) It has been found that, owing to a healthy respect for our eight-gun fighters, enemy fighter formations will usually break up when attacked. [*When the German fighters were engaged in a cross-over turn, it would have looked as though they were breaking formation.*] It is therefore essential to neutralise them with a part of our force, so that the remainder may deliver their attack on the bombers without interference. This is discussed more fully in the following paragraphs, which deal with our tactics.

## THE ATTACK OF ESCORTED FORMATIONS
SEARCH

(12) Fighters in search formation should always patrol higher than the anticipated or reported heights of the enemy if weather conditions permit. The search formation indicated at Appendix 'A' has been found to be successful.

(13) It should be a fundamental principle that the rear units of any formation should be employed solely on look-out duties to avoid any possibility of surprise from astern or above.

(14) Thus the essential 'Upper guard' is supplied, not only in that the second Squadron acts as such, but the rear Section of each Squadron supplies this cover to its own unit.

(15) Whatever the strength of the fighter unit, a proportion of it should always be detailed for this duty.

APPROACH

(16) Upon approaching the enemy bombers, every effort should be made to achieve surprise. If this is successful it may be possible to deliver an attack without interference. The 'Upper' Squadron or Unit may be able to draw off their escort and, if necessary, attack them while the 'Lower' Squadron attacks the bombers. Remembering that the escorts are primarily fixed gun fighters, even a small detachment from our fighters, by attacking one after the other of the enemy fighters quickly from above, without getting closely engaged, may draw large numbers of them off and so enable the remaining fighters to deliver an attack unmolested.

(17) Should our fighter formation be weak in comparison with the enemy's, the guard aircraft may have to be content with engaging their attention as much as possible and warning the fighters attacking the enemy bombers by R/T, when the enemy fighters move in to attack.

(18) Always ensure that the upper guard is in position ready to assist before attacking, or that the enemy has no available protection.

ATTACK

(19) Whenever possible, fighters should attack enemy bomber formations in equal numbers by astern or quarter attacks from the same level, taking care not to cut the corners while closing in to decisive range, and thus presenting a side view target to the bombers' rear guns. They should keep their nose on the enemy and then, when at decisive range, make a deflection if required. If in a good position, a short burst of two or three seconds may well be decisive, but in any case this should not be exceeded without breaking away to ensure that an enemy fighter is not on one's tail. If all is well, the attack can be immediately renewed.

(20) Whenever fighters that are attacking bombers receive warning from their upper guard of an impending attack by enemy fighters, they should immediately break away outwards. The German fighters frequently dive once in such an attack, and carry on away from the combat.

(21) Should the fighters not be numerically strong enough to engage the enemy bombers aircraft for aircraft, it will be necessary to 'nibble' from the flanks. Fighters should be most careful not to approach into the 'Vic' of the bomber formation, as this will expose them to effective cross fire.

(22) French experience has confirmed the doctrine of Fighter Command attacks in that simultaneous attacks

against compact sections have proved most effective. This method distracts the attention of machine gunners and enables the fighters to benefit from superiority of fire. The French prohibit attack in line astern, i.e. No. 1 Attack, against compact sections.

BREAKAWAY

(23) Fighter aircraft, when breaking away from a bomber formation, should endeavour to maintain the maximum relative speed. A steep and violent climbing turn results in the air gunner being given a period in which the only relative movement between himself and the fighter is that of an extension of range, and therefore he has practically a point-blank aim at the fighters.

(24) The best form of breakaway would appear to be a downward turn, thus keeping up maximum speed and gradually changing the angle of flight paths of the bomber and the fighter.

## FIGHTERS V. FIGHTERS

(25) It is probable that the enemy will operate independent fighter formations over this country for the purpose of:

(i) Gaining air superiority.

(ii) Carrying out low attacks on aerodromes and dispersed aircraft.

(iii) Attempting to draw off our fighters prior to bombing attacks, whilst our fighters are re-fuelling and rearming (this latter practice has been frequently carried out in France).

(26) The allocation of forces will be decided by the Group or Sector Commander, but fighter units should always remember that to waste petrol and ammunition under these circumstances may well be playing into the hands of the enemy. It may be necessary, therefore, for our fighters to adopt a purely defensive role for the protection of the aerodrome, and not attack these fighters, who are in the nature of a decoy, so that when the bombing forces arrive they will be able to attack them and shoot them down.

(27) When battle is engaged with fighters, a dog-fight nearly always ensues. It may then be a matter of individual combat, but whenever possible fighters should remain together so that they may afford mutual support.

(28) When a fighter unit is attacking enemy fighters, Sections should be led into the attack together. As already stated, such attacks must invariably develop into a series of dog-fights and whenever possible our fighters should attempt to remain loosely in Section formation, or at least in pairs, so as to afford mutual support and to assist in the reformation of the unit after combat. On no account should individual fighters leave a formation to deliver attacks unless specifically ordered to do so.

## SUMMARY

(29) The following points are again emphasized:

(i) It is essential that leaders should weigh up the situation as a whole before delivering attacks. Rushing blindly in to attack an enemy may have disastrous results, and will certainly be less effective.

(ii) Never fly straight, either in the formation as a whole or individually. When over enemy territory alter course and height with a view to misleading AA.

(iii) Keep a constant watch to the rear of the formation of aircraft.

(iv) Upon hearing close gun fire, turn immediately. Hesitancy in so doing may result in effective enemy fire. Do not dive straight away.

(v) Before taking off, search the sky for enemy fighters, and if they are known to be about, turn as soon as possible after taking off. Enemy fighters have frequently dived on aircraft whilst they were taking off from their aerodromes. Similar remarks apply during approach and landing.

(vi) Conserve ammunition as much as possible. A short burst at effective range is usually decisive, and leave further ammunition for further attacks.

(vii) Exploit surprise to the utmost. The enemy has been taught to do this, and you should be prepared accordingly.

(viii) Always remember that your objective is the ENEMY BOMBER.

# APPENDIX D

# 'BATTLE OF BRITAIN DAY' – THE GERMAN VIEW

Lagebericht No. 376, translated below, gives the German view of the air operations between dawn on 15 September and dawn on 16 September 1940, the date now commemorated as 'Battle of Britain Day'. Although the two daylight attacks on the capital have often been described as 'an all-out effort by the Luftwaffe against London', it is clear from this document that the number of bombers involved fell far short of the number available. Only 148 bombers claimed to have bombed London during the day – this was a large force, but by no means an 'all-out effort'.

It is of interest to note the reference to 'Morane and Curtiss fighters with French Markings' operating over London. No such fighters took part in the Battle of Britain and this was a clear case of misidentification. The German losses admitted in Section III are accurate, but refer only to aircraft that did not regain friendly territory; aircraft that got back to German-occupied territory, in whatever state, were not listed as 'lost'. This conforms with the normal RAF method of stating losses, though other German records gave details of aircraft returning with damage.

Luftwaffe High Command
Department Ic Headquarters, 16 Sept 1940 Nr 17410/40 g

Secret
SITUATION REPORT NR 376
(closed on 16.9 at 1000 hours)

(A.) AIR SITUATION NORTH.
(I.) WEATHER REPORT, see Appendix I.
(II.) BOMBER OPERATIONS ON 15.9 AND DURING THE NIGHT UNTIL DAWN 16.9

(a) Own Territory (Reich and Occupied Territories)

*Air Zone Western France*
(1) At about 13.00 hours 4 bombs were dropped on the island of Alderney, without damage being reported.
(2) During the night the enemy carried out numerous coastal flights and dropped bombs at six points. No damage reported.
*Air Zone Belgium–northern France*
(3) Between 2100 and 0300 hours there were numerous coastal flights of which 14 entered the Reich area. At eight points bombs were dropped. At Antwerp a munitions dump was blown up. At Calais several fires were started and the railway station was destroyed. Flak defences were active and one enemy aircraft was shot down.
(4) Between 2130 and 0430 22 enemy aircraft passed overhead, of which 18 entered the Reich area. Bombs were dropped near Vlissing. One patrol boat was set on fire.

*Reich Area*
(5) Between 2140 and 0415 hours 53 enemy aircraft penetrated to the line Husum–Neumuenster–Luebeck–Schwerin–Oranienburg–Berlin–Tangermuende–Celle–Osnabrueck–Kassel–Duisburg–Muenchen–Gladbach with bombs dropped in 15 places. The main targets for attack were Wilhelmshaven and Krefeld. In Krefeld considerable damage to houses as well as some casualties (2 dead and 7 wounded) were reported. The Flak defences opened fire, but no results were observed.

(b) Great Britain (Luftflotten 2 and 3)

(1) Reconnaissance aircraft observed considerable sea traffic between the Thames and the Humber, moving both directions.
(2) Operations against London.
In the course of 15.9 a total of 148 bombers reached the target; between 1250 and 1600 hours they released 133 tons of high explosive and incendiary bombs (5 SC 1000, 2 SC 500, 246 SC 250, 18 Flambo, 50 LZZ 250 and 967 SC 50) as well as 108 incendiary containers. [*German bombs were designated by type (SC = general purpose, SD = armour piercing, Flambo = 240-pound flame bomb, LZZ = delayed action) with the weight in kilogrammes. Thus the SC 1000 was a general purpose 2,200-pounder; the LZZ 250 was a delayed action 550-pounder.*] Due to thick cloud the results could not be observed. There was one hit (1,000 kg) which caused a fire at Bromley Gas Works and hits were observed on warehouses. The following individual targets were bombed:
The section of the city to the south of the Thames (with 180 SC 50, 6 Flambo, 6 SC 250 and 6 LZZ 250)
The northwestern part of the docks (with 80 SC 250 and 40 LZZ 250)
Part of the city 2 1/2 miles to the south of Battersea Park (with 7 SC 250 and 390 SC 50)
London Main Line Station (with 4 LZZ 250)
Central area of city (with 60 SC 250)
Eastern Edge of London (with 20 SC 50)
Large buildings at the West India Docks (with 3 SC 1000)
Commercial Docks (with 4 SC 250)
London Docks (with 6 SC 250)
Part of the city south of the Thames (with 2 SC 250, 290 SC 50 and 20 incendiary containers)

Over the target large formations of fighters (up to 80 aircraft) intercepted. As well as Spitfires and Hurricanes, Morane and Curtiss fighters with French markings were observed. The fighters pressed home their attacks either singly or in pairs, without regard for the flak, and followed our bombers from the target to the middle of the Channel and in some cases even as far as the French coast. Heavy and at times accurate flak was observed over Chatham, Maidstone and the London dock area. Barrage balloons were raised in the target area; exact details of altitudes and positions not available.

During the night, until dawn on 16.9, a total of 181 bombers reached the target where between 2100 and 0520 hours they dropped 224 tons of high explosive and incendiary bombs (35 SC 1000, 73 SC 500, 236 SC 250, 68 LZZ 250, 163 Flambo and 654 SC 50) as well as 279 incendiary containers. Due to cloudless skies and good visibility it was possible to observe fires in the following areas: the west part of the Woolwich Arsenal; the area to the north and west of the Tower [of London]; the area to the east and southeast of Victoria Park; Piccadilly underground station (two SC 1000 on the target); Tilbury Docks; King George V Docks; West India Docks; London Docks; near Southwark (about 20 bright fires); near Woolwich; at the bend in the Thames [i.e., Millwall] about 20 very bright fires; at the north of the city; at Victoria Station; at St James's Park; at St Paul's Station [i.e., Cannon Street]

About 12 miles from the centre of the city on a bearing of 160 degrees two decoy sites were observed, with fires and simulated explosions. [*This reference to 'decoy sites' is interesting, because it was only at the close of 1940 that the 'Starfish' sites came into use.*] Night fighters were seen (at around 20,000 feet) over the north and north-east of London but there were no attacks. To the east of Harwich four night fighters made attacks at altitudes of around 17,000 feet. The flak defences over the northern and eastern parts of the city, and the city centre, were very heavy. Barrage fire was used. To the south of the city little flak was met. Searchlight activity was weak in the north and the central part of the city, strong in the north-east. Searchlights rapidly found and held aircraft flying at 16,000 feet. In the north-east four barrage balloons were seen, though their height could not be ascertained.

(3) Other attacks were carried out against the following targets:

(aa) by day (between 1037 and 1630 hours) Supermarine Aviation Works at Southampton Woolston, with 20 SC 500 and 3 Flambo. Hits observed on the southern part of the target.

Oil tanks in Portland Harbour, with 61 SC 250, 25 Flambo, 9 LZZ, 16 SD 50 and 16 incendiary containers. Hits were observed on the southern part of the rank area, with flames and smoke.

Portland Harbour, with 16 SC 250, 8 Flambo and 160 SC 50 Hits were observed on the southern part of the target 1 convoy to the north-west of Ireland: 1 merchant ship (8,000 tons) was hit. Fires and explosions were observed and the ship sank. 1 tanker (10,000 tons) was hit and sank. Alternative targets at Hastings and Eastbourne were attacked with 8 SC 250, 2 Flambo, 2 LZZ 250 and 2 incendiary containers. No results were observed.

(bb) at night (between 2225 and 0315 hours) with fires observed: Southampton (4 SC 250), Bournemouth (2 SC 250, 1 Flambo, 12 SC 50), Avonmouth (4 Flambo, 60 SC 50, 16 incendiary containers), Liverpool (11 SC 250, 2 Flambo, 124 SC 50), 1 passenger ship 15–20,000 tons, in the North Channel at the latitude of Rathlin Island (2 SC 500), set on fire. Without results observed: Sheerness (1 SC 1000 and 1 SC 500), Hastings (1 SC 500, 1 SC 250), Worthing (2 SC 250, 2 Flambo), Portsmouth (2 SC 250, 1 Flambo, 12 SC 50), Gloucester (20 SC 50), Cardiff (20 SC 50), Lincoln (2 SC 250), 1 merchant ship (6,000 tons) in the North Channel.

(4) The *9th Fliegerdivision* carried out a night minelaying operation according to plan.

(5) For further particulars of the defences see Appendix 4.

(c) North Sea and Baltic Areas.

(1) During an armed reconnaissance near the Firth of Forth one enemy merchant ship (7,000 tons) was struck by an aerial torpedo. The hit was clearly observed.

(2) Security and anti-submarine patrols off the coast of Holland, and reconnaissance over the Skagerrak, carried out without incident.

(III) TOTAL LOSSES (AIRCRAFT) ON 15.9.40

(a) Own          20 Do 17
                 18 Me 109
                  8 He 111
                  3 Me 110
                  3 Ju 88

Total            52 aircraft

(b) Enemy, in aerial combat

|          | 51 Spitfire |
|----------|-------------|
|          | 26 Hurricane |
|          | 1 Bristol Blenheim |
| by flak  | 1 aircraft (type unknown) |
|          | near Antwerp. |

Total      79 aircraft

# APPENDIX E

# OPERATION 'STEINBOCK', 1944 – GOERING'S ORDER

This document, issued over the signature of Hermann Goering, gives an interesting insight into the background to the series of attacks launched against Britain in the first half of 1944.

3.12.43
State Top Secret
By Hand of Officer Only
To
Chief of Staff Luftlotte 2
Chief of Staff Luftlotte 3
Chief of Staff Bombers
General in charge Equipment, Generalfeldmarschall Milch

(1) To avenge the terror attacks by the enemy I have decided to intensify the air war over the British Isles, by means of concentrated attacks on cities and especially industrial centres and ports.
(2) For the intensifications of the war against England, the following [additional] units are to be committed:

(a) from Luftflotte 2:
KG 30, KG 54, KG 76 each with two Gruppen (of which one Gruppe only temporarily)
(b) from re-equipped units:
II./KG 6 (Ju 88), I./KG 100 (He 177), I./KG 51 (Me 410)

(3) All units are to be concentrated against targets, making use of all the experience gained during the previous months' operations against England. The operations are to be carried out in a manner and frequency depending on casualties and replacements, so that the fighting strength of the units remains absolutely unimpaired. This is in view of the necessity to maintain a permanent defensive capability against the ever-present threat of an attempted enemy invasion in the west.
(4) Operational readiness, and the stocking-up of the units earmarked for the operation, are to be speeded up by all possible means so that the operation can begin at the end of the full-moon period in December. The detailed measures necessary for this are to be ordered by the Quartermaster General.
(5) The necessary preparation, especially those of the ground organisation, are to be initiated without delay. The advanced airfields only are to be used for the attacks; the units' main and reserve staffs are to be moved back. In so far as is necessary, use is to be made of airfields in the Reich area with the agreement of the commander Central Area. On the airfields themselves the aircraft are to be widely dispersed and parked well away from the runways; they are protected by revetments so as to nullify the effect of the anticipated enemy bombing attacks. In addition, a dummy occupation is to be made of those advanced airfields which are not to be used.
(6) Particular attention is to be paid to the selection and preparation of bombs. In general, for all attacks, 70 per cent of the payload is to be used for carrying firebombs; of the high explosive bombs, first and foremost the heaviest types (larger than 1,000 kg) are to be used with the 'England Mixture' [*the 'England Mixture' was a combination of Trialen and Hexogen to form a very powerful if sensitive explosive*], and air mines; types smaller than 500 kg are to be used only to make up the loads to the full capacity of the aircraft. Experts from the office of the Director of Air Armament, Engineer General Marquardt at Marienfeld, are to be available to give advice on this.
(7) Headquarters Fliegerkorps IX is to report via Luftflotte 3 as soon as possible, giving
(a) Its intentions, stating the targets for December and January.
(b) Its intentions for their execution, in general.
(c) The state of the flak and fighter defences to the C-in-C Air Force operations staff.

(8) Express attention is drawn to the need for especial secrecy for all preparations. Only those persons who have an absolute need to know of them are to be briefed. In each case, the scope of the briefing is to be restricted to

the minimum absolutely necessary. Special directives will follow on the security of the transfer operations. C-in-C Luftflotte 2 has already been informed verbally.

(signed) *Goering*
*Reichsmarschall of the*
*Greater German Reich*
*and C-in-C Luftwaffe*

## APPENDIX F

## LUFTWAFFE UNITS COMMITTED TO OPERATION 'STEINBOCK', 20 JANUARY 1944

| Unit | Equipment | Strength | Serviceable |
|------|-----------|----------|-------------|
| Stab. KG 2 | Dornier 217 | 3 | 3 |
| I./KG 2 | Dornier 217 | 35 | 35 |
| II./KG 2 | Junkers 188 | 35 | 31 |
| III./KG 2 | Dornier 217 | 38 | 36 |
| V./KG 2 | Messerschmitt 410 | 27 | 25 |
| Stab. KG 6 | Junkers 88 | 3 | 3 |
| I./KG 6 | Junkers 88 | 41 | 41 |
| II./KG 6 | Junkers 88 | 39 | 39 |
| III./KG6 | Junkers 88 | 41 | 37 |
| II./KG 30 | Junkers 88 | 36 | 31 |
| I./KG 40 | Heinkel 177 | 15 | 15 |
| Stab. KG 54 | Junkers 88 | 3 | 3 |
| I./KG 54 | Junkers 88 | 36 | 25 |
| II./KG 54 | Junkers 88 | 33 | 33 |
| I./KG 66 | Junkers 88, | | |
| | Junkers 188 | 45 | 23 |
| Stab. KG 76 | Junkers 88 | 5 | 4 |
| I./KG 76 | Junkers 88 | 33 | 31 |
| I./KG 100 | Heinkel 177 | 31 | 27 |
| I./SKG 10 | Focke Wulf 190 | 25 | 20 |
| | | 524 | 462 |

## APPENDIX G

## ATTACK ON LONDON, 23 FEBRUARY 1944

Reproduced below is a translation of the operational order to I. Gruppe of Kampfgeschwader 2, for the attack on London on the night of 23 February 1944. The Gruppe was equipped with Dornier 217s.

I./Kampfgeschwader 2 Headquarters, Section Ia [Operations] 23 February 1944

Operations Order for the Night of 23/24 February 1944
(1) I., II. and III./KG 2, combined attack on London. Target area Hamburg [code-name for the Millwall dock area].
(2) Time of attack 2220–2242 hours.
(3) Height of attack 13,000 feet.
(4) Bomb loads:

| | | |
|------|-----------|----------------------------------------|
| AK* | Lt Burgart | 4 SC 500 + 4 BC 50 [incendiary] with delay |
| BK | Oblt Tamm | 1 AB 1000 + 2 AB 500 |
| LK | Lt Tamm | 1 AB 1000 + 2 AB 500 |
| DK | Ofw Stemann | 1 AB 1000 + 2 AB 500 |
| MK | Offz Jakob | 1 AB 1000 + 2 AB 500 |

| HK | Lt Boettger | 1 AB 1000 + 2 AB 500 |
| AL | Lt Ott | 1 AB 1000 + 2 AB 500 |
| CL | Fw Spiering | 1 AB 1000 + 2 AB 500 |
| IL | Fw Moebins | 1 AB 1000 + 2 AB 500 |
| ML | Ofw Jaeger | 1 AB 1000 + 2 AB 500 |
| OL | Lt von Parpart | 1 AB 1000 + 2 AB 500 |
| CB | Fw Kuester | 1 AB 1000 + 2 AB 500 |
| EL | Lt Kuttler | 4 SC 500 + 4 BC 50 instantaneous |
| BA | [reserve aircraft] | 4 SC 500 + 4 BC 50 instantaneous |
| CA | [reserve aircraft] | 4 SC 500 + 4 BC 50 instantaneous |

*Side letters of aircraft.

(5) Route: Villaroche–St Valery-en-Caux–Eastbourne–target–St Valery-en-Caux–Villaroche.

(6) Execution:
(a) Outward Flight: aircraft with high explosive bombs to take-off first. Low level flight at 500 feet to climbing point. From St Valery en Caux maintain a height of 16,500 feet but climb as late as possible. From the English coast onwards descend gradually to attack height, 13,000 feet. Aircraft carrying high explosive bombs to bomb from 2230 to 2233 hours; aircraft with incendiaries to bomb from 2233 to 2242 hours.
(b) Return Flight: reduce height to reach own coast at 650 feet. Convoy route not to be crossed at less than 2,600 feet.
(c) Route markers: none.
(d) Target markers: Yellow flares, at 11,000 feet. II./KG 2 will drop no [high-explosive] bombs.
(e) At the target: left hand turns to be flown.
(7) Times of take-off:
2 Staffel, six aircraft, 2116/2120 hours.
3 Staffel, seven aircraft, 2121/2126 hours.
Sequence of attack: aircraft with high explosive bombs, 2 Staffel, 3 Staffel.
Tankage: Full (fill up where necessary).
(8) [Minimum] Height Crossing Coast: Outward 16,500 feet, Homeward 500 feet.
(9) Co-operating units: II./KG 2, III./KG 2, KG 6, KG 54, KG 100, Operational Staffel IV./KG 101.
(10) Enemy Defences: Known.
(11) Own Defences: Known.
(12) Radio Briefing: see signals order.
(13) Navigational Aids: see signals order.
(14) Radio Procedure: radio silence outward and homeward, except for reports of shipping out of the convoy lane.
(15) Radio tuning and call signs: see signals order.
(16) Direction of Take-off: Runway I from West to East.
(17) Weather: see meteorological report.
(18) Debriefing: Oblt Roessing [Gruppe adjutant].
(19) OC Operation: Major Schoenberger [Gruppe commander].
(20) Navigation Officer: Oblt Roessing.
(21) Controller: Oblt Uebersohn.
(22) Briefing: 1900 hours.
(23) Synchronise Watches.
(24) Dueppel Order: Dueppel to be released at intervals of 30 seconds from 25 miles off the English coast to the target and back to 25 miles off the coast. In the London flak zone it is to be released as rapidly as possible – one packet every 4–5 seconds.
(25) Check-up of crews to prevent their carrying letters, pay books etc.
(26) I shall be at the Gruppe headquarters when crews take-off and return.

(signed) *Schoenberger*
*Major and Gruppe commander*

# Index